ITALIAN VEGAN CUISINE

A JOURNEY THROUGH
ITALY'S RICH PLANT-BASED CUISINE

buon appetito !

This book serves as your compass to mastering vegan Italian cuisine, showcasing exquisite dishes from Italy's twenty renowned culinary regions. Inspired by my comprehensive 'Italy Now and Then' series, it transports the enchantment of Italy's plant-based treasures straight to your kitchen.

If you enjoy the book, please leave a review on Amazon as it will help the book's ranking

For questions, feel free to write me an email to gba@arcaini.com

***

No part of this book may be reproduced, transmitted, or stored in an information retrieval system in any form or by any means without prior written permission from the author.

Foreword

When connoisseurs and enthusiasts ponder the depths of Italian cuisine, their minds invariably drift to quintessential staples such as spaghetti and, more broadly, pasta, along with pizza, extra-virgin olive oil, cheese, wine, tomatoes, espresso, gelato, aromatic herbs, and spices, and the globally celebrated principles of the Mediterranean diet.

In my published series, "Italy Then and Now," I delve into the profound history of Italy's twenty regions. These works explore regional distinctions, with individual chapters dedicated to local culinary delights and esteemed wine specialties native to each area. My latest contribution, "Become a Master of Italian Cooking," ventures further, presenting readers with a comprehensive collection of traditional recipes of Italian heritage. These culinary blueprints, often traced back to eras predating Christ, offer a profound glimpse into authentic regional home cooking practices.

Historically, the genesis of most Italian dishes is humble, born from necessity rather than luxury. Many were the inventions of the country's lower economic strata, families who, bound by financial constraints, ingeniously crafted meals using basic ingredients readily available in their immediate surroundings. This starkly contrasts with the affluent echelons of society, who enjoyed the privilege of incorporating expensive proteins into their diets.

Undoubtedly, Italian cuisine has undergone a remarkable evolution, emerging as a beloved cornerstone of global gastronomy. My travels around the world have reinforced this perception; in numerous countries, Italian eateries often occupy the echelon of top-tier restaurants. These establishments typically present themselves in dual formats: the more casual, often pizzeria-style dining options and their upscale counterparts, characterized by elegant table settings complete with tablecloths and cloth napkins, catering to a fine dining experience.

This culinary diversity underscores the universal appeal and adaptability of Italian cuisine, from simple, rustic dishes that speak to the soulful history of Italy's common folk to the refined complexities favored in haute cuisine, which continues to captivate and satisfy palates worldwide.

Table of Contents

Chapter 1.
Understanding Veganism

Many in my extended family and among my friends have adopted varying vegan lifestyles over the years. Yet, they often choose not to disclose this aspect of their lives to avoid debates. In fact, there is a silent trend indicating an exponential growth of people migrating to a plant-based lifestyle worldwide, and many legitimate studies provide the rationale for such a shift.

A significant reason for misunderstandings about vegan lifestyle choices is that most non-vegans show little interest in learning about it, possibly fearing it might compel them to step out of their comfort zone.

Let's break down the meaning of veganism. Being vegan isn't just about skipping burgers or avoiding leather jackets. It's a lifestyle choice that touches on three major areas: being kind(er) to animals (ethics), looking after your own body (health), and taking care of our planet (environment).

Ethics

Vegans hold the view that, in crucial ways, animals are similar to humans—they experience a range of emotions, including joy, fear, and suffering. This perspective leads vegans to advocate for fair treatment of animals, opposing their use as mere resources for human consumption. The idea of subjecting pets, which many consider family members, to the conditions endured by animals in industrial farming is inconceivable to them. This stance underlines a fundamental vegan belief: animals aren't commodities but beings deserving of respect and compassion.

Think about it: many farms where they raise animals for food don't provide the best living situations. It can be pretty rough, with animals all crammed together and not living natural lives at all. Vegans don't support this kind of setup, so they avoid products from animals to show they don't agree with those practices.

Health

At seventy-five and deeply rooted in my Italian culinary traditions, I'm not inclined to alter my eating habits drastically. However, my investigations indicate that opting for a vegan diet has positive implications for one's health. While I cherish my customary cuisine, I recognize that embracing veganism can be a beneficial choice for personal well-being.

Veganism can offer several health benefits, primarily due to its focus on plant-based foods, often lower in saturated fat and calories and higher in certain nutrients. Here's why a well-planned vegan diet can be healthy for your body:

1. **Rich in Nutrients**: A vegan diet tends to be high in fiber, antioxidants, beneficial plant compounds, vitamins C and E, potassium, magnesium, folate, and other key nutrients. These are more abundant in whole plant foods than in meats and dairy.
2. **Weight Management**: People following vegan diets tend to have lower body weights and body mass indexes (BMIs). This may be due to a higher dietary fiber intake, which can help you feel fuller longer, and a lower calorie intake.
3. **Heart Health**: Vegan diets can be beneficial for heart health. Several studies suggest that vegans may have up to a 75% lower risk of developing high blood pressure and a 42% lower risk of dying from heart disease. This is partly due to an intake of significantly fewer saturated fats and more heart-healthy fruits, vegetables, legumes, and whole grains that can promote good cholesterol levels, lower blood pressure, and support overall heart health.
4. **Cancer Prevention**: Some research suggests that a vegan diet could help prevent certain types of cancer.

The World Health Organization has pointed out that about one-third of all cancers can be prevented by factors within your control, including diet. For instance, eating legumes regularly may reduce your risk of colorectal cancer, and a diet rich in fruits and vegetables is linked to a lower risk for several types of cancer.

5. **Lower Risk of Type 2 Diabetes**: Vegan diets are known to be more effective for blood sugar control than diets with which they are compared. They can improve insulin sensitivity and reduce the risk of developing type 2 diabetes. The high fiber content of a vegan diet can also contribute to better glycemic control.

6. **Possible Reduction in Arthritis Symptoms**: Some studies have reported that a vegan diet can significantly reduce pain, swelling, and morning stiffness for people with different types of arthritis.

That said, ditching animal products also means you miss out on some nutrients, so vegans must ensure they're getting important enrichments like Vitamin B12, iron, and omega-3s from other foods or special vitamin supplements.

Environment

Here's the shocker - raising animals for food takes up a lot of resources. We're talking huge amounts of water massive spaces of land, and, as we all know, it contributes to pollution. While I don't intend to politicize the narrative, a solid argument can be made that all the world's cows, pigs, and chickens are like a squad of nature troublemakers, helping to mess up the climate. That's because of all the gases they produce, and the natural areas destroyed to create space for them. Vegans argue that by eating plants instead of animal products, they're cutting out the middle animal. This means using fewer resources and causing less pollution, which is obviously a win for Earth.

So, there you have it! Veganism, in a nutshell, is about making choices that aim to reduce harm to animals, stay healthy, and look after the world. It's like casting a vote for what you care about every time you eat or buy something. And with the world facing some pretty hefty challenges right now, this whole vegan trend seems like it's giving people a way to make a positive change.

Chapter 2.
The Italian Vegan Pantry

Let me share a little-known secret. Italian cuisine enjoys its premier status in global favorability not because the beef, chicken, pork, or fish used are superior to those found elsewhere in the world. The secret lies in the meticulous preparation and the balanced, sophisticated blend of spices and vegetables that characterizes Italian cooking.

So, embarking on a vegan journey doesn't mean you must forsake your love of traditional Italian cuisine. In fact, Italian cooking, known for its robust flavors, simple ingredients, and deeply satisfying dishes, can be a playground for vegan cooking. Focusing on fresh vegetables, aromatic herbs, and rich grains forms a solid foundation for Italian vegan cuisine. Here's how to master Italian vegan cooking with essential ingredients and clever substitutes.

Essential Ingredients for the Base

Italian cuisine starts with fresh, quality ingredients, and this doesn't change when you're cooking vegan. Staples include:

- **Tomatoes:** a staple in many Italian dishes, whether they're fresh, canned, or sun-dried. They're vegan-friendly and add a rich, tangy flavor to sauces and soups. Since I retired, I've taken over dinner duties. It's not just because I'm a genius in the kitchen but also because I help my wife with the daily workload. We have tomatoes in some form almost every day, like a simple tomato salad, a base for sauces, or mixed into various dishes. They're versatile and an essential part of our meal routine.
- **Olive Oil:** This is perhaps the most crucial component. A good quality extra-virgin olive oil can transform a simple dish into something sublime. It's used for sautéing, in dressings, and even drizzled over food before serving.
- **Garlic and Onions:** fundamental ingredients in Italian cuisine, providing essential flavor to a wide range of dishes, from a basic bruschetta to a more elaborate marinara sauce. Besides its distinctive taste, garlic serves an additional purpose as a natural remedy, particularly known for its ability to help lower high blood pressure. This makes these ingredients not only valuable for their culinary contributions but also for their health benefits.
- **Fresh Herbs:** Basil, oregano, rosemary, and thyme are just a few herbs that are paramount in your

Italian vegan pantry. Of course, if you can't get your hands on "fresh" herbs, you can use dried substitutes. However, fresh herbs contribute vibrant flavors that dried herbs cannot match.

- **Vegetables:** Beyond tomatoes, vegetables like eggplant, zucchini, bell peppers, and leafy greens are central to Italian vegan cooking, often making up the bulk of a dish. It is important to use ripe veggies. Using ripe vegetables and fruits in vegan cuisine, as in all types of cuisine, is preferred for several important reasons related to flavor, texture, and nutritional content. This preference is even more significant in vegan cooking because plant-based ingredients are central to the cuisine, and their qualities greatly influence the outcome of the dish. Here's why ripe produce is favored:

  - **Flavor:** Ripe fruits and vegetables are at their peak flavor. Sugars have fully developed, making them taste sweeter, and the natural aromas are more vibrant. This is particularly important in vegan cuisine, where the natural flavors of fruits and vegetables are often the stars of a dish. Unripe produce can be more bitter or astringent and lack the nuanced flavors they develop when fully ripe.
  - **Texture:** The texture of fruits and vegetables significantly changes as they ripen. Ripe fruits and veggies are often more tender and easier to chew and digest. In contrast, unripe ones can be hard and tough. The pleasant, palatable texture of ripe produce can be crucial in vegan cuisine, especially in raw preparations.

8

- **Nutritional content**: As fruits and vegetables ripen, their nutritional content can change. While the patterns can vary (for instance, vitamin C content may decrease in some fruits as they ripen), some ripe fruits and vegetables can be richer in antioxidants and certain other nutrients than their unripe counterparts.
- **Digestibility**: Ripe fruits and vegetables are generally easier to digest. For example, unripe bananas contain more resistant starches, which can be difficult for some people to digest and cause discomfort. As they ripen, these starches turn into easily digestible sugars.
- **Culinary versatility**: Ripe fruits and vegetables are more versatile in cooking. They can be used in various ways, including eating raw, cooking, and blending. Their flavors are also more likely to blend well with other ingredients, allowing for a harmonious dish.
- For these reasons, using ripe vegetables and fruits is often recommended in cooking, particularly in vegan cuisine, which relies heavily on the inherent flavors and qualities of plant-based ingredients. However, there are specific recipes or culinary traditions that may use unripe produce to achieve a particular flavor or texture in a dish (like the tartness and crunch of green papayas in certain Southeast Asian salads), so the choice can also depend on the desired outcome for the dish.

Substitutes for Common Ingredients:

Several substitutes can be used to maintain the authenticity of flavors without compromising vegan values.

- **Cheese:** One of the most missed items when one switches to veganism is cheese. However, there are several vegan alternatives available. Nutritional yeast provides a cheesy flavor, perfect for sprinkling on pasta and pizza. Vegan parmesan can be homemade by blitzing nuts (usually cashews or almonds) with nutritional yeast, garlic powder, and salt. Vegan mozzarella, often made from coconut oil and starches, melts beautifully on pizzas.

- **Pasta:** Indeed, while a range of pasta options are inherently vegan, certain types do contain eggs. For those committed to authentic Italian vegan cooking, it's advisable to choose egg-free pasta varieties, often made from ingredients like wheat, rice, quinoa, or lentils. It's essential to read the labels carefully to ensure they meet vegan standards.

Interestingly, in Italian cuisine, the secret to a delicious dish often doesn't lie in the pasta itself. Regardless of its shape or composition, the true magic is in the sauces and spices accompanying it. The flavors infused with a well-prepared sauce, combined with carefully selected spices, truly elevate a dish. This highlights the beauty of Italian cooking — it's not merely about the individual ingredients but the culinary alchemy that happens when blended with skill and tradition.

- **Meat:** Italian recipes often call for meat. Vegan dishes like lasagna, Bolognese, meatballs, lentils, mushrooms, and eggplants offer the hearty texture you want. Textured vegetable protein (TVP) and tempeh are also excellent for mimicking ground meat.

- **Cream and Milk:** Italian dishes known for their creaminess can still be enjoyed by using coconut milk, soy milk, almond milk, or oat milk. For thicker cream, cashew cream made from soaked and blended cashews is an excellent dairy substitute in recipes.
- **Eggs:** In recipes that use eggs for binding (like meatballs or frittatas), ground flaxseeds or chia seeds mixed with water create a gelatinous consistency similar to eggs. Applesauce and mashed bananas can work as binders in baked goods.

Italian vegan cooking is about embracing the rich tapestry of Italian cuisine while aligning with ethical eating practices. By substituting wisely and not compromising on the freshness and quality of ingredients, you can enjoy the health benefits and deliciousness of Italian food without any animal products. Whether you're a long-time vegan or just starting, these ingredients and substitutes are essential in recreating your favorite Italian dishes with a vegan twist.

Chapter 3
Mastering Italian Vegan Cooking

Embracing veganism in the culinary realm, especially in cuisine as rich and regionally diverse as Italy's, requires creativity and an understanding of authentic flavors. Italian cooking is revered for its simplicity, the quality of ingredients used, and the comforting flavors it embodies. Transitioning this cuisine into a completely plant-based one allows not only for the preservation of tradition but also for an exploration of a variety of textures, flavors, and nutrients. Here's how to master the art of Italian vegan cooking:.

Tips for Preparing Authentic Italian Vegan Dishes

- **Freshness is Key:** One secret behind the deliciousness of Italian food is the commitment to fresh ingredients. Whether it's tomatoes, basil, or other produce, fresh ingredients contribute significantly to flavor. Shop locally and seasonally, which is traditional in Italian cooking, to ensure your ingredients are at their peak.
- **Understand the Basics:** Master the basic recipes and techniques, such as making a perfect marinara sauce, sautéing vegetables until they're just right, or

preparing homemade vegan pasta. Once you understand the foundations, you can build and adapt most Italian recipes to suit your vegan needs.

- **Simmer and Slow Cook:** Many Italian sauces develop their flavors over low heat and prolonged cooking. Techniques such as simmering ingredients in a soffritto (a mixture of sautéed vegetables, usually onion, garlic, and celery) can create a depth of flavor that forms the base of many dishes.

- **Roasting Vegetables:** To achieve a rich flavor, consider roasting your vegetables. This technique caramelizes the natural sugars in vegetables, leading to a robust and intensified flavor profile that can mimic the heartiness often associated with meat.

- **Herbs and Spices:** While not known for its spiciness, Italian cuisine deeply cherishes a variety of herbs. Essentials such as basil, oregano, rosemary, thyme, and sage should be staples in your culinary toolkit. Rarely does a day pass without me reaching for several, if not all, of these seasonings. Cultivating your own selection of basic herbs is straightforward, requiring minimal space. Using fresh herbs is desirable and incorporating them at the precise cooking moment is crucial for unleashing their complete aromatic potential.

- **Balancing Flavors:** Balancing the five essential flavors (sweet, sour, salty, bitter, and umami) is crucial in Italian cooking. For instance, I avoid adding any sugars and prefer adding a carrot to balance the acidity in tomato-based sauces.
- **Vegan Cheese and Cream:** Learn to make vegan parmesan using nuts such as cashews or almonds mixed with nutritional yeast. For creamy dishes, ingredients like cashew cream, vegan mascarpone, or coconut cream can provide the richness you seek.

Achieving Italian Flavors with Plant-Based Ingredients

- **Umami Bomb:** Traditional Italian cuisine often draws umami flavors from parmesan, anchovies, or meat (umami, known as the fifth basic taste, is characterized by a savory, meaty flavor, often associated with broths and cooked meats and is attributed to the taste of glutamates). Vegan umami can be achieved through ingredients like tomatoes, mushrooms, red wine, balsamic vinegar, soy sauce, ripe olives, nutritional yeast, and seaweed. These add depth and savoriness to your dishes.
- **Quality Olive Oil:** Olive oil, fundamental to Italian cooking, serves multiple purposes, including cooking, garnishing, and composing dressings.

Opting for a superior grade of olive oil is essential as it significantly elevates the taste, especially noticeable in dressings or when drizzled atop dishes. In my specialty book, "Become a Master of Italian Cooking," (available in the Amazon Kindle store), I challenge the common misconception surrounding the use of "extra-virgin olive oil" for cooking. Contrary to popular belief, "extra-virgin olive oil" is the right choice for cooking and salad dressings. While its cost is slightly higher than its standard counterpart, it is the optimal selection for both health benefits and flavor richness.

- **Garlic is Gold:** Italian cooking celebrates garlic, particularly for its capacity to significantly elevate flavor. Whether it's employed raw, lightly sautéed, thoroughly roasted, or infused into oil, garlic stands out in its versatility. It's crucial to heat garlic until it releases its inviting aroma, avoiding burning, which can introduce a bitter note. Moreover, it's worth noting that garlic is a potent natural solution for managing high blood pressure.

- **Stocks and Broths:** A robust vegetable stock is essential in all kinds of culinary traditions, particularly in vegan cuisine, where it lays the foundational taste for numerous soups, stews, and sauces. Preparing stock with vegetable remnants is not only cost-effective but also guarantees a depth of flavor that surpasses that of commercial alternatives.

- **Nutritional Yeast for Cheesiness:** Nutritional yeast, a deactivated yeast, is a vegan staple, offering a cheese-like flavor rich in protein, vitamins, especially B-complex, and minerals. It has a cheesy flavor and is a fantastic addition to many dishes requiring cheese replacement. It can be used in pesto, cheese sauces, risottos, and as a topping for pasta.

- **Incorporate Nuts:** Nuts can be used for more than just making vegan cheese. They add creaminess, texture, and richness to various dishes. Think about toasting pine nuts for garnish or using blended almonds to thicken a sauce.

- **Wine and Vinegar:** Don't overlook the power of good quality red or white wine to deepen flavor profiles, especially in risottos and stews. Similarly, balsamic and red wine vinegar can add necessary acidity to dishes. A word about balsamic vinegar. Many vineyards compete for a market share of vinegar products. However, as a native Italian, only balsamic vinegar from the Modena region makes it to my pantry. Balsamic vinegar is a renowned product from Modena, Italy, known for its rich flavor and velvety black color. It's used in various dishes and is prized in the culinary world. There are specific classifications of balsamic vinegar from Modena based on quality, aging process, and production methods. The two primary types of balsamic vinegar are Traditional Balsamic Vinegar (Aceto Balsamico Tradizionale, the most prestigious and best vinegar), aged for at least 12 years, and highly regulated, and Balsamic Vinegar of Modena (Aceto Balsamico di Modena), a commercial version aged minimally 60 days, often incorporating wine vinegar and colorants. For use in raw form (salads), I strongly recommend using the higher-grade Traditional Balsamic Vinegar. In contrast, for use in cooking, the better alternative is the more fluid regular Balsamic Vinegar.

Mastering Italian vegan cooking involves respecting the simplicity of traditional recipes and the quality of your ingredients while being willing to experiment with plant-based substitutes that still pay homage to authentic flavors. It's about balancing innovation and tradition to create dishes that satisfy both the body and soul. The reward is a rich, diverse, and ethical culinary experience that honors Italy's storied culinary heritage while celebrating a compassionate, vegan lifestyle.

Chapter 4.
A Tour of Italy Through Vegan Cuisine

This chapter delves into a comprehensive guide filled with recipes and culinary insights, providing elaborate directions to animate your Italian vegan creations. Italian cuisine's rich mosaic differs significantly from one region to another. In this journey, we will traverse various Italian regions, highlighting distinct vegan delights and local produce that shape each locale's food culture.

Northern Italy

Aosta Valley

The Aosta Valley, known as Valle d'Aosta in Italian, is a mountainous region in the northwest of Italy, bordering France and Switzerland. Surrounded by the Alps, it's known for its picturesque landscapes and hearty cuisine. While the traditional local cuisine heavily features meat and dairy, the move towards plant-based eating has encouraged a delightful vegan reinterpretation of some of these dishes, using the rich array of local produce.

Here are some vegan dishes and adaptations from the Aosta Valley:

Valle d'Aosta-style Soup (Zuppa Valdostana)

Traditionally, this soup includes cabbage, bread, and fontina cheese. A vegan version would replace the cheese with a nutritional yeast-fortified cashew cream for the cheesy flavor and texture. The main ingredients remain savoy cabbage and stale whole-grain or sourdough bread, layered in a casserole with vegetable broth, onions, and the cashew cream, then baked to perfection.

Ingredients:

- 6-8 slices of stale whole-grain or rustic bread
- 4 tablespoons of olive oil, divided
- 1 large onion, thinly sliced
- 2 cloves of garlic, minced
- 1/2 teaspoon of dried thyme
- 1/2 teaspoon of dried rosemary
- 4 cups of vegetable broth (preferably homemade)
- Salt and black pepper, to taste
- 1 1/2 cups of vegan cheese (opt for varieties that melt well, like vegan mozzarella or vegan fontina)
- Fresh parsley, chopped (for garnish)

Instructions:

Preheat the Oven and Prepare Bread:

- Preheat your oven to 350°F (175°C).
- Brush both sides of each bread slice with 2 tablespoons of olive oil and place them on a baking sheet.
- Toast in the oven for about 5-10 minutes or until they're crisped to your preference, then set aside.

Sauté Onions and Garlic:

- In a large pot, heat the remaining 2 tablespoons of olive oil over medium heat.
- Add the sliced onions, stirring occasionally, until they become soft and translucent, around 5-7 minutes.

- Add the minced garlic, dried thyme, rosemary, and sauté for another 1-2 minutes until the garlic is fragrant, ensuring it doesn't burn.

Prepare the Soup Base:

- Pour in the vegetable broth and bring the mixture to a boil.

- Once boiling, reduce the heat to a simmer and season with salt and pepper to taste.

- Let the soup simmer for about 20-30 minutes to allow the flavors to meld.

Assemble the Soup:

- Place a layer of the toasted bread slices at the bottom of a casserole dish or individual oven-safe soup bowls.

- Sprinkle a generous amount of vegan cheese over the bread.

- Ladle some hot soup over the layers, then repeat the layering process until all ingredients are used, ending with a layer of vegan cheese.

Bake:

- Transfer the casserole dish or soup bowls into the oven and bake for about 20 minutes, or until the cheese is bubbly and golden brown.

Serve:

- Carefully remove from the oven, let it stand for a few minutes to cool slightly, then garnish with fresh chopped parsley.

- Serve hot, enjoying the melded flavors of the broth-soaked bread, aromatic herbs, and melted vegan cheese.

This vegan take on Zuppa Valdostana offers the same heartwarming and comforting eating experience as the traditional version but aligns with vegan dietary preferences.

Polenta Concia

Polenta is a versatile, comforting staple, and 'Polenta Concia' is a traditional preparation involving butter and cheese. For a vegan twist, cook polenta with a rich vegetable broth and stir in a vegan cheese substitute and a bit of olive oil or vegan butter for creaminess. Adding roasted vegetables or sun-dried tomatoes, which are not traditional but add depth, can make it even more flavorful.

Ingredients:

- 1 cup of polenta (coarse cornmeal)
- 4 cups of water or vegetable broth (for more flavor)
- 1 teaspoon of salt (or to taste)
- 1/4 cup of nutritional yeast (for a cheesy flavor)
- 1/4 cup of vegan butter (you can adjust the amount to your preference)
- 1/2 cup of vegan cheese (something that melts well, like a vegan cheddar or mozzarella) Optional: sautéed vegetables, mushrooms, or vegan sausage for an extra layer of flavor

Instructions:

Prepare the Polenta:

- Bring the water or vegetable broth to a boil in a large pot.

- Add salt to taste.

- Gradually whisk in the polenta to prevent any lumps from forming.

- Reduce the heat to a low simmer and continue to cook the polenta, stirring frequently, for about 25-30 minutes until it's thickened and the cornmeal is tender.

Add Flavors:

- Once the polenta is cooked, turn off the heat. Stir in the vegan butter until completely melted and mixed through the polenta.

- Add the nutritional yeast and half of the vegan cheese, stirring until everything is well combined and creamy.

- Ensure the residual heat is melting the cheese and incorporating it into the polenta.

- For additional flavor, you can fold in sautéed vegetables, mushrooms, or crumbled vegan sausage at this stage.

Bake the Polenta (Optional):

- Preheat your oven to 375°F (190°C).

- Pour the creamy polenta into a baking dish and sprinkle the remaining vegan cheese on top.

- Bake in the preheated oven for about 20 minutes or until the cheese on top has melted and is turning golden.

Serve:

- Allow the polenta to sit for a few minutes after removing it from the oven. It will continue to set a bit more.

- Spoon onto plates or into bowls and serve warm, possibly with a side of roasted vegetables or a green salad.

This vegan Polenta Concia recipe retains the creamy, comforting essence of the dish while ensuring it's completely plant-based. The nutritional yeast and vegan cheese impart a cheesy flavor without any dairy, keeping the dish authentic to its roots.

Chestnut Stew (Marroni)

Chestnuts are popular in the region and used in various dishes. A vegan stew with chestnuts, root vegetables like carrots and parsnips, wild mushrooms, and perhaps some locally sourced red wine can make for a warming, hearty dish.

Fresh herbs like rosemary and thyme add aromatic depth. As a side note, if you ever wander through any major Italian cities during winter, you will find many small stands on the street that grill chestnuts on an open fire. Try them; they are delicious.

Ingredients:

- 1 pound (approx. 450 grams) of fresh chestnuts (you can use canned or vacuum-packed for convenience)
- 2 tablespoons olive oil
- 1 large onion, finely chopped
- 2 medium carrots, diced
- 2 celery stalks, diced
- 2-3 cloves garlic, minced

- 1 teaspoon fresh rosemary, finely chopped (or 1/2 teaspoon dried rosemary)
- 1 teaspoon fresh thyme leaves (or 1/2 teaspoon dried thyme)
- 1/2 teaspoon ground nutmeg
- Salt and black pepper, to taste
- 1/2 cup red wine (optional, can be substituted with vegetable broth or omitted)
- 2-3 cups vegetable broth
- 1 bay leaf
- Fresh parsley, chopped (for garnish)

Instructions:

Prepare the Chestnuts (skip this step if using pre-prepared chestnuts):

- Preheat your oven to 400°F (200°C).
- Using a sharp knife, make a small incision in each chestnut to prevent them from bursting.
- Place chestnuts on a baking sheet and roast for about 30 minutes or until the shells crack open.
- Once cool enough to handle, peel and chop the chestnuts. Set aside.

Sauté the Vegetables:

- Heat olive oil in a large pot over medium heat.
- Add the onions, carrots, and celery, cooking until the onions become translucent and the vegetables start to soften, around 5-7 minutes.
- Stir in the garlic, rosemary, thyme, nutmeg, salt, and pepper, allowing the mixture to cook for another 2 minutes.

Deglaze the Pot:

- Pour in the red wine (if using), stirring to loosen any bits stuck to the bottom of the pot. Let it simmer for a couple of minutes.

Add the Chestnuts:

- Add the prepared chestnuts to the pot, followed by the vegetable broth and bay leaf.
- Bring the stew to a boil, then reduce the heat to allow it to simmer.
- Cover the pot and let it cook for approximately 20-30 minutes, stirring occasionally, allowing the flavors to meld and the chestnuts to soften.

Adjust Consistency and Seasoning:

- If you prefer a thicker stew, you can use an immersion blender to slightly blend part of the stew or mash some of the chestnuts.
- Taste and adjust the seasoning with more salt and pepper, if necessary.

Serve:

- Discard the bay leaf and serve the stew hot, garnished with fresh parsley.
- This dish goes well with a slice of rustic bread or sautéed greens.

This vegan Chestnut Stew offers a delightful combination of earthy flavors and satisfying heartiness, perfect for a cozy meal.

Farinata

This chickpea pancake, also known as "Cecina" or "socca," is more common in the coastal regions of Italy but can be adapted to Aosta's high-altitude environment. It requires only chickpea flour, water, and olive oil, seasoned simply with salt and pepper. It can be embellished with fresh local herbs or a sprinkle of nutritional yeast and served with dark leafy greens sautéed in garlic.

Ingredients:
- 1 cup chickpea flour (also known as gram flour or besan)
- 1 cup water (room temperature)

- 1 1/2 tablespoons extra-virgin olive oil, plus extra for the pan and drizzling on top
- 1 teaspoon salt, or to taste
- Black pepper to taste (optional)
- Rosemary (fresh or dried) or other herbs of choice (optional)

Instructions:

Mix the Batter:

- In a bowl, whisk together the chickpea flour, water, olive oil, and salt until smooth.
- Let the mixture rest at room temperature for at least 2 hours or up to 12 hours. This resting time allows the batter to thicken and the flavors to meld.

Preheat the Oven and Pan:

- Place a 10-inch cast-iron skillet or a round metal baking pan in the oven.
- Preheat the oven as hot as it will go (450-500°F or 230-260°C). The high heat will help to create a crispy crust.

Prepare the Pan:

- Once the oven is hot, carefully remove the pan (it will be extremely hot), and add a couple of tablespoons of olive oil, ensuring it covers the bottom of the pan.
- Pour the rested batter into the pan. It should sizzle as it hits the hot oil, indicating the pan is hot enough.

Season and Bake:

- Sprinkle the top with black pepper and herbs if you're using them.

- Carefully place the pan back in the oven and bake for 20-30 minutes, depending on how thick the batter is. You're looking for a crisp, golden-brown crust and a soft center.

Slice and Serve:

- After baking, remove the pan from the oven and let it cool for a few minutes.

- Use a spatula to gently loosen the edges of the farinata from the pan. Slide it onto a cutting board.

- Cut it into wedges or squares, drizzle with more extra-virgin olive oil if desired, and serve warm.

Serving Suggestions:

- Farinata is versatile and can be topped with various ingredients, much like a flatbread or pizza. Consider fresh herbs, sautéed vegetables, vegan cheese, or even a sprinkle of coarse sea salt and cracked black pepper.

- It's best enjoyed fresh and hot from the oven while the edges are still crispy.

This simple, flavorful recipe is a great introduction to a classic Italian dish. It can easily be adapted with additional toppings or seasonings to suit your taste.

Apple Strudel (Strudel di mele)

Though originally from the neighboring region of Trentino-Alto Adige, apple strudel is also found in Valle d'Aosta due to the Austro-Hungarian influence on northern Italian cuisine.

A vegan version uses dairy-free pastry and margarine instead of butter, stuffed with spiced apples, raisins, and pine nuts or walnuts.

When adapting traditional dishes to vegan versions, the key is maintaining the essence of the dish's flavors and presentation. These adaptations respect local culinary traditions while offering healthful, plant-based alternatives that can be enjoyed by vegans and non-vegans alike. They showcase the versatility of vegan cooking and the rich culinary tapestry of regions like the Aosta Valley.

Ingredients:

For the dough:

- 1 1/2 cups all-purpose flour
- 1/2 teaspoon salt
- 1/3 cup olive oil or vegetable oil
- 1/2 cup water (more if needed)

For the filling:

- 5-6 large apples, preferably tart ones like Granny Smith
- 3/4 cup raisins
- 1/2 cup finely chopped walnuts or almonds (optional)
- 2 teaspoons cinnamon
- 1/2 cup brown sugar (can adjust based on sweetness preference)
- Juice and zest of 1 lemon
- 1/2 teaspoon nutmeg (optional)
- 3-4 tablespoons breadcrumbs (to soak up the juice from the apples)

To finish:

- Powdered sugar for dusting
- Soy or almond milk for brushing (optional)

Instructions:

Prepare the Dough:

- In a large mixing bowl, combine the flour and salt. Mix the oil with a fork or pastry blender until the mixture resembles coarse crumbs.

- Gradually add water, mixing until you can form the dough into a ball. If the dough is too dry, add more water, a tablespoon at a time.
- Knead the dough on a lightly floured surface until it is smooth, about 5-10 minutes.
- Wrap it in cling film and let it rest at room temperature for at least 30 minutes.

Prepare the Filling:

- Peel, core, and thinly slice the apples.
- In a large bowl, combine the apples, raisins, nuts (if using), cinnamon, brown sugar, lemon juice, lemon zest, and nutmeg. Mix well, ensuring the apples are well coated.

Roll the Dough:

- Preheat your oven to 375°F (190°C).
- On a lightly floured surface, roll out the dough into a thin rectangle, about 16x24 inches. It should be thin enough to see your hand through it.
- Sprinkle breadcrumbs over the dough, leaving a margin around the edges. This helps to absorb the juices released by the apples during baking, preventing the bottom from getting soggy.

Assemble the Strudel:

- Arrange the apple filling evenly over the breadcrumb-covered dough, leaving a clean edge.
- Lift the towel and use it to help roll the dough over the apples, jelly-roll style, starting from the longer side. Tuck in the ends and seal the seam well.
- Carefully transfer the strudel to a baking sheet lined with parchment paper, with the seam side down. You can shape it into a crescent or leave it straight.

- If desired, brush the top with soy or almond milk for a golden color.
- Bake for about 35-40 minutes or until the strudel is golden brown.

Serve:

- Allow the strudel to cool slightly before dusting with powdered sugar.
- Slice it into portions and serve warm or at room temperature.

This vegan apple strudel keeps the traditional flavors of the classic recipe, substituting regular strudel dough with an olive oil-based version. It's a delightful, cruelty-free dessert that can warm up a cold evening, especially when served with a scoop of dairy-free ice cream or a dollop of vegan whipped cream.

Piedmont

The Piedmont region, located in the northwest corner of Italy, is renowned for its sophisticated cuisine and is often considered a haven for food enthusiasts. While the area is historically known for rich dishes that incorporate a variety of meats and cheeses, there is a growing trend and appreciation for vegan cuisine, and many traditional dishes can be adapted to a vegan lifestyle.

Here are some vegan-friendly dishes and specialties that you might encounter in Piedmont:

Bagna Cauda

Traditionally, bagna cauda is made with garlic, anchovies, and olive oil and served as a warm dip with various vegetables.

The vegan version omits anchovies, focusing on the richness of garlic and high-quality olive oil, providing a simple but robust flavor profile.

Ingredients:

- 1/2 cup extra-virgin olive oil
- 6-8 cloves garlic, finely minced or grated
- 1 tablespoon capers, rinsed and chopped
- 1-2 tablespoons of nori seaweed flakes (or another seaweed type) to mimic the fishy taste of anchovies
- 1/2 cup unsweetened almond milk or soy milk (for creaminess)
- 1 tablespoon fresh lemon juice
- Salt, to taste
- Black pepper, to taste
- Assorted raw vegetables (like bell peppers, carrots, endive, zucchini, and celery) for dipping
- Crusty bread, cut into pieces (optional)

Instructions:

Prepare the Garlic Oil:

- In a small saucepan or skillet, warm the olive oil over low heat. Don't let it get too hot; it should be warm to the touch.

- Add the minced garlic to the warm oil. Cook it gently on low heat for about 10-15 minutes or until it's soft and fragrant but not browned. Stir occasionally to ensure the garlic doesn't stick to the pan.

Add the 'Fishy' Element:

- Stir in the chopped capers and nori flakes (or your choice of seaweed). The seaweed helps mimic the ocean flavor traditionally provided by the anchovies. Allow these to infuse in the oil for another 5 minutes, keeping the heat low.

Add Creaminess and Seasonings:

- Slowly pour the almond or soy milk, stirring continuously to create a creamy, emulsified sauce. It's important to keep the heat low so the mixture doesn't boil.

- Let the mixture gently simmer until it's heated through and has a slightly thickened consistency, about 5-7 minutes.

- Add the lemon juice, then season with salt and black pepper to taste. Remember, the capers and seaweed add some saltiness, so be cautious with additional salt.

Serving the Bagna Cauda:

- Once your Bagna Cauda reaches a smooth, dip-like consistency, transfer it to a serving bowl or a traditional fondue pot to keep it warm.

- Serve with a platter of fresh, raw vegetables and crusty bread, using them to dip into the warm, flavorful oil mixture.

This vegan Bagna Cauda provides the warm, savory experience of the original dish without using animal products, respecting the dietary choices of those who prefer plant-based options. It's the perfect centerpiece for a communal dining experience, where everyone can dip their favorite veggies into the savory sauce.

Peperonata

It's one of my family's favorites during cooler weather. Although originally from the southern regions but enjoyed throughout the country, Piedmont has its own local variations.

Naturally vegan, Peperonata is a celebration of garden flavors. It can be served with bread or as a topping for polenta or rice.

Ingredients:

- 4 large bell peppers (a mix of red, yellow, and/or green for color)
- 2 tablespoons olive oil
- 1 large onion, thinly sliced
- 2-3 garlic cloves, minced
- 1 can (400g) of diced or whole tomatoes, or 2-3 fresh ripe tomatoes, diced
- 1-2 tablespoons of capers (optional)
- 1 tablespoon balsamic vinegar or red wine vinegar
- Salt, to taste
- Black pepper, to taste
- A handful of fresh basil leaves, torn, or 1 teaspoon dried basil
- A pinch of sugar (optional, to balance the acidity of the tomatoes). I prefer one minced carrot.

Instructions:

Prepare the Peppers:

- Core and seed the bell peppers, cutting them into strips or squares, depending on your preference.

Sauté Onions and Garlic:

- In a large skillet or sauté pan, heat the olive oil over medium heat. Add the sliced onions, cooking until they become soft and translucent, about 5-7 minutes.

- Add the minced garlic to the onions, cooking for another minute until the garlic is fragrant but not browned.

Cook the Peppers:

- Add the sliced bell peppers to the pan. Cook, stirring occasionally, until they start to soften, about 5-10 minutes. You want the peppers to be tender but not mushy, retaining a slight bite.

Add the Tomatoes and Seasonings:

- If using canned tomatoes, include their juice for extra flavor. If using fresh tomatoes, they'll start to break down and release their juices once in the pan.

- Stir in the capers and minced carrots if you're using them. They'll add nice bursts of briny flavor that complement the sweetness of the peppers and onions.

- Allow the mixture to simmer for 10-15 minutes or until the tomatoes have broken down into a sauce and the peppers are thoroughly tender.

- Pour in the balsamic or red wine vinegar. Add salt and black pepper to taste. If the mixture seems too acidic, consider adding a pinch of sugar to balance it out.

Finish with Basil:

- Just before you're ready to serve, stir in the fresh basil leaves. If you're using dried basil, add it a bit earlier, letting it simmer with the peppers and tomatoes.

Serve:

- Serve your Peperonata warm, at room temperature, or even cold. It's extremely versatile: it works beautifully as a side dish, tossed with pasta, spooned over crusty bread, or as a topping for grilled tofu or seitan steaks.

This simple, flavorful dish celebrates the taste of bell peppers, enhanced with the savory depth of tomatoes and the fragrant sweetness of basil. It's a delicious way to enjoy a taste of Italian cuisine in a vegan-friendly way. I usually prepare twice or three times the single-dinner portion as the peperonata gets better each time you warm it up.

Risotto

While many risottos are made with butter and cheese, they can be adapted to vegan preferences using olive oil and cheese substitutes. Piedmont, with its ample supply of rice from the Vercelli area, is famous for its risottos, often flavored with local herbs, wild mushrooms, or wine. I do not use butter or cheese in preparing risotto; rather, I use vegetable broth instead of water.

Using high-quality vegetable broth instead of water is a fantastic way to infuse the risotto with a deep, savory flavor.

This method highlights one of the fundamental principles of good cooking: every ingredient, even the cooking liquid, contributes to the overall flavor of the dish.

Ingredients:

- 1 1/2 cups Arborio rice (traditional risotto rice)
- 5-6 cups vegetable broth (you can make this from scratch with fresh vegetables for more flavor)
- 1 cup white wine (a local Piedmontese variety if available)
- 2 tablespoons olive oil
- 1 large onion, finely chopped
- 3-4 cloves garlic, minced
- 1 1/2 cups mixed wild mushrooms (like porcini, which are popular in Piedmont), sliced
- 1 cup fresh peas or asparagus (optional, depending on season)
- Salt, to taste
- Black pepper, to taste
- 1/4 cup nutritional yeast (to mimic the cheesy flavor)

- Fresh herbs (such as thyme or Italian parsley) for garnish
- Truffle oil or freshly shaved truffles for an authentic Piedmontese touch (optional)

Instructions:

Prepare the Broth:

- Heat the vegetable broth in a saucepan and keep it warm on the stove. You'll be adding it to the risotto gradually.

Sauté Onions and Garlic:

- In a large, heavy-bottomed pan, heat the olive oil over medium heat. Add the chopped onion, sautéing until soft and translucent but not browned.

- Add the minced garlic, cooking for another minute until fragrant.

Cook the Rice:

- Add the Arborio rice to the pan with the onions and garlic, stirring for 1-2 minutes until the rice is well-coated with oil and has a slight toasty aroma. This step is crucial for developing the risotto's flavor and texture.

- Pour in the white wine, stirring constantly until the liquid is mostly absorbed by the rice.

Add the Broth Gradually:

- Add the warm vegetable broth one ladle at a time, stirring frequently. Wait to add the next spoon until the liquid has been mostly absorbed. This process helps to gradually release the rice's starches, creating the creamy texture that risotto is known for.

Cook the Vegetables:

- While the risotto is cooking, sauté your mushrooms (and peas or asparagus, if using) in a separate pan with a bit of olive oil until they're cooked through and set aside.

Continue Cooking the Risotto:

- Keep adding broth and stirring the risotto. The process should take about 18-20 minutes. The risotto is done when the rice grains are al dente, meaning they should be cooked but still have a slight bite to them.

Final Additions:

- Stir in the sautéed vegetables, nutritional yeast, salt, and pepper. Combine everything well. The nutritional yeast gives a cheesy flavor to the dish without any dairy.

- If you're using truffle oil, drizzle a small amount into the risotto and gently stir through for an indulgent, earthy flavor typical of Piedmont cuisine.

Serve:

- Spoon the risotto into dishes, garnishing with fresh herbs. If you have fresh truffles, shave a few slices on top of each serving for a truly Piedmontese experience.

- Serve immediately. Risotto is best enjoyed fresh from the stove, as it continues to thicken if left to sit.

This vegan risotto, rich with the flavors of the Piedmont region, offers a compassionate take on a classic dish without compromising on taste or texture.

Minestrone

This hearty vegetable soup is a staple in Italian cuisine, usually served during cold weather. In Piedmont, it's made with seasonal vegetables, beans, and sometimes pasta or potatoes, which is my preference.

By using vegetable broth and avoiding the use of any parmesan cheese, this dish is a fulfilling vegan option.

Ingredients:

- 2 tablespoons olive oil
- 1 large onion, chopped
- 2 cloves garlic, minced
- 2 medium carrots, diced
- 2 celery stalks, chopped
- 1 small leek, sliced (optional, but traditional in some Piedmontese recipes)
- 1 medium zucchini, chopped

- 1 medium potato, peeled and diced
- 1 cup seasonal vegetables (like green beans or peas), chopped
- 1 can (about 400 g) crushed tomatoes or 2-3 ripe tomatoes, peeled and diced
- 5-6 cups vegetable stock
- 1 can (about 400 g) cannellini beans or borlotti beans, rinsed and drained
- 1 cup cabbage or kale, shredded
- 1/2 cup Arborio rice or short pasta (like ditalini or macaroni)
- 1 teaspoon dried Italian herbs (basil, oregano, thyme) or a handful of mixed fresh herbs, chopped
- Salt and pepper, to taste
- Optional: vegan pesto or chopped fresh basil/parsley for garnish

Instructions:

Sauté the Base Vegetables:

- In a large pot, heat the olive oil over medium heat. Add the onions and garlic, sautéing until the onions are translucent.

- Add the carrots, celery, and leeks (if using). Continue to sauté until they start to soften, stirring occasionally.

Add Additional Vegetables:

- Add the zucchini, potato, and any other seasonal vegetables you're using. This is a great opportunity to use whatever fresh, local produce you have on hand – minestrone is all about versatility.

- Sauté for another few minutes, allowing all the vegetables to start cooking down.

Introduce Tomatoes and Broth:

- Add the crushed or fresh tomatoes to the pot, followed by the vegetable stock. The liquid should be enough to cover all the vegetables in the pot; if not, add a bit more.
- Bring the mixture to a boil, then reduce the heat to a simmer.

Simmer the Soup:

- Add the canned beans and shredded cabbage or kale. Stir to combine.
- Cover and let the soup simmer for about 20-30 minutes until the vegetables are tender.

Add Rice or Pasta:

- Add the Arborio rice or pasta, ensuring there's enough liquid in the pot for them to cook and expand.
- Simmer the soup until the rice or pasta is cooked, about 10-15 minutes, depending on what you're using.

Season and Serve:

- Stir in the dried or fresh herbs, then season with salt and pepper to taste. Let it cook for another couple of minutes to melt the flavors.
- Serve hot, garnished with a dollop of vegan pesto or a sprinkle of fresh basil or parsley if desired.

This Piedmont-style vegan minestrone celebrates the simplicity of fresh, plant-based ingredients. It's warming, nutritious, and flavorful, making it a comforting meal, especially during cooler weather. Since it's a flexible recipe, feel free to incorporate any of your favorite vegetables or those in season locally.

Grissini

Grissini are thin, crisp breadsticks from Piedmont, and they're a popular accompaniment to meals in Italy. They can be flavored with various ingredients, though the classic version uses flour, water, yeast, salt, and olive oil.

Of course, you can buy grissini online, and making them vegan is straightforward, as traditional grissini don't contain any animal products. If you want to venture into making your own grissini, here is how:

Ingredients:

- 1 cup warm water (about 110 degrees Fahrenheit)
- 1 package (2 1/4 teaspoons) active dry yeast
- 1 tablespoon sugar (optional, but helps to activate the yeast)
- 2 1/2 to 3 cups all-purpose flour
- 2 tablespoons extra-virgin olive oil, plus extra for brushing
- 1 teaspoon salt
- Optional toppings: sesame seeds, poppy seeds, dried herbs (like rosemary or thyme), coarse sea salt

Instructions:

Activate the Yeast:

- In a large bowl, combine the warm water and sugar, stirring to dissolve the sugar. Sprinkle the yeast over the water and let it sit for about 5-10 minutes until it dissolves and starts to foam, indicating it's active.

Make the Dough:

- Once the yeast is activated, add 2 1/2 cups of flour, olive oil, and salt to the bowl. Mix with a wooden spoon or your hands until the dough comes together.

- Transfer the dough to a lightly floured surface. Knead it by hand for about 10 minutes, adding more flour as necessary to prevent sticking, until the dough is smooth and elastic.

First Rise:

- Shape the dough into a ball and place it in a clean, oiled bowl. Cover with a damp cloth or plastic wrap and let it rise in a warm place for about 1-1.5 hours or until it has doubled.

Shape the Grissini:

- After the dough has risen, punch it down to release air bubbles. Transfer it to a lightly floured surface.

- Divide the dough into small pieces. The traditional grissini are thin, so aim for pieces about the size of a walnut.

- Roll each piece of dough into a long, thin stick, about 6-8 inches long. If you want your grissini to be super thin, you can make them even longer and thinner. They will puff up a bit as they bake.

Second Rise:

- Place the rolled-out grissini on baking sheets lined with parchment paper, ensuring they are not touching, as they will stick together during baking if they are too close.

- Cover with a clean kitchen towel and let them rise again in a warm place for about 15 minutes. They won't double in size this time but will puff up a little.

Prepare for Baking:

- Preheat your oven to 400 degrees Fahrenheit (about 200 degrees Celsius).

- If you're using them, sprinkle your toppings (seeds, herbs, coarse salt) on the grissini at this point. You should lightly brush the sticks with olive oil to help the toppings stick.

Bake the Grissini:

- Bake in the oven for 10-15 minutes or until crispy and golden brown. If your grissini are thicker, they might need a few extra minutes.

- Remove the grissini from the oven and cool on a wire rack.

Enjoy your homemade vegan grissini as a snack, an appetizer, or alongside your main meal. Grissini are perfect for dipping in soups, pairing with dips, or accompanying a cheese-like spread.

Focaccia

Piedmont is famous for its various focaccia breads, which are usually vegan. These are often flavored with rosemary or other herbs and can be found in most regional bakeries.

In my family, focaccia is an almost daily must, and my son and his friends usually ask if there is any focaccia as soon as they get to our home.

One important suggestion is to always using fresh herbs as a topping for your focaccia. They are the central ingredients for a good focaccia. I usually combine rosemary, oregano, and thyme and chop them very small.

The vegan version omits traditional dairy ingredients, offering a delightful treat everyone can enjoy. Below is a simple recipe for vegan focaccia:

Ingredients:

- 1 1/2 cups warm water (around 110 degrees Fahrenheit)
- 1 package (2 1/4 teaspoons) active dry yeast
- 1 tablespoon sugar (to help activate the yeast)
- 4 cups all-purpose flour (plus more for handling the dough)
- 1/4 cup extra-virgin olive oil (plus more for drizzling)
- 2 teaspoons salt (plus coarse sea salt for topping)
- Optional toppings: rosemary, oregano, thyme, cherry tomatoes, olives, or sliced onions

Instructions:

Prepare the Yeast:

- In a bowl, mix the warm water and sugar, stirring until the sugar dissolves. Sprinkle the yeast on top and let it sit for about 5-10 minutes until it becomes frothy. This indicates the yeast is active.

Make the Dough:

- In a large mixing bowl, combine the flour and 2 teaspoons of salt.

- Add the yeast mixture and 1/4 cup of olive oil. Mix until all the ingredients are well combined. If the dough seems too dry, add a bit more warm water; if it's too sticky, add more flour.

- Transfer the dough to a floured surface. Knead for about 5-7 minutes until it becomes smooth and elastic. I have to admit I am usually using my KitchenAid mixer,

- If you use the mixer, after the dough is smooth, remove it from the mixer and transfer it to a floured surface. Kneed for an additional minute or two.

- Shape the dough into a ball.

First Rise:

- Place the dough in a clean, oiled bowl, cover it with a damp cloth or plastic wrap, and let it rise in a warm, draft-free area for around 1-1.5 hours or until it has doubled in size.

Shape the Focaccia:

- After the first rise, gently punch the dough down to release air bubbles.

- Using a rolling pin, flatten the dough to fit the size of the baking sheet.

- Create dimples in the dough by pressing down with your fingertips. This characteristic texture ensures pockets to hold the oil and toppings.

- Transfer the flattened dough to a (very) lightly oiled or parchment-lined baking sheet (approximately 9x13 inches).

Second Rise:

- Cover the shaped dough with a damp cloth or plastic wrap, and let it rest for another 20-30 minutes. It should be notably puffy but not necessarily doubled in size.

- Preheat your oven to 400 degrees Fahrenheit (200 degrees Celsius).

- If using, prepare your toppings (like mince the combined de-stemmed rosemary, oregano, thyme, slice the onions, or wash cherry tomatoes).

Top and Bake:

- Just before baking, drizzle and distribute a thin layer of olive oil over the dough, ensuring it pools in the dimples. Sprinkle coarse sea salt and add your chosen toppings, pressing them slightly into the dough.

- Bake in the oven for 12-15 minutes until the focaccia has a golden-brown crust. If you insert cherry tomatoes, they should be wrinkly and slightly dried.

Serve:

- Remove your focaccia from the oven and allow it to cool slightly before slicing and serving. It's best enjoyed warm but is also delicious at room temperature.

This vegan focaccia is a treat that can be enjoyed as a side dish, appetizer, or even a main course with some accompaniments. The key to great focaccia is high-quality olive oil, so make sure you choose a good one. It's all about simplicity and the harmony of flavors!

Panna Cotta

Panna cotta is a traditional Italian dessert originating from the Piedmont region; it is known for its rich, creamy consistency and is typically served with caramel, chocolate sauce, or fruit compotes.

The classic recipe uses heavy cream, sugar, and gelatin. However, it's possible to make a vegan version of this delightful dessert by substituting a few ingredients. Here's how you can prepare vegan panna cotta:

Ingredients:

- 2 1/2 cups of coconut milk or almond milk (or another plant-based milk, but full-fat coconut milk gives the creamiest result)
- 1/4 cup of agave syrup or maple syrup (or to taste, depending on your preferred level of sweetness)
- 1 tablespoon of vanilla extract

- 2 teaspoons of agar-agar powder (a vegan gelatin substitute made from seaweed)
- Optional: Fresh berries, fruit puree, or vegan caramel sauce for serving

Instructions:

Mix the Ingredients:

- In a saucepan, whisk together the plant-based milk, agave or maple syrup, and agar-agar powder. Ensure the agar-agar is fully dissolved in the mixture to avoid lumps.

Heat the Mixture:

- Place the saucepan over medium heat and bring the mixture to a simmer. Reduce the heat to maintain a gentle simmer.

- Continue to whisk the mixture constantly and allow it to simmer for approximately 5 minutes. This process helps the agar-agar to activate and the mixture to thicken slightly.

- After simmering, remove the pan from the heat and whisk in the vanilla extract.

Set the Panna Cotta:

- Pour the mixture into ramekins, molds, or small glasses. Be careful, as the mixture will be hot.

- Let the panna cotta cool down to room temperature. Once cooled, cover the ramekins with plastic wrap (without touching the panna cotta).

Refrigerate:

- Place the panna cotta in the refrigerator to set. It will need at least 4 hours, but it's best to leave it overnight. The agar-agar will help the panna cotta to firm up during this time.

Serve:

- Once set, the panna cotta should be firm but still have a slight jiggle. You can serve it in the ramekin or un-mold it onto a plate.

- To un-mold, run a thin knife around the edge of the ramekin. Briefly dip the ramekin base in hot water to loosen the panna cotta. Invert it onto a plate, giving it a gentle shake if necessary.

- Serve with your choice of toppings, such as fresh berries, fruit puree, or a drizzle of vegan caramel sauce.

This vegan panna cotta is not only a delicious dessert but also a testament to the versatility of vegan cooking, proving that with the right ingredients, you can recreate classic textures and flavors without animal products.

Farinata

A thick pancake or crepe made from chickpea flour, water, olive oil, and salt. It's baked in the oven, traditionally in a large, round copper pan.

Naturally vegan and gluten-free, farinata can be enjoyed plain or with added toppings like rosemary or vegetables.

As veganism becomes more popular worldwide, many restaurants in Piedmont now offer vegan options, and specialty vegan restaurants are also opening up.

Whether by adapting traditional recipes, utilizing the rich array of local produce, or creating innovative new dishes, Piedmont's food scene caters to a diverse range of dietary preferences while maintaining its deep-rooted culinary heritage.

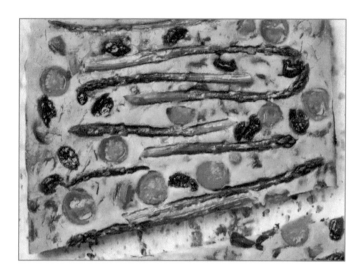

Ingredients:

- 1 cup chickpea flour (also known as gram flour or besan)
- 2 cups water
- 1 1/2 teaspoons sea salt (or to taste)
- 1/4 cup extra-virgin olive oil (plus more for drizzling)
- Black pepper (to taste)
- Optional: Rosemary (fresh or dried), thinly sliced onions, or other herbs/spices of your choice

Instructions:

Prepare the Batter:

- In a bowl, whisk together the chickpea flour and salt. Gradually add the water while whisking to create a smooth, lump-free batter.

- Stir in the 1/4 cup of olive oil. This step is essential for the farinata's characteristic texture.

- Cover the bowl with a cloth and let the batter rest at room temperature for at least 2 hours. However, some recipes recommend resting for up to 12 hours for a fermented taste.

Preheat the Oven and Pan:

- Position a rack in the upper third of your oven and preheat it to 450 degrees Fahrenheit (230 degrees Celsius). If you have a pizza stone, put it in the oven now; otherwise, a large cast-iron skillet or a baking sheet will work.

- Once the oven is hot, place the skillet or baking sheet to preheat for 5 minutes. You want it piping hot before adding the batter.

Bake the Farinata:

- Carefully remove the hot skillet or baking sheet from the oven. Add a couple of tablespoons of olive oil, ensuring it covers the entire surface.

- Pour the batter into the skillet or onto the baking sheet to a thickness of about 1/4 inch. If using, sprinkle your additional toppings (rosemary, black pepper, onions) over the top.

- Place it in the oven and bake for 10 to 15 minutes, or until the edges are crispy and golden and the center is firm and no longer jiggly.

- Once done, remove the farinata from the oven and let it cool for a few minutes before slicing it into wedges or squares.
- Drizzle with a little more extra-virgin olive oil and add a sprinkle of sea salt or any finishing herbs or spices as you like.
- Serve warm or at room temperature as a snack, appetizer, or side dish.

Farinata is delicious and satisfying, offering a unique flavor thanks to the chickpea flour. It's perfect for sharing and pairs wonderfully with fresh salads, soups, or any assortment of antipasti. Enjoy this piece of Italian culinary tradition right from your kitchen!

Lombardy

Lombardy, the region of my birthplace, Milan, boasts a rich culinary heritage shaped by its varied terrains, from majestic mountains to fertile plains. Though local gastronomy is characterized by the prominent use of meat and dairy, numerous traditional Lombard recipes can be creatively reimagined to fit a vegan lifestyle.

Here are some vegan-friendly interpretations of Lombard cuisine:

Risotto alla Milanese

One of the most famous dishes from my hometown, Milan, the capital of Lombardy, is Risotto alla Milanese, known for its creamy texture and signature golden color from saffron.

You can buy saffron online. Since adding saffron to the rice only requires a minuscule amount, a small can will last you a lifetime.

A vegan version can easily be made by substituting a few ingredients without compromising the authentic taste. Use high-quality Arborio rice, vegetable broth, vegan butter or olive oil, and a good pinch of saffron.

Nutritional yeast or vegan parmesan can be added at the end for a cheesy flavor. My personal recipe includes porcini mushrooms.

Ingredients:

- 1 1/2 cups Arborio rice (or another risotto rice such as Carnaroli or Vialone Nano)
- 1 small onion, finely chopped
- 2 cloves garlic, minced (optional)
- 1 cup porcini mushrooms chopped (optional)
- 5 cups vegetable stock (you might not use all of it)
- 1 cup dry white wine (vegan-friendly)
- A pinch of saffron threads (about 1/4 to 1/2 teaspoon)
- 3 tablespoons olive oil or vegan butter
- Salt, to taste
- Black pepper, to taste
- Nutritional yeast or vegan Parmesan cheese for that cheesy flavor (optional)
- Fresh parsley, chopped (for garnish, optional)

Instructions:

Prepare the Saffron:

- Warm a little bit of the vegetable stock in a pan or microwave. Add the saffron threads to the warm stock to release the color and flavor. Set aside.

Cook the Onions:

- In a large, heavy-bottomed saucepan or a deep skillet, heat the olive oil or vegan butter over medium heat.

- Add the chopped onion (garlic and porcini mushrooms, if using), cooking until they are translucent and tender, which should take about 3-4 minutes.

Toast the Rice:

- Add the Arborio rice to the pan with the onions. Stir for about 1-2 minutes until the rice is well-coated and slightly toasted (it will become translucent around the edges).

Deglaze with Wine:

- Pour in the white wine, stirring constantly until the rice has absorbed most of the wine.

Add the Stock:

- Reduce the heat to a simmer. Start adding the warm vegetable stock one ladle at a time, allowing the rice to absorb the liquid slowly. Stir often to prevent sticking.

- After the first few ladles of stock have been absorbed, stir in the saffron-infused stock. Continue adding the remaining stock, one ladle at a time, letting the liquid absorb before adding more. This process should take about 18-20 minutes. The rice should be tender but still have a slight bite to it (al dente).

Season and Serve:

- When the risotto is cooked to your liking, season with salt and pepper. If you're using nutritional yeast or vegan parmesan, stir it in now.

- Remove from heat, cover, and let it sit for a few minutes. This resting period helps to achieve the perfect creamy consistency.

- Garnish with chopped parsley if desired and serve your vegan Risotto alla Milanese warm.

Creating a vegan version of this classic dish still captures the essence and depth of flavor that Risotto alla Milanese is known for. It makes for a comforting meal and serves well with vegan scallops or a fresh salad. Enjoy your compassionate culinary adventure!

Ossobuco

Traditional Ossobuco, a hallmark of Milanese cuisine, is a braised veal shank, but a plant-based version can mimic the heartiness of this dish without meat.

Thick slices of king oyster mushrooms, seitan or soy-based meat can be seared and then slow-cooked with vegetables, white wine, and vegetable broth, served with gremolata made from lemon zest, garlic, and parsley.

Ingredients:

- 4 large king oyster or portobello mushrooms (stems removed) or 1 to 1.5 pounds of seitan (in thick slices or chunks)
- 2 tablespoons extra-virgin olive oil
- 1 large onion, finely chopped
- 2 carrots, peeled and finely chopped
- 2 celery stalks, finely chopped
- 3 cloves garlic, minced
- 1 teaspoon fresh thyme leaves (or 1/2 teaspoon dried thyme)
- 1 teaspoon fresh rosemary, finely chopped (or 1/2 teaspoon dried rosemary)
- 1 cup dry white wine (vegan-friendly)
- 3 cups vegetable broth
- 1 tablespoon tomato paste
- 2 bay leaves
- Salt and pepper, to taste
- All-purpose flour for dusting (optional, especially if using seitan)
- Fresh parsley, chopped (for garnish)
- Zest of 1 lemon (for garnish, optional)

Instructions:

Prepare the "Shanks":

- If using mushrooms, clean them with a damp cloth. If using seitan, pat the chunks dry with a paper towel. Optionally, lightly dust the seitan with flour.

- Heat 1 tablespoon extra-virgin olive oil in a large skillet over medium-high heat. Add the mushrooms or seitan and sear until they are golden brown on both sides. Remove from the skillet and set aside.

Sauté the Vegetables:

- In the same skillet, add another tablespoon of extra-virgin olive oil. Add the onions, carrots, celery, and sauté until the onions become translucent and the vegetables soften.
- Add the garlic, thyme, and rosemary, and cook for another minute until fragrant.

Deglaze the Pan:

- Pour in the white wine, stirring well to lift any browned bits off the bottom of the skillet. Let it simmer for a few minutes to reduce slightly.

Build the Sauce:

- Stir in the tomato paste and cook for another minute to blend the flavors.
- Return the mushrooms or seitan to the skillet, adding the vegetable broth and bay leaves. Ensure that the "shanks" are mostly submerged in the liquid.
- Bring the mixture to a boil, then reduce the heat to low, covering the skillet with a lid. Let it simmer for about 30-40 minutes, allowing the flavors to meld and the sauce to thicken. If using mushrooms, check them periodically to ensure they are not becoming too soft.

Final Seasoning:

- Taste the sauce and adjust the seasoning with salt and pepper as needed. Remove the bay leaves and discard them.

- Plate the vegan "Ossobuco" with a generous amount of sauce. Garnish with chopped parsley and, if desired, a sprinkling of lemon zest for an added layer of flavor.

- Traditional Ossobuco is often served with risotto alla Milanese or creamy polenta, making either option an excellent side for this dish.

This vegan take on Ossobuco stays true to the comforting, complex nature of the Lombardian culinary heritage while embracing a plant-based ethos. It's perfect for a cozy night or a dinner party with friends.

Pizzoccheri

Pizzoccheri is a traditional dish from the Valtellina valley in Lombardy.

Bordering Switzerland, the valley is known for its stunning mountainous scenery, historical significance, and rich cultural heritage, particularly in food and wine production. Pizzoccheri is a type of short tagliatelle or ribbon pasta made from buckwheat flour, traditionally cooked with potatoes, Swiss chard, or cabbage and layered with pieces of cheese. However, we can make a delightful vegan version by substituting a few ingredients. Here's how you can prepare vegan Pizzoccheri:

Ingredients:

For the Pasta:

- 300g (around 2 1/3 cups) buckwheat flour
- 100g (around 3/4 cup) white flour (optional, can be replaced with buckwheat flour for gluten-free option)
- Approx. 3/4 cup water (as needed for the dough)

For the Dish:

- 2 medium-sized potatoes, peeled and cut into small cubes
- 1 large head Swiss chard or Savoy cabbage, trimmed and cut into strips
- 2 cloves garlic, minced
- 1/2 cup vegan butter (you can reduce this amount for a lighter version)
- 200g (7 oz.) vegan cheese (choose one that melts well, like a vegan Fontina or vegan mozzarella)

- Salt, to taste
- Black pepper, to taste
- Optional: nutritional yeast or vegan Parmesan cheese for sprinkling

Instructions:

Prepare the Pasta Dough:

- Mix the buckwheat flour with the white flour in a bowl, add a pinch of salt, then slowly add water, mixing continuously until you have a firm dough.
- Knead the dough on a lightly floured surface until smooth.
- Roll out the dough until it's about 3 mm thick, then cut it into strips approximately 7 cm long and 1 cm wide.

Cook the Vegetables and Pasta:

- Bring a large pot of salted water to boil. Add the potatoes and cook for about 4 minutes.
- Add the Swiss chard or cabbage to the pot. Let these vegetables cook until they start to become tender (approximately 3 minutes).
- Add the pizzoccheri pasta to the pot and cook everything for an additional 7-8 minutes or until the pasta is cooked through.

Prepare the Vegan "Butter" Sauce:

- While the pasta cooks, melt the vegan butter in a small pan over medium heat.
- Add the minced garlic to the melted butter, cook for a couple of minutes, then remove from the heat.

Layer the Dish:

- Drain the pasta and vegetables, reserving a little of the cooking water.

- In a large serving dish, create layers with the pizzoccheri and vegetables, vegan cheese, and a drizzle of the garlic "butter" sauce. If the dish seems a little dry, add some reserved cooking water. Continue until all your ingredients are used up, finishing with a layer of vegan cheese and some sauce on top.

Final Cooking Step:

- Cover the serving dish with a lid or aluminum foil and bake in a preheated oven at 375°F (190°C) for about 10-15 minutes, or until the cheese has melted and the dish is hot and bubbly.

Serve:

- Season with more salt and black pepper to taste. Optionally, you can sprinkle nutritional yeast or vegan parmesan on top for an extra cheesy flavor.
- Serve hot, divided into plates or bowls.

This hearty, comforting dish is perfect for cold weather. It stays true to the flavors of the Lombardy region while being completely vegan. Enjoy your meal (or, as they say in Italian, "Buon appetito!")!

Focaccia Lombarda

Unlike the typical focaccia, the Lombard version is sweet and usually filled with raisins or topped with granulated sugar and anise seeds.

A vegan version replaces regular butter with plant-based butter and uses plant milk instead of cow's milk.

Ingredients:

- 500 grams (approximately 4 cups) all-purpose flour
- 240 ml (1 cup) soy milk or almond milk, lukewarm
- 100 grams (1/2 cup) granulated sugar
- 80 grams (approximately 1/3 cup) unsalted vegan butter, room temperature
- 1 packet (7 grams or 1 1/2 teaspoons) instant yeast or active dry yeast
- 1/4 teaspoon salt
- Zest of 1 unwaxed lemon

- 80 grams (approximately 1/2 cup) raisins (optional)
- Soy milk or almond milk for brushing
- Coarse sugar for sprinkling (optional)

Instructions:

Activate the Yeast:

- If you're using active dry yeast, mix it with the lukewarm plant-based milk and a teaspoon of sugar.

- Let it sit for about 10 minutes until it becomes frothy.

- If you're using instant yeast, you can add it directly to your flour.

Prepare the Dough:

- In a large mixing bowl, combine the flour, the remaining sugar, and salt.

- Add the lemon zest and raisins (if using) and mix well.

- Add the vegan butter into the flour mixture, combining well until you have a crumbly texture.

Form the Dough:

- Pour in the activated yeast mixture or instant yeast.

- Knead the dough until it's smooth and elastic, about 10 minutes by hand or 5 minutes with a stand mixer fitted with a dough hook.

- If the dough is too dry, add a bit more plant-based milk; if it's too wet, add a little more flour.

First Proofing:

- Place the dough in a greased bowl, cover it with a clean kitchen towel, and let it rise in a warm, draft-free area for about 1.5 to 2 hours or until it has doubled in size.

Shape the Focaccia:

- Once risen, punch the dough down to release air bubbles.
- Transfer it to a lined or lightly greased baking sheet, spreading it to form a rectangle or circle about 1/2 inch thick.
- Cover it with a kitchen towel and let it rise again for an additional hour.

Preheat the Oven:

- About 20 minutes before the second rise is complete, begin preheating your oven to 350°F (175°C).

Bake the Focaccia:

- Before baking, gently brush the surface of the dough with some soy or almond milk for a golden color.
- Sprinkle the coarse sugar on top if desired. Bake for 25-30 minutes, or until the focaccia is golden brown and a toothpick inserted in the center comes out clean.

Cool and Serve:

- Remove the focaccia from the oven and let it cool on a wire rack before slicing and serving.

Enjoy your vegan Focaccia Lombarda, a treat that pairs beautifully with a cup of coffee or tea! This sweet bread is perfect for breakfast or as a snack during your day.

Liguria

Liguria, the coastal region known for its stunning shores and the famous Italian Riviera, boasts a cuisine rich in vegetables, fresh herbs, and the sea's bounty. Traditional Ligurian cuisine emphasizes simple ingredients that highlight the flavors of the Mediterranean palate. Here are some traditional dishes from Liguria that are vegan or can be easily adapted for a vegan diet:

Focaccia di Recco

In creating a vegan version, we will substitute the traditional cheese with a plant-based alternative. Here's how you can prepare it:

Ingredients:

For the Dough:

- 500 grams (approximately 4 cups) all-purpose flour
- 60 ml (1/4 cup) extra-virgin olive oil, plus more for drizzling
- 240 ml (1 cup) water, more if needed
- 1 teaspoon salt

For the Filling:

- 400 grams (14 oz) vegan cream cheese (ensure a softer variety for spreading, or use a homemade blend of soaked cashews, lemon juice, water, and salt blended until creamy)

Extra:

- Salt for sprinkling
- Additional olive oil for brushing

Instructions:

Prepare the Dough:

- In a large mixing bowl, combine the all-purpose flour with the salt.
- Add the olive oil and gradually add water, kneading continuously until smooth and elastic.
- Cover the bowl with a damp cloth and rest for about 30 minutes.

Divide the Dough:

- Turn the dough out onto a lightly floured surface.

- Divide it into two equal parts.

Preheat the Oven and Prepare the Baking Sheet:

- Preheat your oven to the highest setting, typically between 450-500°F (230-260°C).
- Prepare a baking sheet by lightly oiling it or lining it with parchment paper.

Roll Out the Dough:

- Roll out one portion of your dough as thinly as possible, aiming for a nearly transparent sheet.
- Lay the thin dough on the prepared baking sheet or pizza stone.

Add the Vegan Cheese:

- Spread the vegan cream cheese evenly over the surface of the dough on the baking sheet.

Top with the Second Layer:

- Roll out the second portion of dough to a very thin layer.
- Place it over the first layer with the vegan cheese, pressing the edges together to seal.

Bake the Focaccia:

- Brush the top layer lightly with olive oil and sprinkle with some salt.
- Bake for 12-15 minutes, until the crust is golden brown and crispy.

Serve:

- Allow the focaccia to cool slightly before cutting and serving. Enjoy it while it's warm.

This vegan Focaccia di Recco is a delightful, cruelty-free way to enjoy a classic Italian dish. The key to success is rolling the dough as thin as possible to achieve the traditional texture and appearance.

Pesto Genovese

The most iconic contribution of Liguria to the culinary world is Pesto Genovese A specially beloved pasta sauce.

The traditional recipe includes basil, garlic, pine nuts, extra-virgin olive oil, Parmesan cheese, and Pecorino cheese. A vegan version can be made by substituting the cheeses with nutritional yeast or a vegan Parmesan alternative to maintain the sauce's creamy, savory quality without compromising flavor.

Ingredients:

- 2 cups fresh basil leaves (preferably young, tender leaves)
- 1/2 cup pine nuts (you can toast them lightly for a deeper flavor)
- 2-3 garlic cloves, adjusted according to your preference
- 1/2 cup extra-virgin olive oil, plus extra for consistency if needed
- Salt, to taste
- 3 tablespoons nutritional yeast (as a cheese substitute, provides a cheesy flavor)
- Optional: 1-2 tablespoons fresh lemon juice (to brighten the flavor and help keep the color vibrant)

Instructions:

1. Prepare the Ingredients:

- Suppose you've opted to toast the pine nuts. Do this first: place them in a dry skillet over medium heat, stirring frequently until golden and fragrant. Be careful not to burn them.
- Remove from heat and let cool.

2. Blend the Base:

- In a food processor or high-powered blender, combine the fresh basil leaves, cooled pine nuts, and garlic cloves.
- Process or blend them until they form a coarse paste.

3. Add the Oil:

- While your processor or blender is running, slowly drizzle in the olive oil.

- This slow incorporation helps to emulsify the oil and ingredients, creating a smoother, unified sauce.
- You may stop and scrape down the sides, as necessary.

4. Season the Pesto:

- Once your pesto has reached your desired consistency, transfer it to a bowl.
- Stir in the nutritional yeast and add salt to taste.
- If you're using lemon juice, add it at this stage.

5. Adjust Consistency and Flavor:

- If your pesto seems too thick, add a bit more olive oil or even a splash of water to thin it out.
- Taste and adjust the seasoning as needed, adding more salt or nutritional yeast if desired.

6. Store or Serve:

- Your vegan Pesto Genovese is now ready to be used immediately, or it can be stored.
- To store, place it in an airtight container, cover the surface with a thin layer of olive oil (to prevent oxidation), and it will keep fresh in the refrigerator for up to a week.
- You can also freeze pesto in ice cube trays for longer storage and defrost as needed.

Enjoy your vegan Pesto Genovese with pasta spread over crusty bread, layered in sandwiches, or however you prefer. This versatile sauce can brighten up any number of vegan dishes with its fresh, herbaceous flavor.

Panzarotti

Panzarotti often confused with calzones, are deep-fried pockets of dough traditionally filled with various ingredients. Variations of this wonderful dish exist all over Italy but is prominent in Liguria.

The traditional filling often includes cheese or meat, but a vegan version can be just as delicious. Below is a recipe for vegan panzarotti.

Ingredients

For the Dough:

- 500g (approximately 4 cups) all-purpose flour, more for dusting
- 1 packet (7g or 1.5 tsp) instant yeast
- 1 tsp sugar
- 1 tsp salt
- 2 tbsp olive oil

- 240ml (1 cup) warm water (you may need slightly more or less)

For the Filling:

- 1 tbsp olive oil
- 1 small onion, finely chopped
- 2 cloves garlic, minced
- 1 cup (150g) mushrooms, chopped (optional)
- 1 cup spinach or other leafy greens, chopped
- Salt and pepper, to taste
- A pinch of chili flakes (optional)
- 1/2 cup vegan cheese, shredded (optional)
- 1/2 cup tomato sauce (homemade or store-bought)
- 1 tsp dried oregano or basil

Instructions:

Prepare the Dough:

- In a large mixing bowl, combine the flour, instant yeast, sugar, and salt.

- Add the olive oil and gradually add warm water, kneading until the dough comes together. You may need slightly more or less water depending on the absorption of the flour.

- Transfer the dough to a lightly floured surface and knead for about 10 minutes or until smooth and elastic. (Add flour if necessary to firm up the dough.)

- Place the dough back in the bowl, cover it with a clean towel, and let it rise in a warm place for about 1-2 hours, or until it has doubled in size.

Prepare the Filling:

- While the dough is rising, heat olive oil in a pan over medium heat. Add onion and garlic, sautéing until soft and translucent.

- Add the mushrooms (if using) and cook until most of the water has evaporated and they begin to brown.

- Add the spinach and cook until just wilted. Season with salt, pepper, and chili flakes (if using). Remove from heat and let the mixture cool.

Assemble the Panzarotti:

- Once the dough has risen, punch it down gently to release air bubbles. Transfer it to a lightly floured surface.

- Divide the dough into golf-ball-sized portions. Roll each portion into a ball, then use a rolling pin to roll out each ball into a thin circle about 5-6 inches in diameter.

- On one half of each circle, spread a thin layer of tomato sauce, leaving a border around the edges. Sprinkle some dried oregano or basil over the sauce.

- Add a spoonful of the spinach-mushroom mixture (and vegan cheese, if using) on top of the sauce.

- Fold the dough over the filling to create a half-moon shape. Press the edges together and then use a fork to crimp the edges, ensuring they are well sealed.

Fry the Panzarotti:

- Heat a deep pan with enough oil for deep frying, bringing it to around 350°F (175°C).

- Carefully place a few panzarotti into the hot oil, avoiding overcrowding. Fry them until golden brown and crispy, about 3-5 minutes, turning them as needed for even browning.

- Once cooked, remove the panzarotti with a slotted spoon and drain them on paper towels to remove excess oil.

Serve:

- Serve your vegan panzarotti hot, with some extra tomato sauce on the side for dipping, if desired.

Enjoy your Ligurian-inspired vegan panzarotti as a snack, appetizer, or main dish!

Ratatouille Ligurian Style (Capon Magro)

Capon Magro is a traditional Ligurian dish, but it's important to note that it's distinct from Ratatouille, which is French. Capon Magro is a layered salad made primarily from vegetable bread and often includes seafood. However, we will exclude that for a vegan version. Here's how you can prepare a vegan Capon

Magro, maintaining the dish's essence while ensuring it's entirely plant-based.

Ingredients:

For the Vegetable Stock:

- 1 onion
- 2 carrots
- 2 celery sticks
- A handful of parsley stems
- Salt, to taste
- 10 cups water

For the Capon Magro:

- 3 cups mixed vegetables (green beans, cauliflower, asparagus, and beets)
- 4 medium potatoes, peeled
- 2 carrots, peeled
- 2 hard bread rolls or slices of stale country bread
- 1 small head of green lettuce (or lettuce of your choice)
- 2 tablespoons capers
- Green olives, as desired
- 1/4 cup chopped fresh parsley
- Extra-virgin olive oil for drizzling

For the Vegan Green Sauce (Salsa Verde):

- 1 cup fresh parsley, tightly packed
- 2 cloves garlic
- 2 tablespoons capers
- 1/2 cup extra-virgin olive oil
- 1 tablespoon white wine vinegar
- Salt, to taste

Instructions:

Prepare the Vegetable Stock:

- Chop the vegetables for the stock.
- In a large pot, combine all the stock ingredients and bring to a boil. Lower the heat and simmer for about 30 minutes.
- Strain the stock, reserve the liquid, and discard the solids.

Prepare the Vegetables:

- Cut the vegetables and potatoes into bite-sized pieces.
- Bring the vegetable stock to a boil and cook each type of vegetable separately in the stock until tender. Use a slotted spoon to remove the vegetables and set aside.

Prepare the Bread:

- Soak the bread in some vegetable stock until moist throughout but not falling apart.
- Press the bread between your hands to remove excess stock.

Assemble the Capon Magro:

- On a large serving dish, create a base layer using the soaked bread.
- Lay the lettuce leaves over the bread, then begin layering the cooked vegetables, potatoes, and carrots. Between layers, sprinkle some capers, olives, and chopped parsley. Continue until all your ingredients are used up, forming a dome or pyramid shape.

Prepare the Vegan Green Sauce:

- Combine parsley, garlic, capers, olive oil, vinegar, and salt in a food processor or blender. Blend until smooth, adjusting seasoning as needed.

- Drizzle the Capon Magro with a generous amount of olive oil.

- Serve the Capon Magro with the vegan green sauce on the side. Guests can spoon the green sauce over their portions as desired.

This dish is traditionally served chilled, so refrigerate it for a few hours before serving. It's a beautiful, healthy, refreshing dish, perfect for warm weather and gathering events. Enjoy your vegan take on this classic Ligurian specialty!

Torta di Verdure

This vegetable tart is made with various seasonal greens, like chard, zucchini, and artichokes, bound with a batter and baked. A vegan version can substitute any dairy in the batter with plant-based milk and use chickpea flour as a binding agent.

Ingredients:

For the Crust:

- 2 1/2 cups all-purpose flour
- 1/2 cup extra virgin olive oil
- 1/2 cup cold water
- 1/2 teaspoon salt

For the Filling:

- 3 tablespoons olive oil
- 1 large onion, thinly sliced
- 2 cloves of garlic, minced
- 1 small zucchini, sliced into thin rounds
- 1 small eggplant, diced
- 1 bell pepper (any color), thinly sliced
- 2 medium ripe tomatoes, chopped
- 1 cup of canned artichokes
- 1 cup of fresh spinach or Swiss chard, chopped
- A handful of fresh basil leaves, chopped
- Salt and black pepper, to taste
- Optional: 2 tablespoons nutritional yeast (for a cheesy flavor)

For Brushing:

- 2-3 tablespoons soy milk or any other plant milk

Instructions:

Prepare the Crust:

- In a mixing bowl, combine the flour and salt. Add the olive oil and mix with a fork or pastry blender until the mixture resembles coarse crumbs.

- Gradually add cold water, stirring until it starts to come together. If needed, add a bit more water until the dough is cohesive but not sticky.

- Form the dough into a ball, wrap it in plastic food wrap, and chill in the refrigerator for at least 30 minutes.

Prepare the Filling:

- Heat the olive oil in a large skillet over medium heat. Add the onion and garlic, sautéing until soft and translucent.

- Add the zucchini, eggplant, artichokes, and bell pepper to the skillet. Cook for 5-7 minutes or until the vegetables start to soften.

- Add the chopped tomatoes and cook for another 5 minutes, allowing the tomatoes to break down.

- Stir in the spinach or Swiss chard and cook until wilted.

- Remove from heat and stir in the fresh basil. Season with salt and black pepper to taste. Let the mixture cool. Stir in nutritional yeast if desired for a cheesy flavor.

Assemble the Torta:

- Preheat the oven to 375°F (190°C).

- Divide your dough into two parts: one for the base and one for the top.

- On a lightly floured surface, roll out the larger piece of dough to fit the bottom and sides of a 9-inch pie or tart pan.

- Transfer the rolled-out dough to the pan, pressing it into the bottom and sides. Trim any excess dough.
- Spoon the vegetable filling into the crust, spreading it out evenly.
- Roll out the second piece of dough and place it over the filling. Trim, seal, and crimp the edges. Make a few small slits in the top to vent steam.
- Brush the top of the pie with soy milk for a golden finish.

Bake:

- Bake in the oven for 30-40 minutes or until the crust is golden brown and the filling is bubbly.
- Allow to cool for a few minutes before slicing and serving.

Enjoy your vegan Torta di Verdure, a dish served warm or at room temperature, making it ideal for any season or occasion!

Emilia-Romagna

Emilia Romagna, often described as the food capital of Italy, is renowned for its decadent cuisine and rich flavors, traditionally characterized by dairy products, cured meats, and exquisite pasta. However, the region's bountiful produce and culinary creativity provide ample opportunities for vegan adaptations. Below are some vegan-friendly dishes from Emilia-Romagna:

Piadina Romagnola

Piadina Romagnola is a thin Italian flatbread that's traditionally made with lard or olive oil and often served filled with various ingredients such as cold cuts, cheese, and vegetables. Originating from the Emilia-Romagna region, this flatbread can be easily made vegan by substituting a few ingredients. Here's how you can make your own vegan Piadina Romagnola.

Ingredients:
- 3 cups all-purpose flour
- 1/2 teaspoon baking soda
- 3/4 teaspoon salt

- 3 tablespoons olive oil (or vegan margarine if you want to mimic the traditional lard used)
- 3/4 cup water (more if needed)

For serving: (Optional filling ideas)

- Vegan cheese
- Sautéed vegetables (spinach, bell peppers, mushrooms)
- Vegan deli slices
- Arugula or mixed greens
- Tomato slices

Instructions:

Make the Dough:

- In a large mixing bowl, whisk together the flour, baking soda, and salt.

- Add the olive oil (or vegan margarine) and rub it into the flour mixture with your fingers until it resembles coarse crumbs.

- Gradually add water, mixing until the dough begins to come together. You may need more or less water depending on the humidity and your flour type. The dough should be soft but not sticky.

- Turn the dough out onto a lightly floured surface and knead it for a few minutes until it's smooth.

- Divide the dough into 4-6 equal portions, roll them into balls, and cover them with a clean kitchen towel. Let them rest for at least 30 minutes.

Roll and Cook the Piadina:

- After the resting period, heat a cast-iron skillet or a non-stick pan over medium heat.

- On a lightly floured surface, roll each dough ball into a very thin circle, about 8-10 inches in diameter, similar to a tortilla.

- Place one rolled-out dough circle into the hot skillet and cook for 1-2 minutes on each side. It should puff up in places and get nice brown spots. Don't overcook, as they should remain soft and pliable.

- Remove from the skillet and place it on a plate, covering it with a kitchen towel to keep warm. Repeat the process with the remaining dough circles.

Assemble the Piadina:

- Once all your piadinas are cooked, you can start to assemble them with your favorite fillings. Place the fillings on half of each piadina, then fold the other half over the top, similar to a half-moon shape.

- Serve while they are still warm.

Enjoy your vegan Piadina Romagnola, a versatile flatbread perfect for lunches, dinners, or even a quick snack. They're delicious and served with a side of marinara for dipping as well!

Pasta e Fagioli

This "pasta and beans" dish is a hearty and rustic choice. While it sometimes includes meat-based broth or pancetta, a vegan version can use vegetable stock and omit the meat, relying on herbs and garlic for flavoring.

The result is a rich, comforting stew.

Ingredients:

- 2 tablespoons olive oil
- 1 medium onion, finely chopped
- 2 medium carrots, diced
- 2 celery stalks, diced
- 3 garlic cloves, minced
- 1 teaspoon fresh rosemary, minced (or 1/2 teaspoon dried)
- 1 teaspoon fresh thyme leaves (or 1/2 teaspoon dried)
- 1 (14.5-ounce) can diced tomatoes
- 4 cups vegetable broth
- 2 (15-ounce) cans of cannellini beans, drained and rinsed

- 1 cup small pasta (like ditalini, small shells, or elbow macaroni)
- Salt and pepper, to taste
- Optional: red pepper flakes, to taste
- Optional: 2 tablespoons fresh basil or parsley, chopped
- Optional: Nutritional yeast or vegan parmesan for serving

Instructions:

Sauté Vegetables:

- In a large pot, heat the olive oil over medium heat.
- Add the onion, carrots, and celery. Cook, stirring occasionally, until the vegetables are softened, about 5-7 minutes.
- Add the minced garlic, rosemary, and thyme. Cook for another minute until fragrant, ensuring not to burn the garlic.

Prepare the Soup Base:

- Stir in the diced tomatoes, including their juices. Cook for a few minutes to combine the flavors.
- Add the vegetable broth and cannellini beans. Increase the heat to bring the mixture to a boil. Once boiling, reduce the heat to a simmer.

Cook the Pasta:

- Add the pasta to the pot. Stir well to ensure the pasta is submerged in the liquid.
- Cook for 10-15 minutes or until the pasta is tender, stirring occasionally to prevent sticking. The beans will break down slightly during this cooking process, which will help thicken the soup. If the soup becomes too thick, you can add a bit more broth or water to reach your desired consistency.

- Season with salt, pepper, and red pepper flakes (if using), adjusting to your preference.

Final Adjustments:

- Once the pasta is cooked to your liking and the soup is heated through, turn off the heat. If you're using fresh basil or parsley, stir them so they wilt into the hot soup.
- Let the soup stand for a few minutes to cool slightly. The flavors will continue to meld and develop as the soup rests.

Serve:

- Ladle the soup into bowls. If desired, sprinkle nutritional yeast or vegan parmesan on top for a cheesy flavor.
- Serve with a side of crusty bread for dipping, if desired.

This vegan Pasta e Fagioli is a comforting, wholesome meal that captures the heartiness of Italian home cooking while being completely plant-based. Enjoy the robust flavors from the simple ingredients characteristic of Emilia Romagna's cuisine.

Stuffed Tomatoes (Pomodori Ripieni)

Stuffed tomatoes, known as "Pomodori Ripieni," are a versatile dish found throughout Italy, with regional variations in the filling. In Emilia Romagna, the cuisine often features a range of deeply flavored and rich ingredients.

Here's a vegan take on the Pomodori Ripieni inspired by the traditional flavors of the Emilia Romagna region.

Ingredients:

- 6 large ripe tomatoes
- Salt and pepper, to taste
- 1 cup cooked rice (like Arborio)
- 2 tablespoons olive oil, plus more for drizzling
- 1 small onion, finely chopped
- 2 garlic cloves, minced

- 1/2 cup finely chopped mushrooms (preferably porcini, if available)
- 1/4 cup finely chopped fresh parsley
- 1 tablespoon fresh thyme leaves
- 1/4 cup nutritional yeast or vegan parmesan
- Optional: 1/4 cup chopped walnuts or pine nuts for added texture
- Optional: balsamic vinegar for a drizzle

Instructions:

Prepare the Tomatoes:

- Preheat your oven to 375°F (190°C).
- Cut the tops off the tomatoes and scoop out the seeds and core, creating a space for the filling. Sprinkle the insides with a little salt and place them upside down on kitchen paper to drain the excess water.

Make the Filling:

- Heat the olive oil in a skillet over medium heat. Add the onion and garlic, sautéing until they are soft and translucent.
- Add the mushrooms to the skillet, cooking until they are soft.
- Remove from the heat and stir in the cooked rice, parsley, thyme, and nutritional yeast (or vegan parmesan). Mix until well combined and season with salt and pepper to taste. If you're using nuts, add them to the mixture now.

Stuff the Tomatoes:

- Fill the tomato shells with the rice and mushroom mixture, pressing down gently to pack the filling without overstuffing.

- Place the stuffed tomatoes in a lightly greased baking dish. Drizzle with a bit more olive oil on top.

Bake:

- Bake in the preheated oven for 25-30 minutes or until the tomatoes are tender and the top of the filling has formed a slight crust.

- Suppose you want a deeper color on top. In that case, you can place the tomatoes under the broiler for a few minutes but watch them carefully to prevent burning.

Serve:

- Let the tomatoes cool for a few minutes before serving, as the insides will be hot.

- If desired, drizzle with a little balsamic vinegar for an extra layer of flavor.

This dish embodies the heartiness and depth of flavors cherished in Emilia Romagna cuisine, all the while keeping it plant-based. It's perfect as a main course served with a side salad or as part of a larger spread.

Tagliatelle al Ragù

Tagliatelle al Ragù is a quintessential dish from Emilia-Romagna, with the classic version featuring a meat-based sauce. However, it's entirely possible to capture the rich and hearty essence of this regional favorite in a vegan rendition.

Here's how you can prepare Vegan Tagliatelle al Ragù, utilizing plant-based ingredients to mimic the texture and depth of traditional ragù.

Ingredients:

- 400g (14 oz) fresh or dried tagliatelle
- 2 tablespoons olive oil
- 1 large onion, finely chopped
- 2 carrots, finely chopped
- 2 celery stalks, finely chopped
- 4 garlic cloves, minced
- 300g (10.5 oz) textured vegetable protein (TVP) or vegan mince
- 2 tablespoons tomato paste

- 800g (28 oz) canned crushed tomatoes
- 1/2 cup red wine (optional; ensure it's vegan)
- 1 cup vegetable broth
- 1 teaspoon dried oregano
- 1 teaspoon dried basil
- Salt and pepper, to taste
- A pinch of sugar (optional to balance acidity)
- Fresh basil or parsley, chopped (for garnish)
- Vegan Parmesan cheese (optional for serving)

Instructions:

Prepare the 'Meat':

- If you're using TVP, rehydrate it according to the package instructions. If you're using vegan mince, ensure it's thawed.

Cook the Base Vegetables:

- In a large skillet or pot, heat olive oil over medium heat. Add the onions, carrots, celery, and garlic. Sauté until the onions become translucent and the vegetables soften about 5-7 minutes.

Add the 'Meat':

- Increase the heat to medium-high and add the rehydrated TVP or vegan mince to the skillet. Cook, stirring frequently, until it's nicely browned. This process can help add a depth of flavor to the vegan "meat."

Deglaze with Wine:

- (Optional) Pour the red wine to deglaze the pan, scraping up any bits stuck to the bottom. Allow the wine to simmer for a few minutes until it reduces slightly.

Add the Tomatoes:

- Stir in the tomato paste, cooking for a minute until it darkens. Then, add the crushed tomatoes, vegetable broth, oregano, and basil. If the sauce is very acidic, add a pinch of sugar to balance the flavors. Season with salt and pepper to taste.

Simmer the Ragù:

- Reduce the heat, allowing the sauce to simmer uncovered for about 30 minutes, stirring occasionally. The ragù should thicken, and the flavors will deepen over time. If the sauce becomes too thick, add a bit more vegetable broth.

Cook the Tagliatelle:

- While the sauce simmers, prepare the tagliatelle according to the package instructions until it's 'al dente.' Drain, reserving a bit of pasta water.

Combine Pasta and Ragù:

- Add the cooked tagliatelle directly into the skillet with the ragù, tossing to combine over low heat. If needed, add a little pasta water to help the sauce coat the noodles.

Serve:

- Serve hot, garnished with chopped fresh basil or parsley and a sprinkling of vegan Parmesan cheese if desired.

This vegan version of Tagliatelle al Ragù stays true to the flavors of Emilia Romagna by concentrating on the richness of the sauce, ensuring a satisfying, cruelty-free meal.

Cappelletti

Cappelletti is a traditional stuffed pasta dish from Emilia Romagna, often made with a filling of meats and cheese. However, a vegan version of cappelletti can be just as delicious, using plant-based ingredients for the filling without sacrificing flavor.

Here's how you can prepare vegan cappelletti.

Ingredients

for the Pasta Dough:

- 400g (14 oz) of all-purpose flour (plus more for dusting)
- 200ml (approximately 7 fl oz) of water
- A pinch of salt

- (Optional) A pinch of turmeric for color

For the Filling:

- 1 cup of cooked lentils or vegan mince
- 1/2 cup of sautéed mushrooms, finely chopped
- 1/4 cup of nutritional yeast (for a cheesy flavor)
- 2 tablespoons of fresh parsley, finely chopped
- 1 clove of garlic, minced
- Salt and pepper, to taste
- Olive oil

Instructions:

Make the Pasta Dough:

- On a clean surface, make a well with the flour. Add salt and water (and turmeric if desired for color) in the center and slowly start to incorporate the flour into the liquid using a fork, gradually bringing more flour in from the edges until a dough starts to form.

- Knead the dough for about 10 minutes until it is smooth and elastic. If it's too dry, add a little water; if it's too sticky, add some flour. Wrap the dough in plastic wrap and let it rest for 30 minutes.

Prepare the Filling:

- If using lentils, ensure they are well-cooked and drained.

- For sautéed mushrooms, cook them in olive oil with the minced garlic until they're browned, and all their moisture has evaporated.

- In a mixing bowl, combine the lentils or vegan mince, sautéed mushrooms, nutritional yeast, chopped parsley, and salt and pepper.

- Mix until everything is well combined.

- You can use a food processor to obtain a finer texture if desired.

Roll the Pasta:

- After the dough has rested, divide it into four portions.
- Working with one portion at a time (keeping the others covered to prevent drying out), roll the dough into a thin sheet, about 1mm in thickness.
- You can use a pasta machine or a rolling pin, ensuring you have plenty of flour to prevent sticking.

Form the Cappelletti:

- Cut the rolled dough into 2-inch squares.
- Place a small teaspoon of filling in the center of each square.
- Fold the dough over the filling to form a triangle, pressing out any air and sealing the edges well.
- Bring the two bottom corners of the triangle together in front of the filling, overlapping slightly, and press to seal, creating a little "hat" shape.
- Continue this process until all your dough and filling are used.

Cook the Cappelletti:

- Bring a large pot of salted water to a boil.
- Cook the cappelletti in batches to avoid overcrowding, stirring gently to prevent sticking.
- They will generally need about 3-5 minutes to cook and will rise to the surface when ready.
- Use a slotted spoon to remove the cappelletti and drain them well.

- Serve the cappelletti hot, drizzled with olive oil, or tossed in your favorite vegan sauce.
- They are traditionally served in broth in Italy, so you might enjoy them in a clear vegetable broth garnished with fresh herbs.

This recipe embraces the traditional Italian culinary practice, creating a dish full of flavor that honors the vegan dietary choices.

Rice Cake Bolognese (Torta di Riso)

Torta di Riso is a savory rice cake traditionally made with several non-vegan ingredients. Here's a version that maintains the spirit of the classic Emilia Romagna dish while adhering to vegan standards.

Ingredients:

For the Rice:

- 2 cups Arborio rice
- 4 cups vegetable broth
- Salt, to taste

For the Vegan Bolognese:

- 2 tablespoons olive oil
- 1 small onion, finely chopped
- 2 garlic cloves, minced
- 1 carrot, finely chopped
- 1 celery stalk, finely chopped
- 2 cups vegan mince (like textured vegetable protein or lentils)
- 1 can (400g) crushed tomatoes
- Salt and pepper, to taste
- 1 teaspoon dried basil or Italian seasoning
- 2 tablespoons nutritional yeast (optional for cheesy flavor)

For the Cake:

- 1/2 cup breadcrumbs (ensure they're vegan)
- 2 tablespoons vegan butter or olive oil
- Fresh basil leaves for garnish (optional)

Instructions:

Precook the Rice:

- In a large pot, bring the vegetable broth to a boil. Add the Arborio rice and a pinch of salt.
- Reduce the heat to a low simmer. Cook until the rice is tender but still firm, stirring occasionally, about 20-25 minutes.
- Once done, remove from heat and set aside.

Prepare the Vegan Bolognese:

- Heat olive oil in a large skillet over medium heat.
- Add onion, garlic, carrot, and celery; cook until the vegetables are soft, about 5-7 minutes.
- Add the vegan mince to the skillet and cook for another 5 minutes, stirring frequently.
- If using lentils, ensure they are precooked.
- Stir in the crushed tomatoes, salt, pepper, and dried basil or Italian seasoning.
- Reduce the heat to low and simmer the sauce for 15-20 minutes.
- If the sauce becomes too thick, add a small amount of water.
- Adjust seasoning as needed.
- Turn off the heat and stir in nutritional yeast if desired. Set aside.

Assemble the Cake:

- Preheat your oven to 375°F (190°C).
- Grease a 9-inch springform pan or round baking dish with vegan butter or olive oil and coat the bottom and sides with breadcrumbs.
- In a large bowl, combine the precooked rice and half of the vegan Bolognese sauce, mixing well to ensure the rice is evenly coated.
- Place half the rice mixture into your prepared pan, pressing it down to form an even layer.
- Add the remaining vegan Bolognese on top, spreading to cover the rice.

- Finally, add the remaining rice over the Bolognese layer, pressing down gently.
- Sprinkle the top with breadcrumbs and dot with small pieces of vegan butter, or drizzle with a little olive oil.

Bake:

- Place in the preheated oven and bake for 25-30 minutes or until the top is golden and crispy.
- Remove from the oven and allow to cool for a few minutes. Carefully remove the sides of the springform pan if used.

Serve:

- Garnish with fresh basil leaves if desired.
- Cut the rice cake into wedges and serve warm or at room temperature.

This dish is hearty and flavorful, making it a satisfying main course for everyone, not just those following a vegan diet. It captures the essence of Emilia Romagna cuisine with a compassionate twist.

Borlengo

Borlengo, a traditional thin, crepe-like dish from the Emilia Romagna region, is typically filled with savory ingredients.

Here's how you can make a vegan version of Borlengo that still captures the essence of this regional specialty.

Ingredients:

For the Batter:

- 1 cup all-purpose flour
- 1 1/2 cups water
- A pinch of salt
- Olive oil for cooking

For the Filling:

- 2 tablespoons olive oil
- 1 large onion, thinly sliced
- 2 cloves garlic, minced
- 1 cup fresh spinach or arugula (optional)
- Salt and black pepper, to taste
- A pinch of nutmeg (optional)
- Vegan Parmesan cheese for serving (optional)
- Fresh rosemary or thyme leaves (optional)

Instructions:

Prepare the Batter:

- In a mixing bowl, whisk together the flour, water, and salt until you have a smooth, liquid batter. Let it rest for at least 30 minutes to an hour at room temperature. This process allows the flour particles to absorb the water, making the batter more cohesive.

Make the Filling:

- Heat olive oil in a skillet over medium heat. Add the sliced onion, and cook until it begins to soften and caramelize, about 10-15 minutes. If you're using garlic, add it in the last 2-3 minutes of cooking the onions.

- Add the spinach or arugula if you're using it, and cook until just wilted, about 1-2 minutes. Season with salt, black pepper, and a pinch of nutmeg if desired. Remove from heat and set aside.

Cook the Borlengo:

- Heat a non-stick skillet or crepe pan over medium heat and lightly oil it with a brush or paper towel soaked in olive oil.

- Pour a small amount of batter into the center of the pan, tilting and swirling the pan to spread the batter into a thin, even layer, much like making crepes.

- Cook until the edges start to lift from the pan and the bottom is lightly browned, about 2-3 minutes. These are typically not flipped, as they are very thin.

- Once cooked, immediately spread some of the onion and spinach mixture over the Borlengo. Fold it in half or quarters and slide it onto a serving plate.

- Continue cooking the remaining batter, adding more oil to the pan as needed.
- Serve the Borlengo hot, garnished with a sprinkle of vegan parmesan and fresh rosemary or thyme if desired. These are typically eaten by hand, like street food.

Enjoy this vegan take on a traditional Emilia Romagna dish, maintaining the heart and soul of the original recipe without any animal products.

Emilia-Romagna's rich culinary traditions provide a unique opportunity for exploration and vegan innovation. With a bit of creativity, the essential flavors of the region can be enjoyed within the vegan framework, all while honoring the spirit of this Italian food heartland.

Veneto Region

The Veneto region, with its capital in Venice, reflects a diverse culinary landscape. From the seafood-heavy traditions of the coast to the Alpine influences in the north, there's a significant variety of ingredients and dishes.

Transitioning Venetian cuisine to vegan options involves creativity, especially given the region's emphasis on seafood. Still, the rich agricultural offerings and iconic flavors of Veneto provide a solid foundation for plant-based variations.

Here are some examples:

Risotto al Nero di Seppia

Traditionally made with cuttlefish ink, rice, and seafood broth, the vegan version of this dramatic-looking black risotto uses vegetable broth and excludes seafood.

For the distinct black color, edible vegan ink alternatives are available, and finely chopped seaweed can enhance the sea-like flavor without involving seafood.

Ingredients:

- 1 1/2 cups Arborio rice
- 4 cups vegetable broth, warmed
- 1/4 cup olive oil
- 1 small onion, finely chopped
- 3 cloves garlic, minced
- 1/2 cup white wine (vegan brand)
- 2 tablespoons black food coloring (plant-based) or squid ink substitute (available in vegan varieties)
- Salt and black pepper, to taste
- 2 tablespoons vegan butter (optional)
- Fresh parsley, chopped (for garnish)
- Lemon wedges (for serving)
- Vegan Parmesan cheese (optional)

Instructions:

Prepare the Rice:

- In a large pan, heat the olive oil over medium heat. Add the chopped onion and garlic, sautéing until the onion is translucent and the garlic is fragrant.

- Stir in the Arborio rice, ensuring the grains are well-coated in the oil. Toast the rice for a few minutes until it becomes slightly translucent at the edges.

- Pour in the white wine, stirring constantly until it is mostly absorbed by the rice.

Add the Broth:

- Add the warm vegetable broth one ladle at a time, stirring frequently. Wait until most of the liquid is absorbed before adding the next ladle of broth. Continue this process until the rice is al dente (tender but firm to the bite).

- Once the rice is al dente, stir in the vegan black food coloring or cuttlefish ink substitute. This will give the risotto its characteristic black color. Mix thoroughly to ensure the color is evenly distributed.

Season and Finish Cooking:

- Add salt and black pepper to taste. If you're using vegan butter, stir it in now for extra richness. Continue cooking for a couple of minutes until you reach a creamy consistency. If the risotto is too thick, add a bit more broth. The ideal texture is creamy and slightly loose rather than stiff.

Serve:

- Spoon the risotto into dishes, garnishing with chopped parsley and a side of lemon wedges. If desired, sprinkle vegan Parmesan cheese on top.
- Serve immediately, as risotto can lose its creamy texture if left standing too long.

This vegan Risotto al Nero di Seppia retains the visual appeal and luxurious texture of the traditional dish while being completely plant-based.

Bigoli in Salsa

Bigoli in salsa is a traditional dish from Veneto, particularly from Venice.

It's a simple pasta dish with a rich onion and anchovy-based sauce. In this vegan version, we'll substitute anchovies with a plant-based alternative to replicate the unique flavor profile.

Ingredients:

- 400g of Bigoli pasta (or whole wheat spaghetti/linguine if Bigoli is unavailable)
- 1/4 cup of olive oil
- 2 large white onions, thinly sliced
- 4 garlic cloves, minced
- 2 tablespoons of capers, rinsed and chopped
- 1 tablespoon of seaweed flakes (e.g., nori or dulse), optional for a "fishy" taste
- 1/2 cup of white wine (vegan)
- Salt and black pepper to taste
- Fresh parsley, chopped (for garnish)

Instructions:

Prepare the Pasta:

- Cook the bigoli pasta in a large pot of salted boiling water until it is al dente, according to the package instructions.

- Drain the pasta, reserving around 1 cup of water for later, and set aside.

Create the "Anchovy" Base:

- While the pasta is cooking, heat olive oil in a large skillet over medium heat. Add the sliced onions and a pinch of salt, sautéing until completely softened and caramelized, which can take about 15-20 minutes. Stir regularly to ensure they don't burn.

- Add the minced garlic to the caramelized onions and sauté for 1-2 minutes until the garlic is golden and fragrant.

- Introduce the chopped capers and seaweed flakes (if using) to the mixture, stirring well to combine. The seaweed will hint at the ocean flavor typically provided by anchovies.

Deglaze the Pan:

- Pour the white wine into the skillet with the onion mixture, stirring to combine. Allow it to simmer for a few minutes until the alcohol smell dissipates.

Combine Pasta and Sauce:

- Reduce the heat to low and add the cooked Bigoli to the skillet, tossing it with the sauce to combine thoroughly. If the mixture seems dry, add a bit of the reserved pasta water, bit by bit, until it reaches your desired sauce consistency. Allow it to cook together for a few minutes so the pasta absorbs the flavors.

- Taste the sauce and adjust the seasoning with salt and black pepper as needed.

Serve:

- Dish out the Bigoli in salsa into individual serving bowls.
- Garnish with fresh chopped parsley and serve immediately.

Enjoy this hearty, flavorful vegan rendition of Bigoli in Salsa. This dish brings the taste of Veneto to your table without any animal products. The key to the flavor profile is the caramelization of the onions and the briny, ocean-like hint from the capers and seaweed.

Risi e Bisi

"Risi e Bisi" is a classic Venetian dish that translates to "rice and peas."

It is traditionally made with pancetta or meat-based broth, but we can easily make a satisfying vegan version of this comforting dish.

Ingredients:

- 1 cup Arborio rice
- 2 cups fresh or frozen green peas
- 1 large onion, finely chopped
- 2 tablespoons olive oil
- 4 cups vegetable broth (keep it warm on the side)
- 1/2 cup vegan white wine (optional)
- Salt and pepper, to taste
- 2 tablespoons fresh parsley, chopped
- 1/4 cup nutritional yeast or vegan Parmesan cheese, plus more for garnish
- 2 tablespoons vegan butter (optional)

Instructions:

Sauté the Onions:

- In a large, heavy-bottomed saucepan, heat the olive oil over medium heat.
- Add the chopped onion to the oil, sautéing until it is soft and translucent, about 5-7 minutes. You want the onion to be very tender without taking on any color.

Toast the Rice:

- Add the Arborio rice to the saucepan with the onions, stirring for about 1-2 minutes to toast the rice.
- The grains should become slightly translucent around the edges without browning.

Deglaze with Wine:

- Pour in the vegan white wine (if using), and let it simmer until it has mostly evaporated.

- This step is traditional and adds depth, but it can be omitted if you prefer.

Cooking the Rice:

- Add a ladle of warm vegetable broth to the rice mixture, stirring often, until the liquid is almost fully absorbed.

- Then, add another ladle of broth, repeating this process of adding and stirring.

- After about 10 minutes of cooking, add the green peas to the mixture.

- Continue to add broth, one ladle at a time, and stir, allowing the liquid to be absorbed before adding more.

- This process should take about 18-20 minutes.

- The rice should be al dente and creamy, not mushy.

Final Touches:

- When the rice is cooked to your preference, remove the pan from the heat.

- Stir in the nutritional yeast or vegan parmesan, vegan butter (if using), and chopped parsley.

- This step will introduce an extra layer of creaminess and flavor akin to the traditional cheese and butter used in non-vegan versions.

- Season with salt and pepper to taste.

- Remember, the vegan parmesan and broth already have salt, so taste as you season.

- Spoon the creamy risi e bisi into bowls, garnishing with more nutritional yeast or vegan parmesan if desired.
- Serve immediately, as risi e bisi is best enjoyed hot.

This vegan take on the classic Venetian comfort dish retains the creamy, rich flavors and textures of the original, ensuring it can be enjoyed as part of a plant-based diet without missing out on the traditional taste experience.

Frittata di Verdure

Frittata di Verdure is a traditional Italian dish, often made with eggs, vegetables, and sometimes cheese.

However, creating a vegan version of this popular dish is simple and equally delicious, replacing eggs with a chickpea flour-based mixture that cooks similarly to a traditional frittata. Below is a recipe for a vegan Frittata di Verdure inspired by the culinary delights of the Veneto region.

Ingredients:

- 1 cup chickpea flour (also known as gram or besan flour)
- 1 1/4 cups water
- 1/4 cup nutritional yeast (for a cheesy flavor)
- 1/2 tsp turmeric (for color)
- Salt and black pepper, to taste
- 1 small zucchini, sliced
- 1 red bell pepper, sliced
- 1 small onion, thinly sliced
- A handful of cherry tomatoes, halved
- 2-3 tablespoons of olive oil
- Fresh herbs (like basil or parsley), chopped for garnish

Instructions:

Prepare the Batter:

- In a mixing bowl, combine the chickpea flour, water, nutritional yeast, turmeric, salt, and pepper.

- Whisk until you have a smooth batter.

- Set aside at least 30 minutes for the chickpea flour to absorb the water.

Sauté the Vegetables:

- Heat a tablespoon of olive oil in a non-stick or cast iron skillet over medium heat.
- Add the sliced onions, cooking until they start to become translucent.
- Introduce the zucchini and bell pepper and cook until they start to soften.
- Add the cherry tomatoes and cooking for another couple of minutes. The vegetables should be tender but not too soft.
- Season with salt and pepper to taste, then remove the vegetables from the skillet and set aside.

Cook the Frittata:

- Preheat your oven to 375°F (190°C) if your skillet isn't oven-safe.
- Using an oven-safe skillet, you'll finish cooking the frittata under the broiler.
- Heat another tablespoon of oil in the skillet over medium-low heat, ensuring the base is fully coated.
- Pour the batter into the skillet, making sure it's evenly distributed.
- Evenly place the sautéed vegetables into the batter, pressing them in slightly.
- Allow the frittata to cook for 5-7 minutes until the edges start to look set. Be patient, as the chickpea flour takes a while to cook through.

Finish Cooking:

- If your skillet is oven-safe, place it under the broiler for 2-3 minutes until the top is set and starts to golden.

- If not, transfer the frittata carefully into a baking dish and bake in the preheated oven for 10-15 minutes.

Serve:

- Allow the frittata to cool for a few minutes before slicing. It should be firm and sliceable, just like a traditional frittata.

- Garnish with fresh herbs and enjoy hot or at room temperature.

This vegan version of the Frittata di Verdure keeps the heart and soul of the dish alive, celebrating the flavors of the Veneto region without the need for eggs or dairy. It's perfect for breakfast, brunch, or a light dinner, and it's healthy, too!

Marinated Radicchio Salad

Radicchio, a type of chicory, is particularly popular in Italian cuisine, especially in the Treviso (Veneto) region. Its distinct bitter and spicy taste, combined with a hint of sweetness, makes it perfect for a variety of dishes, including a simple, refreshing salad. Here's how you can make a Vegan Marinated Radicchio Salad, a twist on a traditional dish from Treviso.

Ingredients:

- 1-2 heads of radicchio from Treviso (depending on size)
- 1/4 cup of olive oil, extra virgin
- 2 tablespoons of balsamic vinegar
- 1 teaspoon of agave syrup or maple syrup
- 1 clove of garlic, minced
- Salt and pepper to taste
- Optional: toasted walnuts or pine nuts for some crunch
- Optional: orange segments or pomegranate seeds for a sweet contrast

Instructions:

Prepare the Radicchio:

- Wash the radicchio heads, then pat them dry with a clean towel.
- Cut the radicchio into quarters or eighths, depending on size, keeping the stem intact so each piece holds together.
- If you prefer a milder flavor, you can soak the radicchio in cold water for 30 minutes to reduce its bitterness. Drain well if you choose this step.

Make the Marinade:

- In a bowl, combine the olive oil, balsamic vinegar, agave or maple syrup, and minced garlic. Whisk until well blended.
- Taste the marinade and adjust the sweetness or acidity as needed. Season with salt and pepper to your preference.

Marinate the Radicchio:

- Place the radicchio pieces in a large, sealable bag or a shallow dish.

- Pour the marinade over the radicchio, ensuring all pieces are well coated.
- Seal the bag or cover the dish, then let it marinate for at least 30 minutes to an hour in the refrigerator, turning the radicchio occasionally for even marinating.

Optional - Add Extra Flavor:

- If you're using nuts, toast them lightly in a dry skillet until they're golden and fragrant. Set them aside to cool.
- If you're using fruit, prepare your orange segments or pomegranate seeds.

Assemble the Salad:

- Once marinated, remove the radicchio from the refrigerator. You can serve it cold or at room temperature.
- Arrange the radicchio pieces on a serving platter or individual plates.
- Drizzle with a bit of the remaining marinade and top with your toasted nuts or fruit if using.
- For an extra touch, you can sprinkle a little coarse sea salt over the top before serving.

This Vegan Marinated Radicchio Salad is simple yet full of contrasting flavors, with the bitterness of the radicchio balanced by the sweet and tangy marinade. It's a wonderful way to start a meal or accompany a main dish, embracing the unique produce of the Treviso region.

Gnocchi di Patate

While certain gnocchi recipes include egg, many traditional Venetian versions do not, focusing instead on the potato, flour, and salt.

However, when served with a marinara sauce or a vegan pesto, potato gnocchi can be a delightful vegan dish.

Ingredients:

- 2 pounds (about 1 kg) starchy potatoes (like Russets)
- 1 to 1 1/2 cups all-purpose flour, plus more for dusting
- Salt to taste
- Optional: A pinch of nutmeg for extra flavor

Instructions:

Cook the Potatoes:

- Wash the potatoes, leaving their skins on, and place them in a large pot filled with cold water. Salt the water, then bring to a boil.

- Reduce the heat and simmer until the potatoes are tender when pierced with a fork (about 30-40 minutes, depending on their size).

- Once cooked, drain the potatoes and let them cool slightly. While still warm, peel the potatoes.

Prepare the Potato Dough:

- Use a potato ricer or masher to mash the potatoes until smooth, ensuring there are no lumps. It's important to do this while the potatoes are still warm.

- Spread the mashed potatoes out on a flat surface and let them cool completely. This step helps to ensure your gnocchi isn't gummy.

- Sprinkle the all-purpose flour over the potatoes, along with salt to taste and nutmeg if using.

- Gently mix with your hands until a dough starts to form.

- Be mindful not to overwork the dough; otherwise, your gnocchi will be tough.

- If the dough is sticky, add a bit more flour, but do so sparingly.

Shape the Gnocchi:

- Dust a clean surface with flour. Divide the dough into several pieces, and roll each one into a long, sausage-like shape about 3/4-inch in diameter.

- Cut the rolls into 1-inch pieces to form the gnocchi.

- If you want the traditional gnocchi shape, gently press each piece against the tines of a fork or a gnocchi board, rolling it slightly to create the classic ridged pattern.

- This isn't just for aesthetics; it helps the gnocchi catch and hold the sauce.

Cook the Gnocchi:

- Bring a large pot of salted water to a boil. Carefully drop in the gnocchi, working in batches so as not to crowd the pot.

- Cook the gnocchi until they float to the surface, indicating they're done, which typically takes about 2-3 minutes.

- Remove the floating gnocchi with a slotted spoon and drain them well.

Serve:

- Serve your vegan gnocchi hot with your choice of vegan sauce, such as a marinara, pesto, or a simple mixture of vegan butter and fresh herbs.

- You can also sauté the boiled gnocchi in a pan with olive oil until golden for a different texture.

Enjoy your homemade Vegan Gnocchi di Patate, a dish that's as fun to prepare as it is delicious to eat. It's a versatile meal that can pair with a variety of sauces and toppings, allowing you to adapt it for different occasions or seasons.

Venetian-style Tofu (Tofu alla Veneziana)

This isn't a traditional dish but rather an innovation for vegans.

Inspired by Venetian flavors, tofu can be marinated in herbs typical of the region, sautéed with onions and a splash of white wine, and served over polenta or pasta.

Ingredients:

- 1 block (about 14 oz or 400 g) of firm tofu
- 2 tablespoons olive oil
- 1 large onion, thinly sliced
- 2 cloves garlic, minced
- 1/2 cup white wine (a vegan brand)
- 2 tablespoons soy sauce
- 1 teaspoon Italian seasoning (or a mix of dried basil, oregano, and thyme)
- Salt and black pepper to taste

- 2 tablespoons fresh parsley, chopped (optional for garnish)
- Optional: 1 tablespoon capers or green olives, chopped

Instructions:

Prepare the Tofu:

- Drain the tofu and press it by placing it between two kitchen towels and setting a heavy object on top (like a skillet or cutting board).
- Leave it for 15-30 minutes to extract excess water.
- Once pressed, cut the tofu into cubes or slices, as per your preference.

Sauté Onions and Garlic:

- Heat the olive oil in a large pan over medium heat.
- Add the sliced onions, stirring occasionally, until they become soft and translucent, which should take about 5-7 minutes.
- Add the minced garlic to the pan and sauté for another minute until fragrant, ensuring it doesn't burn.

Cook the Tofu:

- Increase the heat to medium-high and add the tofu to the pan.
- Sauté it with the onion and garlic mixture, stirring frequently until it starts to turn golden on the edges.
- Pour in the white wine and soy sauce, and sprinkle the Italian seasoning, salt, and black pepper.
- If using, add the capers or olives here. Stir well to combine all the ingredients.

Simmer:

- Reduce the heat, cover, and let your tofu simmer for about 10-15 minutes.
- This process allows the tofu to absorb the flavors thoroughly. If the pan gets too dry, you can add a few tablespoons of water to help the tofu cook without sticking.

Serve:

- Once the tofu is nicely browned and has absorbed most of the sauce, turn off the heat.
- Taste the mixture and adjust the seasoning if needed.
- Garnish with fresh parsley before serving.

Presentation:

- Serve your Tofu alla Veneziana hot, ideally with a side of traditional Venetian polenta, crusty Italian bread, or overcooked pasta.
- A fresh salad also pairs well to add a refreshing contrast to the dish.

This dish is a celebration of Venetian cuisine's simplicity and flavor, using tofu as a versatile canvas for its aromatic herbs and spices. It's perfect for both everyday meals and special occasions when you want to serve something uniquely flavorful.

Trentino-Alto Adige Region

Trentino-Alto Adige, a region in Northeastern Italy, is unique for its Austro-Hungarian influences and mountainous terrain, which heavily influence its culinary tradition. This area is known for dishes that are often hearty and satisfying, with dairy products, cured meats, and hardy vegetables featuring prominently.

Adapting Trentino-Alto Adige's traditional cuisine to a vegan diet invites creativity and a chance to explore new ingredients and flavors while still enjoying the culinary delights of this culturally rich region.

Canederli

Canederli, also known as "Knödel," are traditional bread dumplings that are popular in the Trentino-Alto Adige region of Italy, a place with strong Austrian and Central European influences in its cuisine. Since my mother was originally from Bavaria (Southern Germany), Knödel was often on the menu at our home.

The original recipe often includes ingredients like milk, eggs, and sometimes speck or sausage.

Here's how you can make a vegan version that maintains the heartiness and flavor of the traditional dish.

- 250g (about 2 1/2 cups) of stale bread, cubed
- 1/2 cup of soy milk (or any plant-based milk)
- 1 tablespoon olive oil (additional for frying)
- 1 large onion, finely chopped
- 2 cloves garlic, minced
- 2 tablespoons fresh parsley, chopped
- 1 teaspoon dried marjoram (optional)
- 1/2 teaspoon nutmeg

- Salt and black pepper to taste
- 70g (about 1/2 cup) all-purpose flour
- Vegetable broth (for boiling the canederli)
- Optional: Vegan cheese or nutritional yeast for added flavor

Instructions:

Bread Preparation:

- In a large bowl, soak the cubed bread with soy milk and let it sit for about 30 minutes to an hour, allowing the bread to fully absorb the milk.

Sauté Onions and Garlic:

- While the bread is soaking, heat olive oil in a skillet over medium heat.
- Add the onions and garlic, sautéing until the onions are translucent and slightly golden. Remove from heat.

Prepare the Dumpling Mixture:

- Add the sautéed onions and garlic, parsley, marjoram (if using), nutmeg, salt, and pepper to the bowl of soaked bread.
- If you choose to add vegan cheese or nutritional yeast, incorporate it into the mixture now.
- Use your hands or a spoon to mix the ingredients until well combined.
- Gradually add the flour, stirring continuously, until the mixture holds together. It should be sticky but formable.

Form the Canederli:

- Wet your hands to prevent sticking and form the mixture into round dumplings about the size of a golf ball.

Cook the Canederli:

- Bring a large pot of vegetable broth to a boil. Carefully drop the dumplings into the broth, reducing the heat to a gentle simmer.

- Cook the canederli for about 15-20 minutes until they float to the surface and are firm to the touch.

- Avoid overcrowding the pot; work in batches if necessary.

Optional Browing:

- For a richer flavor and firmer texture, you can optionally brown the boiled canederli.

- To do this, heat a bit of olive oil in a frying pan and gently sauté the cooked dumplings until they're golden brown on all sides.

Serving:

- Serve the canederli hot, traditionally as a standalone dish, or you can include them in a hearty vegan soup.

- They're often served with a salad or sauerkraut on the side.

This vegan version of Canederli allows you to enjoy a dish that stays true to the culinary traditions of the Trentino-Alto Adige region without using any animal products.

Barley Soup (Orzotto)

Orzotto, a comforting barley soup, is a naturally vegan-friendly dish, especially when prepared with vegetable broth. It features pearl barley, potatoes, carrots, celery, and onions.

It is often seasoned with bay leaves, rosemary, and garlic for a robust flavor.

In its original form, it might contain meat-based broths and cheese, but it can easily be adapted for a vegan diet. Here's a vegan version of this delightful barley soup.

Ingredients:

- 1 cup pearl barley, rinsed and drained
- 2 tablespoons olive oil
- 1 large onion, finely chopped
- 2 garlic cloves, minced
- 2 medium carrots, diced
- 2 celery stalks, diced
- 1 medium zucchini, diced (optional)

- 1/2 cup of diced tomatoes (canned or fresh)
- 4-5 cups vegetable broth (or more as needed)
- 1 teaspoon thyme (dried or fresh)
- 1 tablespoon parsley, chopped (additional for garnish)
- Salt and black pepper to taste
- Optional: Nutritional yeast or vegan cheese for garnish

Instructions:

Sauté Vegetables:

- Heat the olive oil in a large pot over medium heat.
- Add the onion and garlic and sauté until the onion is translucent.
- Add the diced carrots and celery, cooking for about 5-7 minutes until they start to soften.
- If using zucchini, add it at this stage.

Toast Barley:

- Add the pearl barley to the pot with the vegetables and stir well, allowing the barley to toast slightly in the oil and vegetable mixture.
- This step helps to enhance the nutty flavor of the barley.

Add Liquids and Seasoning:

- Pour in the diced tomatoes and about 4 cups of vegetable broth, enough to cover the mixture in the pot.
- Add the thyme, parsley, salt, and pepper.
- Bring the mixture to a boil, then reduce the heat to low, covering the pot with a lid.
- Let it simmer for about 30-40 minutes, stirring occasionally to prevent sticking.

- Check the barley for doneness. It should be tender but still have a slight chew to it, similar to risotto.
- If the mixture is too thick or the barley is not fully cooked, you can add more broth and continue simmering. Adjust the seasoning as per your preference.

Final Touches:

- Once the barley is cooked to your liking and the orzotto is creamy, turn off the heat.
- If you're using nutritional yeast or vegan cheese, stir it in now or use it as a garnish on top.

Serve:

- Ladle the orzotto into bowls, garnishing with extra chopped parsley or any preferred fresh herb.
- Serve hot as a comforting main dish.

This vegan orzotto maintains the creamy, satisfying texture of the traditional dish while ensuring it's completely plant-based. It's perfect for cozy dinners, especially in the colder months, and offers a nutritious balance with the inclusion of various vegetables.

Potato Gnocchi with Vegan Ragù

While traditional Trentino-Alto Adige ragù includes meat, vegan versions use lentils or textured vegetable protein to simulate the texture and richness of meat.

When served with locally favored potato gnocchi, this dish remains true to the region's tastes.

Ingredients

for the Potato Gnocchi:

- 2 lbs. (about 1 kg) starchy potatoes
- 1 to 1.5 cups all-purpose flour, plus extra for dusting
- Salt to taste

For the Vegan Ragù:

- 2 tablespoons olive oil
- 1 onion, finely chopped
- 2 carrots, finely chopped
- 2 celery stalks, finely chopped

- 2 garlic cloves, minced
- 1 cup (175 g) textured vegetable protein (TVP) or vegan mince
- 1 cup (240 ml) vegetable broth
- 2 cups (480 ml) tomato sauce or crushed tomatoes
- 1 teaspoon dried basil
- 1 teaspoon dried oregano
- Salt and black pepper to taste
- Optional: Red wine, fresh herbs, or vegan Worcestershire sauce for additional flavor

Instructions for the Gnocchi

Prepare the Potatoes:

- Boil the potatoes with their skins on until tender. Drain and, when cool enough to handle, peel them.
- Pass the peeled potatoes through a potato ricer or mash them thoroughly, ensuring there are no lumps.

Make the Dough:

- On a clean work surface, knead together the mashed potatoes, flour, and a pinch of salt until a smooth but still slightly sticky dough forms. Be careful not to over-knead.

Form the Gnocchi:

- Divide the dough into several pieces and roll each piece into a long, thin rope.
- Cut into 1-inch pieces.
- To give them the classic gnocchi shape, gently press each piece against a fork or gnocchi board with a thumb and roll to make ridges.

Cook the Gnocchi:

- Bring a large pot of salted water to a boil.

- Drop in the gnocchi and cook until they float to the surface, then wait another 10-20 seconds before removing them with a slotted spoon.
- Set aside.

Instructions for Vegan Ragù:

Sauté the Vegetables:

- Heat the olive oil in a large pan over medium heat.
- Add onion, carrots, celery, and garlic, sautéing until the vegetables are soft and the onion is translucent.

Prepare the Vegan Mince:

- If using TVP, rehydrate it according to package instructions (usually soaking in hot water).
- Drain and squeeze out any excess water.
- Add the rehydrated TVP or vegan mince to the pan and stir well, cooking for a few minutes.

Simmer the Ragù:

- Pour in the vegetable broth, tomato sauce, basil, oregano, and any optional ingredients (like a splash of red wine or Worcestershire sauce).
- Stir everything together, then reduce the heat to low and simmer for 20-30 minutes.
- If the sauce becomes too thick, add a little more broth. Season with salt and pepper to taste.

Combine Gnocchi and Ragù:

- Once the ragù is thick and rich in flavor, add the cooked gnocchi to the pan, gently stirring to coat them in the sauce.

- Serve hot, garnishing with fresh herbs or vegan parmesan if desired.
- Enjoy your comforting, hearty Veneto-style vegan meal!

This dish maintains the traditional flavors and textures you'd expect from gnocchi with ragù, all while keeping the ingredients plant-based.

Sauerkraut with Potatoes

Reflecting the region's Germanic influences, this simple dish of sautéed sauerkraut and potatoes is naturally vegan, offering a satisfying blend of tangy and savory flavors. "Sauerkraut und Kartoffeln" was one of the dishes that made into the Arcaini family table on a regular basis.

- 1 lb (450 g) sauerkraut, drained
- 1 lb (450 g) potatoes, peeled and cubed
- 1 large onion, finely chopped
- 2-3 garlic cloves, minced
- 2 tablespoons olive oil
- 1 cup (240 ml) vegetable broth (more if needed)
- Salt and pepper to taste
- Optional: 1 teaspoon caraway seeds for an authentic flavor twist
- Optional: Fresh parsley, chopped, for garnish

Instructions:

Prepare the Ingredients:

- Rinse the sauerkraut in cold water to remove some of the brine, then drain it.
- If you prefer a milder taste, you may also squeeze out excess liquid.
- Peel and chop the potatoes into even cubes to ensure they cook uniformly.

Sauté Onions and Garlic:

- Heat the olive oil in a large pot or deep skillet over medium heat.
- Add the chopped onion and minced garlic, sautéing until the onion is translucent and the garlic is fragrant.
- If you're using caraway seeds, add them now.

Cook Potatoes:

- Add the cubed potatoes to the pot, stirring for a couple of minutes to allow them to mingle with the flavors of onion and garlic.

Add Sauerkraut:

- Incorporate the drained sauerkraut into the pot, mixing well with the rest of the ingredients.

Pour in Broth and Simmer:

- Add the vegetable broth and bring the mixture to a simmer.
- If everything isn't covered by the broth, add a bit more until it is just covered.
- Reduce the heat, cover the pot, and let it simmer for about 20-30 minutes until the potatoes are tender.

Season and Serve:

- Once the potatoes are cooked through, uncover the pot and let any excess moisture evaporate if necessary.
- The final dish should be moist but not watery.
- Taste the sauerkraut and potatoes, adding salt and pepper as needed.
- Remember, the sauerkraut brings its own saltiness, so you may need less salt than usual.
- Serve hot, garnished with fresh parsley if desired.

This simple, flavorful dish reflects the hearty comfort food of the Trentino Alto Adige region, offering warmth and nourishment, especially during the colder months. It pairs well with a variety of other dishes and can be enjoyed as a main or a side dish in a broader meal.

Stuffed Cabbage Rolls

Stuffed cabbage rolls, known as "involtini di cavolo," are a dish with many variations across Europe. In the Trentino Alto Adige region, this dish reflects both Italian and Central European influences.

Here's how to make a vegan version that retains all the comfort of the original.

Ingredients:
- 1 large head of green cabbage
- 2 cups cooked rice or quinoa
- 1 cup cooked lentils
- 1 onion, finely chopped

146

- 2 cloves garlic, minced
- 1 carrot, grated
- 1 celery stalk, finely chopped
- 2 tablespoons olive oil
- 1/2 teaspoon smoked paprika (optional)
- Salt and pepper, to taste
- 1-2 cups tomato sauce (depending on how saucy you want your dish)
- Fresh herbs (like parsley or thyme), chopped for garnish

Instructions:

Prepare the Cabbage:

- Bring a large pot of water to a boil.
- Remove the core from the cabbage and place the whole head in the boiling water.
- Boil for around 5-10 minutes or until the leaves are pliable enough to be removed without tearing.
- Carefully remove the cabbage from the water and detach the leaves, setting them aside.
- You'll need about 8-12 leaves, depending on the size.

Prepare the Filling:

- Heat olive oil in a skillet over medium heat.
- Add onion, garlic, carrot, and celery, and sauté until the vegetables are soft.
- In a large bowl, combine cooked rice or quinoa, cooked lentils, and the sautéed vegetables.
- Add salt, pepper, and smoked paprika (if using), then mix well.

Assemble the Rolls:

- Lay a cabbage leaf flat on a work surface.
- Place a generous amount of the filling in the center of the leaf.
- Fold in the sides and roll up the leaf to encase the filling.
- Repeat with the remaining leaves and filling.
- If some leaves are too large, you can cut them in half.
- If they're too small, you can overlap two leaves.

Cook the Rolls:

- Preheat your oven to 350°F (175°C).
- Spread a thin layer of tomato sauce on the bottom of a baking dish.
- Place the cabbage rolls seam-side down in the dish, packed closely together.
- Pour the remaining tomato sauce over the cabbage rolls.
- Cover the dish with foil and bake for 1 hour.

Serve:

- After baking, let the cabbage rolls rest for a few minutes before serving.
- Garnish with fresh herbs and enjoy!

This dish is hearty and flavorful, and it highlights the rustic ingredients typical of the Trentino Alto Adige region. It's perfect for dinner, especially on chilly nights!

Buckwheat Pancakes

Buckwheat is popular in the region's cuisine, and pancakes made from buckwheat flour offer a naturally vegan, gluten-free option.

Vegan Buckwheat Pancakes offer a delightful blend of health and taste. Made from buckwheat flour, a naturally gluten-free and nutrient-dense pseudo-grain, these pancakes are a boon for those seeking gluten-free or plant-based alternatives.

Contrary to its name, buckwheat isn't wheat at all, ensuring these pancakes cater to celiac and gluten-sensitive individuals.

The earthy, slightly nutty flavor of buckwheat provides a unique taste profile, distinct from traditional pancakes.

When combined with non-dairy milk and other vegan-friendly ingredients, the resulting batter fries up into fluffy, tender pancakes that can hold a variety of toppings. From fresh fruit compotes and maple syrup for a sweet touch to vegan cheeses and savory vegetables for a hearty bite, these pancakes serve as a versatile base.

Perfect for breakfast or brunch, vegan buckwheat pancakes are a gastronomic treat, offering both nourishment and indulgence in every bite.

Ingredients:

- 1 cup buckwheat flour
- 1 tablespoon sugar (optional)
- 1 tablespoon baking powder
- 1/4 teaspoon salt
- 1 cup almond milk (or any other plant-based milk)
- 2 tablespoons apple cider vinegar
- 1 teaspoon vanilla extract (optional)
- 3 tablespoons unsweetened applesauce (or a flaxseed egg: 1 tablespoon flaxseed meal + 2.5 tablespoons water, let sit for 5 minutes)
- Vegetable oil or vegan butter for cooking
- Optional toppings: maple syrup, fresh berries, vegan yogurt, or compote

Instructions:

Prepare the Batter:

- In a large mixing bowl, combine the buckwheat flour, sugar (if using), baking powder, and salt.

- In a separate bowl or large jug, mix the almond milk and apple cider vinegar.

- Let it sit for a few minutes to curdle, creating a vegan 'buttermilk.'

- Add the vanilla extract to the 'buttermilk' if using and mix well.

- Pour the wet mixture into the dry ingredients, stirring until just combined.

- Be careful not to over-mix; it's okay if there are a few lumps.

- Fold in the applesauce or prepared flaxseed egg until incorporated.

Cook the Pancakes:

- Heat a large non-stick skillet or griddle over medium heat.

- Add a small amount of vegetable oil or vegan butter to coat the surface.

- Once hot, pour 1/4 cup of batter onto the skillet for each pancake.

- Cook until bubbles form on the surface and the edges start to look set, about 2-3 minutes.

- Gently flip the pancakes and cook for another 2-3 minutes on the other side until golden brown and cooked through.

Serve:

- Serve the pancakes hot, stacked, and with your choice of toppings, such as maple syrup, fresh berries, vegan yogurt, or a fruit compote.

These vegan buckwheat pancakes are not only a nod to Trentino Alto Adige's culinary heritage but also a healthy, energizing way to start the day. They're also versatile, pairing wonderfully with both sweet and savory accompaniments.

Friuli-Venezia Giulia

The Friuli-Venezia Giulia region, nestled in the northeastern corner of Italy, boasts a fascinating mix of cultures and cuisines.

This area, with its complex history and proximity to Eastern Europe, offers a culinary scene that is markedly different from other Italian regions.

Though traditional dishes often incorporate meat, cheese, and seafood, there are several ways to enjoy the essence of Friulian cuisine on a vegan diet.

Jota

Jota is a traditional stew from the Friuli-Venezia Giulia region, known for its comforting and hearty nature.

The dish usually contains beans, sauerkraut or sour turnip, potatoes, and pork.

Here's how you can make a vegan version that preserves the robust flavors of the classic recipe.

- 2 cups sauerkraut, rinsed and drained
- 1 cup dried borlotti beans (or canned, drained and rinsed)
- 2 medium potatoes, peeled and diced
- 1 large onion, finely chopped
- 2 cloves garlic, minced
- 2 tablespoons olive oil
- 1 bay leaf
- 1 teaspoon dried rosemary
- Salt and pepper, to taste
- 6 cups vegetable broth or water
- Optional: 2 tablespoons tomato paste
- Optional garnish: chopped fresh parsley

Instructions:

Prep the Beans (if using dried):

- Soak the dried borlotti beans in a large bowl of water overnight.
- The next day, drain and rinse the beans, then transfer them to a large pot.
- Cover with water and bring to a boil.
- Reduce the heat and simmer until tender, about 1-1.5 hours, then drain.

Cook the Base:

- In a large pot, heat the olive oil over medium heat.
- Add the chopped onion and minced garlic, sautéing until the onion is translucent and the garlic is fragrant.
- Add the diced potatoes to the pot and sauté for a few more minutes, stirring occasionally to prevent sticking.

Combine the Ingredients:

- To the pot, add the cooked borlotti beans (or drained canned beans), sauerkraut, bay leaf, rosemary, and tomato paste (if using).
- Stir to combine all the ingredients thoroughly.
- Pour in the vegetable broth or water, ensuring that the mixture is fully submerged.
- Increase the heat and bring the stew to a boil.

Simmer the Stew:

- Once boiling, reduce the heat to a low simmer.
- Cover the pot and let it simmer for about 1-2 hours, stirring occasionally.

- The longer it cooks, the more the flavors will meld together.
- If the stew is too thick, add more broth or water as needed.
- About 10-15 minutes before the end of cooking, season with salt and pepper to taste.
- Be cautious with the salt, as the sauerkraut and broth may already contribute a salty flavor.

Serve:

- Remove the bay leaf. Ladle the hot stew into bowls and garnish with fresh parsley if desired.
- For an authentic Friulian experience, serve with a slice of dark, crusty bread on the side.

This vegan Jota maintains the sour, hearty flavor profiles of the traditional stew while ensuring it's fully plant-based. It's perfect for chilly nights when you need something warm and satisfying.

Frico

Frico is a traditional dish from the Friuli region, typically made with cheese (often Montasio) and potatoes, cooked until crispy.

Creating a vegan version of Frico involves substituting regular cheese with vegan cheese that melts well and has a strong flavor.

Below is a simplified version that tries to maintain the spirit of the original dish.

Ingredients:

- 2 large potatoes, peeled and thinly sliced or shredded
- 1 1/2 cups vegan cheese, preferably a type that melts well (like vegan mozzarella or vegan cheddar)
- 2 tablespoons olive oil
- Salt, to taste
- Black pepper, to taste
- Optional: a pinch of nutritional yeast for an extra cheesy flavor
- Optional: chopped fresh herbs (such as rosemary or thyme) for additional flavor

Instructions:

Prepare the Potatoes:

- If you're using large potatoes, peel and thinly slice or shred them using a grater or food processor.

- Soak the potato slices in cold water for 10-15 minutes to remove excess starch, then drain and pat dry with a clean kitchen towel.

Cook the Potatoes:

- Heat 1 tablespoon of olive oil in a large, non-stick skillet over medium heat.
- Add the potatoes, spreading them out in an even layer.
- Cook without stirring for about 5-7 minutes or until the bottom starts to turn golden brown.
- Season with salt and pepper (and herbs if you're using them) before flipping the potatoes over.
- Continue cooking for another 5-7 minutes until they are almost cooked through and have a crispy exterior.
- Reduce heat to low.

Add the Vegan Cheese:

- Sprinkle the grated vegan cheese evenly over the potatoes.
- If you're using nutritional yeast, add it at this stage.
- Cover the skillet with a lid and let it cook for another few minutes until the vegan cheese has melted and become slightly crispy.

Final Crisp:

- For a crispier frico, you can carefully flip the cheese and potato mixture and cook it on the other side for a few more minutes, but this is optional as it can be a bit tricky.
- If the mixture seems like it might break, you can place it under a broiler for a minute or two instead, watching closely to avoid burning.

- Once the frico is crispy and golden to your liking, carefully slide it onto a cutting board. Let it cool for a couple of minutes before slicing it into wedges.
- Serve warm as a snack, appetizer, or side dish.

Enjoy your vegan frico, a dish that's crispy on the outside with a melty, cheesy interior, all without any dairy products!

Friulan Salad

When incorporating the rich array of fresh produce available, local salads can include ingredients like radicchio, arugula, chicory, and beets, all of which are also available in your neighborhood grocery stores.

The salads are dressed simply with pristine extra-virgin olive oil and vinegar, preferably traditional vinegar from Modena.

Ingredients

Vegan Friulan Salad:

- Mixed greens (such as lettuce, arugula, radicchio, chicory, and endive), enough for 4 servings
- 2 medium carrots, thinly sliced or shredded
- 1 small cucumber, thinly sliced
- 1 small red onion, thinly sliced
- Cherry tomatoes, halved, as desired
- 1/4 cup olives, green, black, or a mix (preferably Italian like Taggiasca), pitted
- A handful of fresh basil leaves, roughly torn
- 2 tablespoons capers, drained (optional)
- Salt and freshly ground black pepper to taste

For the Dressing:

- 1/4 cup extra virgin olive oil
- 2 tablespoons white wine vinegar or apple cider vinegar
- 1 teaspoon Dijon mustard (ensure it's a vegan brand)
- 1 garlic clove, minced (optional)
- Salt and freshly ground black pepper to taste

Instructions:

Prepare the Vegetables:

- Wash all the greens thoroughly and tear them into bite-sized pieces.

- Place them in a large salad bowl.

- Add the thinly sliced or shredded carrots, cucumber, red onion, halved cherry tomatoes, olives, capers (if using), and basil to the bowl with the greens.

Prepare the Dressing:

- In a small bowl, whisk together the olive oil, vinegar, Dijon mustard, minced garlic (if using), salt, and pepper until well combined.
- Taste the dressing and adjust the seasoning or acidity as needed by adding more salt, pepper, or vinegar.

Assemble the Salad:

- Pour the dressing over the salad ingredients.
- Using salad tongs or two large spoons, gently toss everything together until all the ingredients are evenly coated with the dressing.

Final Adjustments and Serving:

- Let the salad sit for a few minutes before serving to allow the flavors to meld together.
- Give it one final toss, then taste and adjust the seasoning if necessary.
- Serve the salad in individual bowls or on a large platter.
- If desired, garnish with additional fresh herbs or edible flowers for a touch of Friulan countryside.

This simple yet flavorful salad is perfect as a starter or side dish, especially during warm months when the vegetables are at their peak. It reflects the richness of Friulian produce and the simplicity of Italian countryside cooking, all while adhering to vegan dietary preferences.

In the Friuli-Venezia Giulia region, adopting a vegan approach to traditional dishes means embracing the local fruits, vegetables, grains, and spices, celebrating the area's culinary heritage while adhering to plant-based principles. It's a testament to the versatility and adaptability of Italian regional cuisine.

Central Italy

Central Italy, known for its stunning landscapes, rich history, and renowned culinary traditions, consists of several regions. Each one has its unique cultural attributes and culinary specialties.

Tuscany (Toscana)

Tuscany, known for its breathtaking scenery and rich artistic legacy, also boasts a culinary tradition that perfectly complements a vegan lifestyle, thanks to its emphasis on fresh produce and legumes and its use of a rich array of plant-based ingredients.

Here are some vegan dishes and adaptations from the Tuscany region that capture the essence of its cuisine:

Pappa al Pomodoro

Pappa al Pomodoro is a classic Tuscan dish, traditionally made with ripe tomatoes, bread, olive oil, garlic, and basil.

This hearty dish is already vegan-friendly in its classic form. Below is a recipe that honors its Tuscan roots, ensuring you indulge in the flavors of Italy even on a vegan diet.

Ingredients:

- 1/4 cup extra-virgin olive oil, plus more for drizzling
- 1 medium onion, finely chopped
- 2-3 garlic cloves, minced
- 2 pounds ripe tomatoes, peeled, seeded, and chopped (or 1 large can of quality crushed tomatoes)
- 1 teaspoon salt, or to taste
- 1/2 teaspoon black pepper, or to taste
- 1/2 teaspoon red pepper flakes (optional for heat)
- 3-4 cups stale Tuscan bread (or any rustic loaf), crusts removed, torn into small pieces
- 3-4 cups vegetable broth, warmed
- A bunch of fresh basil leaves, roughly torn

Instructions:

Sauté the Base:

- Heat the olive oil in a large pot over medium heat.
- Add the onion, cooking until it is soft and translucent, usually around 5-7 minutes.
- Add the garlic and red pepper flakes (if using), cooking for another 1-2 minutes until fragrant.

Cook the Tomatoes:

- Stir in the chopped tomatoes.
- Add salt and black pepper.
- Lower the heat and let the mixture simmer.
- Cook for about 15-20 minutes, or until the tomatoes are soft and start to break down into a sauce.

Add the Bread:

- Mix the torn bread pieces into the tomato mixture, ensuring the bread is fully soaked in the tomatoes.

Add the Broth:

- Pour in the warm vegetable broth, a little at a time, stirring well to combine after each addition.
- The amount of broth needed may vary depending on how thick you prefer your Pappa al Pomodoro.

Simmer:

- Let the mixture simmer on low heat for about 10-15 minutes, stirring occasionally, until it thickens to a porridge-like consistency.
- The bread should be very soft.

Adjust the Seasonings:

- Taste the mixture and adjust the salt and pepper as needed.
- If the tomatoes are too acidic, add a pinch of sugar to balance the flavors.

Add Fresh Basil:

- Remove from heat. Stir in the fresh basil leaves, saving a few for garnish.

Serve:

- Transfer the Pappa al Pomodoro to serving bowls.
- Drizzle a generous amount of extra-virgin olive oil over each serving and garnish with the remaining basil leaves.

Optional:

- For an extra layer of flavor, toast some garlic in olive oil and drizzle it over the top before serving.

This rustic, vegan Pappa al Pomodoro is a celebration of simple ingredients and flavors, perfect for any season but especially comforting in colder months. Pair it with a fresh salad and a glass of your favorite Tuscan wine for a complete meal.

Ribollita

Originally a peasant dish, ribollita, meaning 'reboiled,' is a flavorful, hearty soup made from leftover vegetables like carrots, celery, potatoes, onions, kale, and cannellini beans, thickened with bread.

It's a perfect example of Tuscan culinary resourcefulness.

Ribollita is a famous Tuscan soup made from bread and vegetables. Originally a peasant dish, its name literally means "reboiled," as it originated from reheating leftover minestrone or vegetable soup from the previous day, with bread added to it.

Traditional ribollita is a showcase of humble ingredients and resourcefulness in the kitchen, as it's designed to use up leftover bread, beans, and vegetables. Here's how you can make a vegan version of this hearty and rustic dish:

Ingredients:

- 1/4 cup extra-virgin olive oil, plus more for serving
- 1 large onion, chopped
- 2 carrots, chopped
- 2 celery stalks, chopped
- 3-4 cloves of garlic, minced
- 1 teaspoon salt, plus more to taste
- 1/2 teaspoon freshly ground black pepper, plus more to taste
- 1 tablespoon tomato paste
- 1 can (14.5 oz) diced tomatoes
- 4 cups low-sodium vegetable broth
- 2 cups water
- 1 bunch of kale or Swiss chard, stems removed, leaves chopped
- 1 can (15 oz) cannellini beans, drained and rinsed
- 4-6 cups day-old bread, torn into pieces
- 1 sprig of fresh rosemary
- 1 sprig of fresh thyme

- 1 bunch of fresh basil, torn
- Red pepper flakes (optional)

Instructions:

Prepare the Base:

- Heat the olive oil in a large pot over medium heat. Add the onion, carrots, celery, and garlic, seasoning with salt and pepper. Sauté until the vegetables are softened, about 5-7 minutes.

Combine Ingredients:

- Add the tomato paste and stir until the vegetables are well-coated. Cook for another 2 minutes.
- Add the diced tomatoes with their juices, vegetable broth, and water.
- Stir in the rosemary and thyme sprigs. Increase the heat to high and bring the mixture to a boil.

Add Greens and Beans:

- Once boiling, reduce the heat to a simmer.
- Add the chopped kale or Swiss chard leaves and the cannellini beans.
- Cover and simmer for about 15-20 minutes or until the greens are tender.

Bread Addition:

- Add the torn bread into the soup, stirring well so that the bread starts to break down and thicken the soup.
- If your soup is too thick, you can add a bit more water or vegetable broth to reach your desired consistency.
- Simmer for another 10 minutes.

- Remove the sprigs of rosemary and thyme.
- Add most of the torn basil leaves, reserving some for garnish.
- Taste and adjust the seasoning with more salt, pepper, and red pepper flakes (if using).

Serve:

- Ladle the hot ribollita into bowls, drizzle with extra-virgin olive oil and top with the remaining basil.
- Optionally, you can also add a sprinkle of vegan parmesan cheese.

Ribollita is traditionally served reheated, so feel free to make this soup a day in advance and reheat portions as needed, enhancing the flavors and giving a truly authentic experience. It's a filling, comforting, and nutritious meal, perfect for chilly evenings.

Fagioli all'uccelletto

"Fagioli all'uccelletto" is a traditional Tuscan dish. Its name, which translates to "beans in the style of little birds," comes from the way the beans are cooked, similar to how hunters would prepare small game birds.

The beans are typically simmered in a tomato sauce with sage, garlic, and olive oil.

Here's how you can prepare a vegan version of Fagioli all'uccelletto:

- 2 cups of cannellini beans (if dried, they need to be soaked overnight; if canned, they should be drained and rinsed)
- 1/4 cup extra-virgin olive oil
- 3-4 cloves of garlic, finely sliced or minced
- 1-2 sprigs of fresh sage (or 1 tsp of dried sage if fresh is unavailable)
- 1 can (400g or 14 oz) of quality chopped tomatoes or crushed tomatoes
- Salt and freshly ground black pepper to taste
- Optional: red pepper flakes for a bit of heat

Instructions:

Prepare the Beans (if using dried beans):

- If you're using dried beans, after soaking them overnight, drain and rinse them before use.

- Place them in a large pot, cover with water, and bring to a boil.

- Reduce to a simmer and cook until tender (usually around 60-90 minutes, depending on the age of the beans).

- Skip this step if you're using canned beans.

Sauté Garlic and Sage:

- In a large skillet or saucepan, heat the olive oil over medium heat.

- Add the garlic and sage, sautéing until the garlic is golden and fragrant.

- Be careful not to burn the garlic, as it can become bitter.

Add Tomatoes:

- Pour in the chopped or crushed tomatoes and stir well.

- Let it simmer for about 5-10 minutes so that the flavors meld.

- If you like a bit of heat, you can add a pinch of red pepper flakes at this stage.

Combine with Beans:

- Add your prepared or canned cannellini beans to the tomato mixture.

- Stir well to ensure the beans are well-coated with the sauce.

- Reduce the heat, cover, and let everything simmer together for an additional 15-20 minutes.

- If the mixture becomes too thick, you can add a little water.

- Taste the mixture and season with salt and black pepper as needed.
- Let the beans sit for a few minutes off the heat to absorb more flavors before serving.
- Serve hot as a side dish or with slices of crusty bread to soak up the sauce.
- This dish is excellent paired with a fresh salad or roasted vegetables for a complete meal.

This hearty and flavorful dish reflects the simplicity of Tuscan cuisine, where the quality of the ingredients is allowed to shine. It's a versatile side that pairs well with many other dishes.

Crostini con Peperoni

"Crostini con Peperoni is a popular Tuscan appetizer featuring crusty bread slices topped with a flavorful bell pepper mixture.

To craft a vegan rendition, begin with slices of artisanal bread, lightly toasted to perfection. In a pan, sauté a mix of colorful bell peppers with aromatic garlic, luscious olive oil, and a medley of Mediterranean herbs until tender.

To elevate the dish, sprinkle with vegan cheese or perhaps a drizzle of rich balsamic reduction.

This appetizer beautifully marries simplicity with the robust flavors of Tuscany, offering a vegan treat that's sure to impress.

Here's how you can create a vegan version of this delightful starter:

Ingredients:

- 4 large bell peppers (a mix of red, yellow, and/or green for color)
- 3 tablespoons of extra-virgin olive oil, plus more for brushing the bread
- 2-3 cloves of garlic, minced
- 1 tablespoon of capers, rinsed and chopped (optional)
- Salt and freshly ground black pepper to taste
- A pinch of red pepper flakes (optional for a spicy kick)

- 1 small bunch of fresh basil leaves, torn or roughly chopped
- 1 loaf of crusty Italian bread or baguette, sliced into 1/2-inch pieces
- Balsamic vinegar or vegan red wine vinegar (optional)

Instructions:

Prepare the Bell Peppers:

- Preheat your oven's broiler. Place the bell peppers on a baking sheet and broil them, turning occasionally, until they're charred on all sides. This usually takes about 10-15 minutes.
- Once blackened, transfer the peppers to a bowl and cover it with plastic wrap or a plate. Let them steam for 10 minutes to loosen their skin.
- Peel the skin off the peppers, remove their cores and seeds, and then slice them into thin strips.

Sauté the Mixture:

- Heat the olive oil in a large skillet over medium heat.
- Add the minced garlic and sauté until golden and fragrant.
- Add the roasted pepper strips to the skillet.
- If using capers, add them now.
- Stir everything together.
- Season with salt, black pepper, and red pepper flakes (if using).
- Cook for 2-3 minutes, allowing the flavors to meld.
- Remove the skillet from the heat and stir in the fresh basil.
- Set the mixture aside to cool slightly. It should be warm but not hot.

Prepare the Bread:

- Brush each bread slice with olive oil on both sides.
- Arrange the slices in a single layer on a baking sheet.
- Place the baking sheet under the broiler and toast the bread slices until they're golden and crispy. This usually takes about 1-2 minutes per side, depending on your broiler. Watch them closely to prevent burning.

Assemble the Crostini:

- Once your bread is toasted, top each slice with a generous portion of the warm pepper mixture.
- If desired, drizzle a little balsamic vinegar or vegan red wine vinegar over the top for an extra flavor dimension.

Serve:

- Arrange the crostini on a serving platter.
- They're best enjoyed warm, so consider serving them immediately.
- They make a perfect appetizer or addition to a tapas-style meal.

This vegan Crostini con Peperoni keeps the vibrant flavors of the traditional dish while ensuring it's suitable for a vegan diet. The combination of sweet, softened peppers with the crunch of toasted bread is sure to be a hit with everyone.

Farro Soup (Zuppa di Farro)

Embracing farro, an ancient grain that's a staple in Tuscan cuisine, "Zuppa di Farro" is a hearty and rustic soup from Tuscany, known for its nutritious ingredients and comforting flavor.

Here's how you can make a vegan version of this Tuscan specialty:

Ingredients:

- 1 cup farro, rinsed and drained. (The ancient grain farro is very versatile and can be replaced in most recipes with spelt berries, wheat berries, and Kamut® berries. If you want a gluten-free substitute, sorghum, brown rice, or oat groats will all make good replacements in most recipes.)
- 2 tablespoons olive oil
- 1 large onion, finely chopped
- 2 carrots, diced
- 2 celery stalks, diced
- 3-4 garlic cloves, minced
- 1 can (400g or 14 oz) chopped tomatoes, with juice

- 4-5 cups vegetable broth
- 1 teaspoon dried thyme or 1 tablespoon fresh thyme leaves
- 1 teaspoon dried rosemary or 1 tablespoon fresh rosemary, finely chopped
- 2 bay leaves
- Salt and freshly ground black pepper to taste
- 1 can (400g or 15 oz) cannellini beans, rinsed and drained (optional for extra protein)
- Fresh parsley, chopped (for garnish)

Instructions:

Prepare the Farro:

- If using whole farro, consider soaking it overnight in water to reduce the cooking time. Before cooking, drain the farro and set it aside.

Cook the Vegetables:

- Heat olive oil in a large pot or Dutch oven over medium heat. Add the onion, carrots, and celery, sautéing until the vegetables are softened (about 5-7 minutes).

- Add the minced garlic to the pot and sauté for another minute until fragrant.

Build the Soup Base:

- Stir in the chopped tomatoes, including their juices, to add depth to the soup base.

- Add the farro to the pot, stirring it through the vegetables and tomatoes, allowing it to toast slightly (about 1-2 minutes).

- Pour in the vegetable broth, ensuring there's enough liquid to cover the mixture generously, as the farro will absorb a lot of water.

- Season the soup with thyme, rosemary, bay leaves, salt, and pepper. Stir well to combine.

Simmer the Soup:

- Bring the mixture to a boil, then reduce the heat to allow the soup to simmer.
- Cover the pot partially with a lid and let it simmer for about 30-40 minutes, or until the farro is tender but still chewy. If you soaked the farro beforehand, check for doneness around the 20-minute mark.

Add Cannellini Beans (optional):

- If you're using cannellini beans, add them to the pot in the last 10-15 minutes of cooking to heat through.

Final Adjustments:

- Once the farro is cooked to your liking, remove the bay leaves.
- Taste the soup, adjusting the seasoning with more salt and pepper if necessary. If the soup is too thick, add a bit more vegetable broth or water until it reaches your desired consistency.

Serve:

- Ladle the hot soup into bowls, garnishing with fresh parsley.
- For an authentic touch, serve with a drizzle of extra-virgin olive oil over the top and some crusty bread on the side.

Enjoy your nourishing and satisfying bowl of vegan "Zuppa di Farro," perfect for warming up on a chilly day! This dish celebrates the simplicity of Tuscan cuisine, focusing on fresh, high-quality ingredients.

Panzanella

Panzanella is a Tuscan bread salad known for its simple yet flavorful ingredients. A vegan version maintains the integrity of this dish, focusing on fresh vegetables and crusty bread.

Here's how you can make it:

Ingredients:

- 4-6 cups of stale (1-2 days old) crusty Italian or French bread, torn or cut into bite-sized pieces
- 4 large ripe tomatoes, cut into chunks or wedges
- 1 small red onion, thinly sliced
- 1 cucumber, halved lengthwise and sliced

- A handful of fresh basil leaves, roughly torn
- 3-4 tablespoons of extra virgin olive oil
- 2-3 tablespoons of balsamic or red wine vinegar
- Salt and freshly ground black pepper to taste
- Optional: capers or [Kalamata] pitted olives for an extra burst of flavor

Instructions:

Prep the Bread:

- If your bread isn't sufficiently stale, you can dry it out by placing the pieces in a preheated oven at 300°F (150°C) for about 10-15 minutes until hardened but not toasted. Allow it to cool.

Soften the Bread:

- Place the bread pieces in a large bowl. In a small bowl, mix about 1/2 cup of water with a pinch of salt, then sprinkle this over the bread. (Some prefer to quickly dip the bread pieces in water instead.)
- Let them stand for a few minutes until you see the bread start to soften. The goal is to make it just slightly moist, not soggy.

Mix the Salad:

- Add the chopped tomatoes, sliced onion, and cucumber to the bowl with the bread.
- Add the fresh basil leaves. If you're using capers or olives, add them now.
- Drizzle with a generous amount of olive oil and red wine vinegar.
- Add salt and pepper to taste.

- Toss everything well to combine. You want the juices from the vegetables to start melding with the bread.

- Cover the bowl with plastic wrap or a clean kitchen towel and let the salad rest at room temperature for at least 30 minutes to an hour. This resting period allows the flavors to blend and the bread to soak up the juices deliciously.

Final Adjustments:

- Give the salad a quick taste and adjust the seasonings as needed, adding more salt, pepper, vinegar, or olive oil if necessary.
- If the bread has soaked up too much of the dressing and the salad seems dry, you can add an extra drizzle of olive oil and a splash of vinegar.

Serve:

- Toss the salad gently once more before serving.
- Plate it on a serving dish or individual plates, garnishing with a few more fresh basil leaves if desired.

Panzanella is best enjoyed fresh on the day it's made. The simple, refreshing flavors make it a perfect dish for warm summer months, especially as a way to showcase ripe, in-season tomatoes.

Cavolo Nero (Tuscan Kale)

This versatile leafy green can be used in various dishes, including stews, salads, and pastas. It's often sautéed with garlic, chili, and extra-virgin olive oil for a simple, nutritious side.

Cavolo nero, also known as Tuscan kale, black kale, or dinosaur kale, is a type of leafy green that has become increasingly popular due to its rich flavor and nutritional benefits. Suppose you're in the USA and unable to find cavolo nero. In that case, here are a few alternatives you can use that are more commonly found in most grocery stores, i.e., curly kale, collard greens, Swiss chard, or mustard greens.

Ingredients:

- 1 bunch of cavolo nero (about 10-12 leaves) or any of the alternatives listed above
- 2 tablespoons of olive oil

- 2-3 cloves of garlic, thinly sliced or minced
- 1/2 teaspoon of red pepper flakes (optional for heat)
- Salt, to taste
- 1-2 tablespoons of lemon juice (optional for added zest)
- 1/4 cup of vegetable broth or water

Instructions:

Prepare the Cavolo Nero:

- Wash the cavolo nero leaves thoroughly in cold water.
- Strip the leaves from the tough central stem by holding the stem end and pulling off the leaf with your other hand.
- Roughly chop the leaves into smaller, bite-sized pieces.

Cook Garlic:

- In a large skillet, heat olive oil over medium heat.
- Add the sliced or minced garlic (and red pepper flakes if you're using them) to the skillet.
- Sauté for about 1-2 minutes until the garlic is fragrant but not browned.

Sauté the Cavolo Nero:

- Add the chopped cavolo nero to the skillet.
- Stir to coat the leaves in the olive oil and garlic. You'll notice the leaves will start to wilt slightly.

Add Liquid:

- After the cavolo nero has wilted (about 2-3 minutes), add the vegetable broth or water to the skillet. This will help steam the cavolo nero and prevent it from getting too crispy or burnt.

- Continue to cook the cavolo nero, stirring occasionally for about 5-7 minutes or until it's tender and reaches your desired level of doneness.
- Some people prefer it slightly more firm, while others like it very soft.

Season and Serve:

- Remove from heat.
- If using, drizzle with lemon juice and give it a quick stir.
- Season with salt to taste.
- Serve the cavolo nero as a side dish or incorporate it into your main course as desired.
- It goes wonderfully with grains, in pasta, or as part of a vegetable platter.

Enjoy your healthy and flavorful Tuscan-style cavolo nero! This dish is simple, yet it's packed with flavor — a testament to the essence of Italian cooking.

Arista di Seitan alla Toscana (Seitan 'Roast' Tuscan-style)

Arista is a traditional Tuscan pork roast seasoned with herbs and cooked with vegetables. In this vegan version, we're substituting pork with seitan, a versatile, protein-rich meat alternative made from wheat gluten.

This recipe captures the essence of the Tuscan flavors, providing a hearty, satisfying dish without using any animal products.

Ingredients:

- 1-1.5 pounds (about 500-700 grams) of ready-made plain seitan
- 3 tablespoons of olive oil
- 4 cloves of garlic, minced
- 2 tablespoons of fresh rosemary, finely chopped (or 2 teaspoons dried)
- 2 tablespoons of fresh sage, finely chopped (or 2 teaspoons dried)
- Salt and black pepper, to taste

- 1/2 cup of white wine (vegan)
- 1/2 cup of vegetable broth
- Optional: 1-2 tablespoons of balsamic vinegar or lemon juice for extra zest
- Optional: 1 small onion, thinly sliced, and 2 carrots, chopped, for additional flavor and texture

Instructions:

Prepare the Seitan:

- If the seitan is in a large piece, slice it into about 1-inch thick slices. This will allow for more even cooking and better flavor absorption.

Marinate:

- In a bowl, mix 2 tablespoons of olive oil with the minced garlic, rosemary, sage, salt, and pepper.
- Add the seitan slices, ensuring they are well coated with the marinade.
- Let it sit for at least 30 minutes, or even better, overnight in the refrigerator.

Sear the Seitan:

- Heat the remaining tablespoon of olive oil in a large skillet or frying pan over medium-high heat.
- Once hot, add the seitan slices (reserve the marinade) and sear them until they're golden brown on both sides.
- Remove and set aside.

Optional Vegetables:

- If using, sauté the sliced onion and chopped carrots in the same skillet until they're softened, about 5-7 minutes.

Deglaze the Pan:

- Pour the white wine into the skillet, stirring well to lift any browned bits from the bottom of the skillet. This process adds depth of flavor to the final dish.

Simmer:

- Return the seitan to the skillet along with the reserved marinade and vegetable broth.
- Bring to a simmer, then reduce the heat to low, covering the skillet with a lid.
- Let it simmer for about 20-30 minutes, allowing the flavors to meld.

Taste and Adjust Seasonings:

- After simmering, taste the sauce. If desired, add balsamic vinegar or lemon juice for a touch of acidity and brightness.
- Adjust the salt and pepper as needed.

Serve:

- Once everything is well-cooked and flavorful, serve your 'Arista' hot, garnished with additional fresh herbs if desired.
- It pairs beautifully with traditional Tuscan sides like roasted potatoes or a fresh green salad.

This dish brings the aromatic presence of Tuscany to your table, celebrating the richness of Italian herbs and the hearty texture of seitan as a stand-in for traditional meats.

Umbria

Umbria, the green heart of Italy, is renowned for its lush landscapes, historical significance, and culinary delights that emphasize simple ingredients and earthy flavors. The region's cuisine leans heavily on legumes, grains, and vegetables, providing a solid foundation for a variety of vegan dishes. Here are some vegan-friendly dishes from Umbria, along with potential adaptations:

Zuppa di Lenticchie di Castelluccio

Castelluccio is famous for its high-quality lentils, and this soup celebrates them in their purest form.

The vegan version of this hearty dish includes lentils, potatoes, carrots, celery, onions, tomatoes, and aromatic herbs cooked until the ingredients are tender and flavorful.

Ingredients:

- 1 cup Castelluccio lentils (available online, or substitute with another variety)
- 2 tablespoons extra-virgin olive oil
- 1 medium onion, chopped
- 2 garlic cloves, minced
- 1 medium carrot, chopped
- 1 celery stalk, chopped
- 1 potato, diced
- 4 cups vegetable broth or water
- 1 bay leaf
- 1 sprig of fresh rosemary (or 1 teaspoon dried rosemary)
- Salt and freshly ground black pepper to taste
- Optional: Fresh parsley or celery leaves for garnish

Instructions:

Prepare the Lentils:

- Begin by rinsing the lentils under cold water, checking for and removing any small stones or other debris.

- Unlike some other varieties, Castelluccio lentils don't typically require soaking before cooking.

Sauté the Base Vegetables:

- Heat the olive oil in a large pot over medium heat.

- Add the chopped onion and minced garlic, sautéing until they become translucent and fragrant.

- This step helps to build the flavor base of the soup.

Add More Vegetables:

- Next, add the chopped carrot, celery, and diced potato to the pot. These vegetables contribute to the soup's hearty texture and nutritional content.

- Sauté for a few more minutes until they start to soften.

Cook the Lentils:

- Add the rinsed lentils to your pot of vegetables, followed by the vegetable broth or water.

- The liquid should cover the lentils and vegetables by a couple of inches, ensuring they cook evenly.

Herbs and Seasoning:

- Place a bay leaf and rosemary sprig into the pot. These herbs infuse the soup with traditional Italian flavors.

- Bring the mixture to a boil and then reduce the heat to a low simmer.

Simmer the Soup:

- Allow your soup to simmer uncovered for about 30-40 minutes.
- Over this time, the lentils and vegetables will become tender, and the flavors will meld together.
- Stir occasionally and check the lentils for doneness.

Season to Taste:

- After the soup has cooked and the lentils are tender, remove the bay leaf and rosemary sprig.
- Add salt and freshly ground black pepper to taste.
- Adjust the seasoning carefully, as the flavors will have concentrated during cooking.

Serve Your Soup:

- Ladle the soup into bowls, serving it hot.
- For an authentic touch, garnish with fresh parsley or celery leaves and a drizzle of extra-virgin olive oil if desired.

This traditional Zuppa di Lenticchie di Castelluccio recipe brings the authentic taste of the Umbrian region to your table, providing a warm, nourishing meal that showcases the simple yet rich flavors of Italian cuisine.

Crostini con Fave

This appetizer features crusty bread topped with a blend of puréed fava beans, extra-virgin olive oil, garlic, and fresh herbs.

It's a delightful start to any meal and is naturally vegan.

Ingredients:

- 1 lb (450 grams) fresh fava beans (in their pods)
- 1 baguette or rustic Italian bread
- 1-2 cloves of garlic, peeled
- Extra virgin olive oil
- Salt, to taste
- Freshly ground black pepper, to taste
- Vegan cheese (opt for a hard variety to mimic the texture of Pecorino, if available)
- Fresh mint leaves (optional for garnish and an extra layer of flavor)

Instructions:

1. Prep the Fava Beans:

- Begin by shelling the fava beans from their pods.

- Blanch the beans in boiling water for about 30 seconds, then immediately place them into a bowl of ice water to stop the cooking process. This also helps make the beans' outer skins easier to peel.
- Once cooled, peel the skins from the beans.

2. Cook the Fava Beans:

- Place the prepared beans in a pan with a bit of water and bring to a low simmer.
- Cook until they are tender (approximately 10-20 minutes, depending on their size). Make sure to add water as needed to prevent the beans from drying out.
- Once the beans are cooked, drain any remaining water.

3. Mash the Beans:

- While still warm, mash the beans in a bowl with a fork.
- Depending on your preference, you can leave some beans partially whole to add texture.
- Season with salt and freshly ground black pepper to your liking.
- For added richness, mix in a small amount of olive oil.

4. Prepare the Bread:

- Slice your baguette or Italian bread into 1/2-inch slices.
- Toast these in an oven preheated to 375 degrees F (190 degrees C) until they reach a crispy golden brown (about 5-10 minutes).
- Alternatively, grilling the bread adds a nice flavor.

5. Assemble the Crostini:

- Once toasted, while still warm, take a peeled garlic clove and rub it on one side of each slice of bread.

- Drizzle your olive oil generously over the top.

- Spread your warm, mashed fava beans on top of the slices of bread.
- Now, add a slice or a sprinkle of your chosen vegan cheese.
- If you have a block of vegan cheese, use a grater or vegetable peeler to create thin slices or shavings.

7. Garnish and Serve:

- If using, tear up some fresh mint leaves and sprinkle them over the top of your crostini.
- This adds a refreshing, aromatic element that pairs beautifully with the fava beans.
- Serve immediately, enjoying the harmonious blend of flavors and textures.

This vegan take on the classic Umbrian dish still respects the simplicity and freshness of the original recipe while making it accessible to those following a vegan diet.

Gnocchi al Sagrantino

While traditional gnocchi is made with potato and flour, the key to this dish is the sauce — a rich, aromatic concoction made from the famed Sagrantino wine, tomatoes, garlic, and herbs.

Ensure the gnocchi is vegan (made without eggs) and substitute any dairy in the sauce with vegan alternatives.

Ingredients:

For the Gnocchi:

- 2 lbs. (about 1 kg) potatoes, preferably starchy ones like Russets
- 1 to 1 1/2 cups all-purpose flour, plus extra for dusting
- Salt, to taste

For the Sagrantino Sauce:

- 1 cup Sagrantino di Montefalco wine (or another robust red wine if Sagrantino is unavailable)
- 1 small onion, finely chopped
- 2 cloves garlic, minced

- 2-3 tablespoons extra-virgin olive oil
- 1 cup vegetable broth
- Salt and black pepper, to taste
- A pinch of sugar, if needed (to balance the acidity of the sauce)
- Fresh parsley, chopped (for garnish)

Instructions:

Make the Gnocchi:

- Start by boiling the potatoes with their skins on in a pot of salted water.

- Cook them until they are just tender through, which you can test by piercing them with a fork.

- Drain the potatoes and let them cool slightly.

- Peel the skins off while the potatoes are still warm.

- Using a potato ricer, mash the potatoes on a clean, flat surface. If you don't have a ricer, you can mash them until smooth with no lumps remaining.

- Sprinkle the mashed potatoes with flour, using just enough to create a dough that holds together and is not too sticky. Be cautious with adding the flour, as too much will make the gnocchi heavy and dense.

- Gently knead the mixture until uniform, but do not overwork.

- Cut the dough into several pieces and roll into logs about 3/4-inch in diameter.

- Cut the logs into 1-inch pieces, and if you like, press each piece against a fork to create ridges.

- Bring a large pot of salted water to a boil.

- Cook the gnocchi in batches by dropping them into the boiling water. They are done when they float to the surface.
- Remove the floating gnocchi with a slotted spoon and set aside.

Prepare the Sagrantino Sauce:
- In a large skillet, heat the olive oil over medium heat.
- Add the chopped onion and garlic, sautéing until they're soft and translucent but not browned.
- Pour in the Sagrantino wine, letting it simmer, and reduce for a few minutes to cook off some of the alcohol.
- Add the vegetable broth and continue to simmer the sauce until it reduces and slightly thickens. This process concentrates the flavors.
- Season with salt and pepper to taste.
- If the sauce is too acidic, add a pinch of sugar to balance the flavors.

Combine Gnocchi and Sauce:
- Add the cooked gnocchi to the skillet with the sauce, gently tossing to coat them.
- Let them simmer for a minute or two to absorb the flavors.

Serve:
- Serve your Gnocchi al Sagrantino hot, garnished with chopped fresh parsley.
- You can also drizzle a bit more olive oil on top if desired.

Enjoy your vegan version of this flavorful Umbrian specialty! The gnocchi should be light and tender, complemented by the rich, bold flavors of the Sagrantino sauce.

Pizza con Patate e Rosmarino

Though not unique to Umbria, this simple yet satisfying pizza — topped with thinly sliced potatoes, rosemary, garlic, and a drizzle of extra-virgin olive oil — is a vegan favorite and showcases classic Italian flavors.

Ingredients:

For the Dough:

- 2 1/4 teaspoons active dry yeast (1 standard packet)
- 1 1/2 cups warm water (not hot, as it can kill the yeast)
- 3 1/2 to 4 cups all-purpose flour, plus more for dusting
- 2 teaspoons salt
- 1 teaspoon sugar

- 2 tablespoons olive oil, plus more for coating

For the Topping:

- 2 to 3 large potatoes, very thinly sliced (using a mandoline if available)
- Fresh rosemary sprigs, leaves removed and roughly chopped
- Coarse sea salt, to taste
- Freshly cracked black pepper, to taste
- Extra virgin olive oil for drizzling
- Garlic cloves, thinly sliced (optional)
- Red pepper flakes (optional for added heat)

Instructions:

Prepare the Dough:

- In a large bowl, dissolve the yeast and sugar in warm water, and let it sit for 5 to 10 minutes until it starts to froth — a sign that the yeast is active.

- Add the flour, salt, and olive oil to the yeast mixture.

- Mix until the dough starts to come together.

- Transfer the dough to a floured surface and knead for about 10 minutes until it's smooth and elastic.

- Add more flour if the dough is too sticky or a bit of water if it's too dry.

- Shape the dough into a ball and place it in a lightly oiled bowl, rolling the dough to coat it in oil.

- Cover the bowl with a clean towel and let the dough rise in a warm place until it has doubled in size, about 1 to 1.5 hours.

Preheat the Oven:

- If you have a pizza stone, place it in the middle rack of the oven.
- Preheat your oven to its highest setting, usually between 450 to 500 degrees F (230 to 260 degrees C).
- The high heat will give your pizza a crisp, golden crust.

Prepare the Topping:

- While the oven is heating, prepare your toppings.
- Wash the potatoes and slice them very thinly, ideally using a mandoline.
- They should be almost transparent.
- Set the slices in a bowl of cold water to remove excess starch, then drain and pat them dry with a kitchen towel to remove moisture. This step helps the potatoes cook evenly without becoming soggy.

Assemble the Pizza:

- After the dough has risen, punch it down gently to release air bubbles. Transfer it to a floured surface.
- Roll out the dough to your desired thickness, remembering it will rise quite a bit in the oven.
- If you don't have a pizza peel for transferring pizza to the oven, you can use a piece of parchment paper on a baking sheet.
- Transfer your rolled-out dough onto the parchment paper.
- Arrange the potato slices on the dough in a single layer, slightly overlapping.
- Sprinkle the chopped rosemary, salt, and pepper evenly over the top. If you're using garlic, scatter the slices over the potatoes.

- Drizzle generously with olive oil, which will help the potatoes crisp up and add flavor.
- If you like a bit of heat, sprinkle some red pepper flakes over the top.

Bake the Pizza:

- Carefully transfer the pizza (with the parchment paper, if using) to the preheated pizza stone or onto a baking sheet in the oven.
- Bake for about 10-15 minutes, depending on your oven's heat, until the crust is golden and the potatoes are cooked and slightly crispy.
- The high heat is key to a crispy crust, but keep an eye on it to avoid burning.

Serve:

- Remove the pizza from the oven and let it cool for a few minutes.
- This resting time helps the crust set and become even crispier.
- Slice and serve hot, enjoying the harmonious blend of the simple flavors.

This type of pizza really celebrates the ingredients' natural flavors, with the rosemary providing an aromatic hint that complements the earthiness of the potatoes. It's a beautiful example of traditional Italian simplicity in cooking.

Torta al Testo con Verdure

Torta al Testo is a traditional flatbread from the Umbria region, often enjoyed with various fillings, including meats, cheeses, and vegetables.

However, you can easily make a vegan version of Torta al Testo, also known as "Torta al Tegamino," filled with a medley of seasoned vegetables.

Here's how:

Ingredients:

For the Torta al Testo:

- 400g (approximately 3 cups) all-purpose flour, plus extra for dusting
- 1 packet (7g) instant yeast
- 1/2 teaspoon sugar
- 1 teaspoon salt
- About 250 ml (1 cup) warm water (adjust as needed)
- 2 tablespoons extra-virgin olive oil

For the Vegetable Filling:

- 1 medium eggplant, sliced into rounds
- 1 red bell pepper, sliced into strips
- 1 zucchini, sliced into rounds
- 1 yellow squash, sliced into rounds
- 1 red onion, sliced
- 2-3 tablespoons extra-virgin olive oil
- Salt and pepper, to taste
- A small bunch of fresh basil, roughly torn
- Optional: garlic powder, balsamic vinegar

Instructions:

Prepare the Dough:

- In a large mixing bowl, combine the flour, instant yeast, sugar, and salt.
- Gradually add warm water to the dry ingredients, mixing them continuously until you form a dough. You may need slightly more or less water, depending on the flour type.
- Add the olive oil and knead the dough on a lightly floured surface for about 10 minutes until it's smooth and elastic.

- Place the dough in a lightly oiled bowl, cover with a clean kitchen towel, and let it rise in a warm place for approximately 1 hour or until doubled in size.

Cook the Vegetables:

- While the dough is rising, you can start on the vegetables.
- Heat a grill pan or a regular pan over medium heat with some olive oil.
- Grill the eggplant, zucchini, yellow squash, red bell pepper, and onion in batches until they're nicely browned and softened.
- You can season them with salt, pepper, and optional garlic powder as they cook.
- Once cooked, you can drizzle the vegetables with a bit of balsamic vinegar for extra flavor, but that's entirely optional.
- Set the cooked vegetables aside.

Shape and Cook the Torta al Testo:

- After the dough has risen, punch it down to release the air and divide it into two equal parts.
- On a lightly floured surface, roll each part into a circle about 1/2 inch thick.
- Heat a large non-stick pan or a flat skillet over medium heat (do not oil it).
- Place one dough circle in the pan and cook for about 5-6 minutes until the bottom is golden brown and the top starts to form bubbles.
- Flip and cook for another 5-6 minutes.
- Repeat with the second dough circle.

- Remove the cooked bread from the pan and allow it to cool slightly.

Assemble the Torta al Testo:

- Take one piece of the warm bread and arrange a layer of the grilled vegetables on top. Sprinkle with fresh basil for an extra burst of flavor.
- Top with the second piece of bread, press down gently and cut into wedges or slices.

Serve:

- Serve warm or at room temperature.
- This dish is great for picnics, and the leftovers are delicious the next day.

This vegan Torta al Testo con Verdure offers a fantastic way to enjoy a medley of grilled vegetables encapsulated in a traditional Umbrian flatbread, making for a satisfying meal that highlights the simplicity and freshness of Italian cooking.

Brustengolo

Brustengolo is a traditional cake from the Umbria region, specifically known in the area around Perugia.

This dish, often prepared in the autumn months, was originally made by the poorer classes with the most readily available ingredients: cornmeal, nuts, and dried fruits. It's naturally dairy-free, and we can easily make a vegan version by ensuring all the accompanying ingredients are plant-based.

Here's how you can make a vegan Brustengolo:

Ingredients:

- 300g (approximately 1 1/2 cups) cornmeal
- 200g (approximately 1 cup) sugar
- 800ml (approximately 3 1/3 cups) water
- 4 tablespoons extra-virgin olive oil, plus extra for greasing
- A pinch of salt
- 1 teaspoon cinnamon
- 1/2 teaspoon nutmeg
- Zest of 1 orange or lemon (based on preference)
- 100g (approximately 1 cup) raisins or sultanas
- 100g (approximately 1 cup) pine nuts or chopped walnuts (or a mix of both)
- 2 medium apples, peeled, cored, and diced

- Optional: 100g (approximately 3.5 oz) of dark chocolate chips (ensure they are vegan)

Instructions:

Prepare the Fruit and Nuts:

- Place the raisins in a small bowl and cover them with warm water (or you could use apple juice for extra flavor) to plump them up.
- Set aside for about 20 minutes, then drain.
- If you're using walnuts, you can lightly toast them in a dry pan for a few minutes until they become fragrant. This step is optional but enhances the flavor.

Make the Batter:

- In a large pot, mix the cornmeal with sugar, then gradually add water, stirring continuously to prevent lumps from forming.
- Add the olive oil and a pinch of salt.
- Cook over medium heat, stirring constantly, until the mixture thickens (usually takes about 10-15 minutes).
- It should be a porridge-like consistency.
- Remove from the heat and let it cool down a bit.

Add Flavors and Textures:

- Once the mixture has cooled slightly, stir in the cinnamon, nutmeg, and citrus zest.
- Add the drained raisins/sultanas, pine nuts or walnuts (or both), and diced apples.
- If you're using chocolate chips, add them at this stage.
- Mix everything together until well combined.

- Preheat your oven to 180°C (approximately 350°F).
- Grease a round cake pan (around 20cm/8 inches in diameter) with a bit of olive oil, or line it with parchment paper.
- Pour the batter into the pan, smoothing the top with a spatula.
- The mixture will be quite thick and chunky because of all the added fruits and nuts.
- Bake in the preheated oven for about 40-45 minutes or until the top is golden and a toothpick inserted into the center comes out clean.

Serve:

- Allow the cake to cool in the pan before turning it out onto a serving plate.
- Brustengolo is delicious and served slightly warm or at room temperature.
- Optional: Dust with a bit of powdered sugar before serving (ensure it is vegan) or serve with a scoop of vegan ice cream.

This hearty, rustic cake is a celebration of the autumn harvest and is perfect for enjoying on a crisp fall day, possibly paired with a warm cup of apple cider or a robust red wine. Its rich textures and flavors make Brustengolo a unique and satisfying treat, offering a taste of Umbria's culinary heritage.

These dishes highlight the rich agricultural bounty of Umbria and can be a seamless part of a vegan diet, emphasizing healthful, plant-based ingredients that don't compromise on flavor. As always, it's essential to ensure that all individual ingredients meet vegan standards.

Marche (Le Marche)

Le Marche, a region celebrated for its beautiful coastlines, mountainous landscapes, and artisanal food production, offers a unique culinary journey.

The traditional fare of Le Marche emphasizes fresh, local produce, a variety of grains, and an abundance of herbs, all of which lend themselves beautifully to vegan adaptations.

Here are several dishes from the region that can be enjoyed by those following a vegan lifestyle:

Olive all'Ascolana

Though traditionally stuffed with meat and deep-fried, there's a vegan twist to these famous Ascoli Piceno olives.

The stuffing can be made from a flavorful blend of breadcrumbs, garlic, herbs, and chopped walnuts or almonds, all encased in large, juicy olives, breaded and fried to golden perfection.

Ingredients:

For the Filling:

- 100g (approximately 1/2 cup) cooked chickpeas
- 1 small carrot, cooked and finely chopped
- 1 small celery stalk, cooked and finely chopped
- 1/2 small onion, finely chopped
- 1 garlic clove, minced
- 50g (approximately 1/3 cup) breadcrumbs

- A handful of fresh parsley, chopped
- Salt and pepper, to taste
- Olive oil

For the Olives:

- 30 large green olives, pitted
- Flour for dusting
- Plant-based milk
- Breadcrumbs, for breading

For Frying:

- Vegetable oil for frying

Instructions:

Prepare the Filling:

- In a food processor, blend the chickpeas into a rough paste, leaving some smaller chunks for texture.
- In a pan, heat some olive oil over medium heat. Add the onion, garlic, and sauté until they're soft and golden.
- Add the carrot and celery and continue cooking for a few more minutes.
- Remove from the heat and transfer the mixture to a large bowl.
- Add the chickpea paste, breadcrumbs, chopped parsley, salt, and pepper.
- Mix well until everything is combined and holds together.
- If the mixture seems too dry, you can add a bit of plant-based milk; if it's too wet, add more breadcrumbs. Let it cool.

Stuff the Olives:

- Carefully stuff each olive with the filling.

- Be gentle to prevent the olives from breaking apart. It's a meticulous process, but the end result is worth it.

Bread the Olives:

- Set up three separate bowls: one with flour, one with plant-based milk, and one with breadcrumbs.
- Roll each stuffed olive in the flour, dip it in the plant-based milk, and then roll it in the breadcrumbs, ensuring it's well-coated.

Fry the Olives:

- In a deep frying pan or pot, heat the vegetable oil to 170–180°C (338–356°F). You need enough oil to completely submerge the olives.
- Fry the olives in batches to avoid overcrowding, which can lower the oil's temperature too much.
- Each batch should take about 2-3 minutes until golden and crispy.
- Use a slotted spoon to remove the olives from the oil and drain them on paper towels.

Serve:

- Serve your vegan Olive all'Ascolana hot, ideally with some marinara sauce or your choice of a vegan dip and perhaps a slice of lemon on the side.

By substituting a plant-based filling, this recipe respects the essence and preparation method of the traditional Olive all'Ascolana while making it accessible for a vegan diet. It's a meticulous dish, but the unique and delicious result is certainly rewarding.

Vincisgrassi

Vincisgrassi is a traditional baked pasta dish from the Marche region, similar to lasagna. It typically includes pasta, a meat sauce, and béchamel sauce, all layered and baked to perfection.

However, creating a vegan version involves substituting the meat and dairy with plant-based alternatives without compromising the depth of flavor that Vincisgrassi is known for. Here's how you can do it:

Ingredients:

For the Pasta:

- 400g (about 14 oz) of vegan lasagna sheets (check the ingredients to ensure they're egg-free)

For the Vegan "Meat" Sauce:

- 2 tablespoons olive oil
- 1 large onion, finely chopped
- 2 carrots, finely chopped
- 2 celery stalks, finely chopped
- 3-4 garlic cloves, minced

- 400g (about 14 oz) of vegan mince (textured vegetable protein, seitan, or a similar product)
- 1 cup red wine (ensure it's a vegan brand)
- 800g (about 28 oz) of crushed tomatoes
- 2 tablespoons tomato paste
- 1 teaspoon brown sugar (optional)
- Salt and black pepper, to taste
- A handful of fresh basil, chopped
- 2 teaspoons dried oregano

For the Vegan Béchamel Sauce:

- 4 tablespoons olive oil or vegan margarine
- 4 tablespoons all-purpose flour
- 4 cups unsweetened plant-based milk (such as almond, soy, or oat milk)
- 1 teaspoon ground nutmeg
- Salt and white pepper, to taste

For the topping (optional):

- Vegan cheese (optional for topping)
- Fresh basil leaves for garnish

Instructions:

Prepare the Vegan "Meat" Sauce:

- Heat the olive oil in a large skillet over medium heat.
- Add the onion, carrots, celery, and garlic, and sauté until the vegetables are soft, about 5-7 minutes.
- Increase the heat to medium-high and add the vegan mince to the skillet.
- Cook it with the vegetables until it's nicely browned, mimicking the texture of ground meat.

- Pour in the red wine and let it simmer until the alcohol has evaporated about 4-5 minutes.
- Stir in the crushed tomatoes, tomato paste, sugar (if using), salt, and pepper.
- Add the basil and oregano.
- Reduce the heat and let your sauce simmer for about 30-40 minutes, stirring occasionally. It should be thick and rich.

Prepare the Vegan Béchamel Sauce:
- In a saucepan, heat the olive oil or vegan margarine over medium heat.
- Add the flour, whisking continuously to create a smooth roux.
- Cook for 1-2 minutes without letting it brown.
- Gradually pour in the plant-based milk, whisking constantly to avoid lumps.
- Continue to cook and whisk until the sauce thickens, about 7-10 minutes.
- Season with salt, white pepper, and nutmeg.
- Remove from heat once thickened.

Assemble the Vincisgrassi:
- Preheat your oven to 180°C (356°F).
- In a large baking dish, start with a thin layer of the "meat" sauce.
- Place a layer of lasagna sheets over the sauce, then pour and spread some of the béchamel sauce over the pasta.
- Repeat the layers (meat sauce, pasta, béchamel), ending with a layer of béchamel on top.

- If you're using vegan cheese, sprinkle it on top of the final layer.

Bake:

- Cover the baking dish with aluminum foil and bake in the preheated oven for 25 minutes.
- After 25 minutes, remove the foil and continue to bake for another 10-15 minutes or until the top is golden and bubbly.

Serve:

- Remove from the oven and let it sit for a few minutes before slicing and serving.
- Garnish with fresh basil leaves if desired.

This vegan Vincisgrassi keeps the heart and soul of the classic dish alive, offering layers of flavor that are deeply satisfying and comforting. It's a sumptuous meal that can be enjoyed by everyone, regardless of dietary preferences.

Crescia sfogliata

Crescia sfogliata is a culinary gem originating from the picturesque Marche region of Italy. Characterized by its multiple flaky layers, this flatbread is reminiscent of a delicate pastry yet remains savory at heart. The base ingredients—fine flour, rich extra-virgin olive oil, and a hint of salt—come together to form a dough that's meticulously folded and rolled to achieve its signature layers.

Once cooked on a grill or a traditional griddle, it acquires a crispy exterior that contrasts beautifully with its soft, airy interior.

While delicious on its own, crescia sfogliata truly shines when paired with accompaniments.

This flatbread serves as a testament to Marche's rich culinary heritage, blending tradition with timeless flavors.

Ingredients:

- 500g (approximately 4 cups) all-purpose flour, plus extra for dusting
- 200ml (approximately 3/4 cup plus 1 tablespoon) water
- 10g (2 teaspoons) salt
- 50g (approximately 1/4 cup) sugar
- 7g (1.5 teaspoons) dry yeast

- 50ml (approximately 3.5 tablespoons) olive oil, plus extra for brushing
- 200g (approximately 7 oz) vegan butter or margarine, cold and cut into small pieces (for laminating)
- 100g (approximately 1 cup) nutritional yeast flakes (optional, for a cheesy flavor)
- Additional herbs or spices, like black pepper or rosemary (optional)

Instructions:

Prepare the Dough:

- In a large bowl, mix the flour, salt, and sugar together.
- Dissolve the yeast in a little warm water and add it to the flour mixture along with the olive oil.
- Gradually add the remaining water while kneading until you obtain a smooth and elastic dough.
- Shape the dough into a ball, cover the bowl with a cloth, and let it rise in a warm place for about 1-2 hours or until it has doubled in size.

Laminate the Dough:

- Once the dough has risen, place it on a lightly floured surface and deflate it gently.
- Roll it out into a large rectangle, about 1 cm thick.
- Distribute the cold vegan butter pieces over 2/3 of the dough's surface, leaving a small border around the edges.
- If you're using nutritional yeast for a cheesy flavor, sprinkle it over the butter.
- Fold the dough into thirds, like a letter, starting with the part without butter. This creates the first layer.
- Seal the edges by pressing down lightly.

- Roll out the dough again into a rectangle and fold it into thirds once more.
- Cover the dough and let it rest in the refrigerator for about 30 minutes. This process creates layers in the dough, similar to making puff pastry.

Shape and Second Rise:

- After resting, roll out the dough one more time on a floured surface, then fold it again.
- Repeat this process 3-4 more times to create several layers.
- If the dough becomes too sticky or warm, return it to the fridge to cool down for a few minutes.
- Once you've completed the layers, shape the dough into a round loaf or the traditional shape you prefer.
- Place it on a baking sheet lined with parchment paper.
- Cover it with a cloth and let it rise again for about 1 hour.

Preheat the Oven and Prepare the Dough:

- Near the end of the rising time, preheat your oven to 200°C (390°F).
- Before baking, brush the surface of the dough with a little olive oil and sprinkle some salt, nutritional yeast, or herbs on top for extra flavor.

Bake:

- Place the Crescia in the oven and bake for about 30-40 minutes, or until golden brown on top and hollow-sounding when tapped on the bottom.
- If you notice the top browning too quickly, you can cover it with aluminum foil midway through baking.

- Remove the bread from the oven and let it cool on a wire rack to maintain the crust's crispness.
- Slice and serve with your favorite vegan dishes.

This vegan version of Crescia Sfogliata maintains the traditional method of lamination, giving you a flaky, rich final product without using any animal products. It's a versatile bread that pairs well with a variety of meals.

Verdure in Potacchio

"Verdure in Potacchio is a simple, rustic dish featuring vegetables braised in a flavorful tomato sauce with herbs and olive oil, known as "potacchio."

Originating from the Marche region, this method of cooking is typically applied to meat, but it's easily adapted for a vegan diet by using vegetables. The result is a hearty, rustic dish that's full of flavor. Here's how you can make Vegan Verdure in Potacchio:

Ingredients:

- 2 tablespoons olive oil
- 1 medium onion, finely sliced
- 2-3 garlic cloves, minced
- 1 medium carrot, sliced into rounds
- 1 medium celery stalk, finely chopped
- 1 medium bell pepper (any color), sliced into strips
- 1 medium zucchini, sliced into rounds
- 200g (about 7 oz) fresh ripe tomatoes, chopped, or 150g (about 5.3 oz) canned crushed tomatoes
- 1-2 medium potatoes, cubed (optional)
- 120ml (1/2 cup) dry white wine (vegan-friendly)
- 120ml (1/2 cup) vegetable broth or water
- Salt and pepper, to taste
- 1-2 teaspoons fresh rosemary or 1/2 teaspoon dried rosemary
- Fresh basil or parsley, chopped (for garnish)

Instructions:

Sauté the Vegetables:

- In a large pan or skillet, heat the olive oil over medium heat.
- Add the onion and garlic, sautéing until the onion is translucent and the garlic is fragrant about 2-3 minutes.

- Add the carrot and celery to the pan, cooking for another 2-3 minutes until they start to soften.

Add the Rest of the Vegetables:

- Introduce the bell pepper and zucchini to the pan, continuing to sauté until all the vegetables are slightly softened but still have some bite to them.
- If using, add the cubed potatoes to the mix, ensuring they are evenly distributed among the other vegetables.

Deglaze the Pan:

- Pour in the white wine, stirring well to lift any bits stuck to the bottom of the pan.
- Allow the wine to simmer until it's reduced by about half, which should take around 2-3 minutes.

Add Tomatoes and Broth:

- Stir in the chopped or crushed tomatoes, mixing well to combine with the vegetables.
- Pour in the vegetable broth or water and give the mixture a good stir.

Season the Dish:

- Sprinkle in the salt, pepper, and rosemary, adjusting the quantities to suit your taste preferences.
- Stir well to distribute the seasonings evenly.

Braise the Vegetables:

- Reduce the heat to low, cover the pan with a lid, and let the vegetables braise for 20-30 minutes. This process allows the vegetables to become tender and absorb the flavors of the sauce.
- If you included potatoes, they might need a bit longer to cook through, depending on their size.

- If the mixture appears too dry, you can add a bit more broth or water.

Check and Adjust Seasonings:

- After the braising period, check the vegetables for doneness; they should be tender but not mushy.
- Taste the sauce and adjust the salt, pepper, or herbs if necessary.

Serve Your Dish:

- Once everything is cooked to your liking, remove the pan from heat.
- Sprinkle the chopped basil or parsley over the top for a fresh, herby garnish.
- Serve your Verdure in Potacchio hot, ideally with crusty bread, polenta, or rice to soak up the delicious, rich tomato sauce.

This vegan version of a classic dish from the Marche region is simple and adaptable. You can change the vegetables according to the season or your preferences, ensuring it's a recipe you can return to all year round.

Frittata di Asparagi Selvatici

Frittata di Asparagi Selvatici is a traditional regional dish often made with wild asparagus and eggs. The frittata, similar to an omelet, is enjoyed for its rich flavor and simplicity. To create a vegan version of this dish, we'll use chickpea flour and other ingredients to mimic the texture and taste of a traditional egg-based frittata.

This substitution keeps the dish plant-based while remaining true to the spirit of the flavors of spring in Le Marche.

Ingredients:

For the Vegan Frittata Mixture:
- 1 cup chickpea flour (also known as gram or besan flour)
- 2 cups water
- 1/4 cup nutritional yeast (optional, for a cheesy flavor)
- 1/2 teaspoon turmeric (for color)
- 1/2 teaspoon baking soda
- Salt and black pepper, to taste
- A pinch of Kala Namak (Indian or Himalayan black salt, optional, for an egg-like flavor)

For the Asparagus Preparation:
- 1-2 tablespoons olive oil

- 1 small onion, finely chopped
- 2-3 garlic cloves, minced
- 250g (about 9 oz) wild asparagus (trim the woody ends and chop into 2-inch pieces). Actually, for cooking, I prefer using all-white asparagus in a glass jar, available at most US grocery stores.
- Salt and black pepper, to taste
- Fresh herbs (such as parsley or basil), chopped for garnish

Instructions:

Prepare the Vegan Frittata Mixture:

- In a bowl, whisk together the chickpea flour, water, nutritional yeast (if using), turmeric, baking soda, salt, and black pepper until smooth.
- Let the batter sit for at least 30 minutes to an hour at room temperature to thicken slightly.

Cook the Asparagus:

- While the batter is resting, heat the olive oil in a non-stick or cast-iron skillet over medium heat.
- Add the chopped onion and minced garlic to the skillet, sautéing until the onion is translucent and the garlic is fragrant.
- Add the chopped asparagus, and cook for 5-7 minutes, or until they're tender but still bright green. Season with salt and pepper to taste.

Combine Asparagus and Batter:

- Once the asparagus is cooked, you can either add it to the frittata batter or leave it in the pan to pour the batter over, ensuring an even distribution of asparagus throughout the frittata.

Cook the Frittata:

- If you've added the asparagus to the batter, pour the mixture into the same skillet, ensuring it's evenly spread.

- If the asparagus is in the pan, pour the batter over it.

- Cook over low-medium heat for approximately 10-15 minutes with the pan covered until the edges are set and the top is just about firm.

- During this process, avoid stirring; like an omelet, the frittata should be set in a solid, cohesive layer.

Flip and Cook the Other Side:

- Once the top is almost set, carefully flip the frittata using a plate or by sliding it onto a plate and then inverting it back into the pan.

- If this step seems tricky, you can also finish cooking the top under a broiler for a few minutes instead of flipping.

- If flipped, cook the other side for another 5-7 minutes until it's firm and golden.

Serve Your Vegan Frittata:

- Remove the frittata from the pan and let it cool for a few minutes. Sprinkle with fresh herbs before slicing.

- Serve warm or at room temperature with a side salad or your choice of bread.

This vegan Frittata di Asparagi Selvatici maintains the heart of the traditional dish, celebrating the fresh, earthy flavor of wild asparagus without the use of eggs or dairy. It's a versatile recipe where you can add other vegetables or herbs based on your preference or season availability.

When adapting regional specialties, it's crucial to respect the essence of the original recipe, substituting non-vegan ingredients with plant-based alternatives that mimic the flavors and textures of traditional fare. This allows vegans to appreciate the culinary heritage of Le Marche without compromising their dietary principles.

Southern Italy

Lazio

Lazio, the region that includes Rome, is a treasure trove of historical, cultural, and culinary richness. The traditional cuisine here is often referred to as "Cucina Povera" (poor kitchen) because of its simple, wholesome ingredients - often plant-based - that are native to the Mediterranean diet. This makes it relatively straightforward to find or adapt dishes within a vegan regimen. Here are some vegan delights from Lazio:

Carciofi alla Romana (Roman-style Artichokes)

Carciofi alla Romana are tender artichokes cooked with garlic, mint, and parsley, typically braised in extra-virgin olive oil and white wine.

They're a springtime favorite and are naturally vegan. Lazio and particularly Rome are famous for their artichokes. I found a supplier (Piancone) for **canned** Roman-style artichokes I can highly recommend (available online). However, you can use any brand that indicates "Roman Style" if you want to replace the raw, whole artichokes with pre-cooked ones.

Ingredients:

- 6 fresh whole artichokes (or canned Roman-style)
- 2 lemons
- 1/3 cup fresh parsley, finely chopped
- 4 cloves garlic, minced
- 2 tablespoons fresh mint, finely chopped
- Salt and black pepper, to taste
- 1/2 cup extra virgin olive oil, plus extra for finishing
- 1 cup water, or as needed
- Optional: 1 tablespoon nutritional yeast (for a cheesy flavor)

Instructions:

Prepare the Artichokes:

- Fill a large bowl with water and squeeze the juice of 1 lemon into it, dropping the squeezed lemon halves into the water as well.

- Working with one artichoke at a time, remove the tough outer leaves to reveal the tender, lighter-colored leaves inside.

- Use a sharp knife to cut off the top 1-1.5 inches of the artichoke, removing the pointy, inedible parts.

- Trim the stem, leaving about an inch, and peel it to remove the tough outer layer.

- Use scissors to trim the pointy tips of the remaining artichoke leaves.

- Immediately place the prepared artichoke in the lemon water to prevent browning. Repeat with the remaining artichokes.

Prepare the Stuffing:

- In a bowl, combine the minced garlic, chopped parsley, and mint. Add salt and black pepper to taste.
- If you're using nutritional yeast for a cheesy flavor, add it now.
- Drain the artichokes from the lemon water.
- Gently spread open the leaves of each artichoke and stuff them with the herb mixture.
- Make sure the stuffing gets into the middle of the artichoke and between the leaves.

Cook the Artichokes:

- In a large pot (large enough to fit all the artichokes snugly), pour in the 1/2 cup of olive oil and place the artichokes stem-side-up. They should be almost like they're standing up in the pot.
- Squeeze the juice of the remaining lemon over the artichokes and add a bit of salt.
- Pour the water into the bottom of the pot, being careful not to pour directly onto the artichokes, and wash away the stuffing.
- The water should come up to about 1 inch deep, but not submerge the artichokes.

Simmer the Artichokes:

- Bring the water to a boil, then reduce the heat to low and cover the pot.
- Let the artichokes simmer for about 45 minutes to 1 hour.

- Check them occasionally to ensure the pot doesn't run dry, adding more water, as necessary.

- The artichokes are done when the leaves can be easily pulled away, and the heart is tender when pierced with a knife.

Serve Your Dish:

- Once cooked, remove the artichokes from the pot and let them drain or pat them dry gently with a clean towel.

- Drizzle with a little extra virgin olive oil and a squeeze of lemon if desired, and serve them warm or at room temperature.

Enjoy your vegan Carciofi alla Romana as a flavorful appetizer or side dish, offering a genuine taste of Roman cuisine without any animal products. They can be eaten leaf-by-leaf, dipped in a bit of oil or your favorite vegan sauce, with the tender heart and stem as the prized final bites.

Pomodori con Riso

Pomodori con Riso (Tomatoes Stuffed with Rice) is a traditional dish from the Lazio region, specifically Rome, often prepared in the summer months when tomatoes are at their peak.

This classic meal is naturally vegan, offering a delicious combination of baked tomatoes and savory rice.

The dish is typically served with potatoes, which cook alongside the tomatoes, absorbing their flavorful juices.

foto di Ada Parisi

Here's how you can make it:

Ingredients:

- 6 large, ripe tomatoes
- 3/4 cup Arborio rice or another type that you prefer
- 2 cloves garlic, minced
- A handful of fresh basil, chopped, plus extra for garnish
- 2 tablespoons fresh parsley, chopped (optional)

- Salt and pepper, to taste
- 1/4 cup olive oil, plus extra for drizzling
- 1-2 cups water or vegetable broth
- 3-4 potatoes (medium-sized), cut into wedges (optional)

Instructions:

Prep the Tomatoes:

- Preheat your oven to 180°C (350°F).

- Cut the tops off the tomatoes and set them aside (they'll be your lids later). Scoop out the pulp and seeds from the inside, being careful not to break the shell. Save the pulp.

- Sprinkle the insides of the tomatoes with a bit of salt and place them upside down on a wire rack to drain for about 15 minutes.

Prepare the Filling:

- While the tomatoes are draining, prepare the filling. Put the tomato pulp in a sieve over a bowl and press to drain the liquid. Keep the liquid for later.

- Chop the strained pulp and put it in a large bowl.

- Add the uncooked rice, minced garlic, chopped basil, parsley, salt, and pepper to the bowl with the tomato pulp. Mix well, letting the rice absorb the flavors.

Stuff the Tomatoes:

- Pat the insides of the tomatoes dry with a paper towel and arrange them in a baking dish. If you're using potatoes, place them in between the tomatoes.

- Fill each tomato with the rice mixture, but don't pack it too tightly, as the rice will expand as it cooks. Replace the tops of the tomatoes.

- Pour the reserved tomato liquid into the bottom of the baking dish, around the tomatoes, not on top.
- If there isn't enough liquid, add water or vegetable broth so there's enough liquid to partially submerge the rice-stuffed tomatoes.

Bake:

- Drizzle olive oil over the tomatoes and potatoes and add some more salt and pepper.
- Bake in the preheated oven for about 1 hour or until the rice is cooked through and the tomatoes are soft.
- If you notice the tomatoes or potatoes browning too quickly, you can cover the dish with aluminum foil.
- Also, check occasionally to ensure there is still liquid in the dish, adding more as needed to prevent burning and to ensure the rice cooks properly.

Serve:

- Once ready, remove from the oven and let them cool for a few minutes. They can be served hot or at room temperature.
- Garnish with additional fresh basil and a final drizzle of olive oil if desired.

Pomodori con Riso is a celebration of simple, natural flavors. It serves as a wonderful main dish or as part of a larger meal. The contrast of textures and the richness of the flavors, especially when the tomatoes are at their ripest, are quintessentially Italian summer eating.

Spaghetti Aglio, Olio e Peperoncino

Spaghetti Aglio, Olio e Peperoncino, one of my family's absolute favorites, is a classic Italian pasta dish from the Lazio region. It is loved for its simplicity and delightful flavors.

It's easy to make vegan, as the traditional recipe itself is almost vegan, excluding the occasional addition of cheese and anchovy. Here's how you can prepare it:

Ingredients:

- 400g Spaghetti
- 1/3 cup Extra Virgin Olive Oil
- 6-8 large Garlic cloves, thinly sliced
- 1-2 teaspoons Red Pepper Flakes (or 1-2 fresh red chili peppers, chopped)

- Salt (as needed)
- Fresh Parsley, chopped (optional, for garnish)
- Vegan Parmesan cheese (optional for serving)

Instructions:

Cook the Spaghetti:

- Bring a large pot of salted water to a boil.
- Add the spaghetti and cook according to the package instructions until it is 'al dente' (cooked to be firm to the bite).
- Reserve about 1 cup of the pasta cooking water for later, then drain the spaghetti.

Prepare the Sauce:

- While the pasta is cooking, heat the olive oil in a large pan over low-medium heat.
- Add the sliced garlic to the oil.
- Sauté gently until the garlic is fragrant and lightly golden. Be careful not to burn it, as burnt garlic will add a bitter taste.
- If you're using fresh chili, add it along with the garlic.
- If you're using red pepper flakes, add them after the garlic is golden.

Combine Pasta and Sauce:

- Add the drained spaghetti directly to the pan with the garlic oil or transfer to a larger pot if needed.
- Stir well to coat the pasta in the garlic oil.
- If the mixture seems dry, add a little bit of the reserved pasta water, just enough to allow the sauce to cling to the pasta nicely.

- The starchy pasta water will help create a cohesive, glossy sauce.

Season and Garnish:
- Taste and add a bit more salt if needed.
- Remember, the flavors should be bold - garlicky, spicy, and rich with olive oil.
- Remove from heat. If you're using parsley, now's the time to stir some in, saving a bit for garnish.

Serve:
- Serve hot, garnished with more parsley and vegan Parmesan cheese if you like.

This dish is all about the freshness of the ingredients and the balance of flavors. Each simple component plays a crucial role, so use the best quality olive oil and freshest garlic you can find. Enjoy your meal, or as the Italians would say, "Buon appetito!"

Caponata di Melanzane

Caponata is originally a Sicilian dish, but it's enjoyed throughout Italy, with variations in preparation from region to region.

In Lazio, the recipe might be adjusted according to local tastes and available ingredients.

Caponata di Melanzane (eggplant caponata) is inherently vegan, boasting a rich, sweet, and sour flavor profile.

Here's a version you might find in Lazio, with some regional touches:

Ingredients:

- 2 large eggplants, cut into cubes
- Salt
- Olive oil (enough for frying the eggplant and some extra for the sauté)
- 1 large red onion, chopped
- 2 celery stalks, sliced into small pieces
- 3-4 ripe tomatoes, peeled, deseeded, and chopped (or 1 small can of chopped tomatoes)
- 2 tablespoons tomato paste (optional for richer flavor)
- 3 tablespoons red wine vinegar

- 2 tablespoons sugar (or a sweetener of your choice)
- 1/3 cup green olives, pitted and chopped
- 2 tablespoons capers, rinsed and drained
- Fresh basil leaves, torn
- Black pepper (to taste)

Instructions:

Prepare the Eggplants:

- Sprinkle the cubed eggplants with a generous amount of salt, put them in a colander, and let them drain for about 1 hour.
- This process removes the bitterness.
- After an hour, rinse them with water and pat dry with a towel.

Fry the Eggplants:

- In a large skillet, heat enough olive oil for frying over medium-high heat.
- Once hot, add the eggplant cubes and fry until they are golden brown and tender.
- You may need to do this in batches.
- Remove the eggplants from the skillet and set them aside on a plate lined with paper towels to drain the excess oil.

Sauté the Vegetables:

- In another pan, heat a few tablespoons of olive oil over medium heat.
- Add the chopped onion and celery, sautéing until they begin to soften.

- Add the chopped tomatoes (and tomato paste, if using) to the pan, and cook for a few more minutes until the tomatoes are tender.

Combine and Simmer:

- Add the fried eggplants to the pan with the sautéed vegetables.
- Add the red wine vinegar and sugar, then stir well.
- The mixture should have a characteristic sweet and sour flavor.
- Add the olives and capers, then allow the caponata to simmer over low heat for about 15-20 minutes, stirring occasionally.
- If it looks too dry, you can add a few tablespoons of water.
- The vegetables should be tender but not mushy.

Season and Rest:

- Stir in the fresh basil and season with salt and pepper to taste. Remove the pan from heat.
- Allow the caponata to cool to room temperature.
- Traditionally, caponata is left to rest for at least an hour to enhance the flavors.
- It's often served cool or at room temperature rather than hot.

Serve:

- Caponata can be served as a side dish, as an appetizer on slices of bread, or as a main dish.
- For a touch of Lazio, you can serve it with local bread, making bruschetta.

Remember, like many traditional dishes, caponata invites a personal touch. Some versions might include pine nuts, raisins, or bell peppers, and each cook decides on the precise balance of sweet and sour that suits their palate. Feel free to adapt this base recipe to your taste!

Pizza Bianca

Pizza Bianca, or "white pizza," is a beloved street food in Rome, the capital city of the Lazio region.

It's a simple, focaccia-like flatbread coated in olive oil, coarse salt, and sometimes rosemary. The traditional Pizza Bianca doesn't contain any animal products, making it inherently vegan. However, various toppings can be added to suit your preferences. Here's how you can make classic Lazio-style Pizza Bianca:

Ingredients:

- 500g (approximately 4 cups) all-purpose or bread flour, more for dusting
- 1 teaspoon sugar
- 2 teaspoons salt
- 1 1/2 cups warm water (approximately 110 degrees Fahrenheit)
- 1 packet (2 1/4 teaspoons) active dry yeast or instant yeast
- 1/4 cup extra-virgin olive oil, plus more for drizzling
- Coarse sea salt for sprinkling
- Fresh rosemary leaves, chopped (optional)

Instructions:

Prepare the Dough:

- In a large bowl, whisk together the flour, sugar, and salt.
- In a separate bowl, mix the warm water with the yeast. Let it sit for about 5 minutes until it starts to froth, indicating the yeast is active.
- Pour the yeast mixture and 1/4 cup olive oil into the dry ingredients.
- Mix until the dough starts to come together, then knead on a lightly floured surface for about 10 minutes until smooth and elastic.
- You can also use a stand mixer with a dough hook for this process.

First Rise:

- Shape the dough into a ball and place it in a lightly oiled bowl, turning it to coat all sides with a bit of oil.

- Cover the bowl with a clean kitchen towel or plastic wrap.

- Let the dough rise in a warm, draft-free area for about 1-1.5 hours or until doubled in size.

Shape and Second Rise:

- Punch down the dough gently to deflate it and transfer it to a lightly oiled or parchment-lined baking sheet.

- Shape it into a rectangle or oval, pressing it out to about a 1/2-inch thickness.

- Cover with a lightly greased piece of plastic wrap, and let it rise again for another 30 minutes to an hour until puffy and doubled.

Preheat the Oven:

- While the dough is on its second rise, start preheating your oven to 450 degrees Fahrenheit (230 degrees Celsius).

- If you have a baking stone or steel, put it in the oven now to heat up.

Season:

- Remove the plastic wrap and use your fingertips to poke dimples all over the surface of the dough, preventing air bubbles during baking.

- Drizzle the top generously with olive oil, letting it pool in the dimples. Sprinkle with coarse sea salt and rosemary (if using).

- Place the baking sheet in the oven (or directly on the stone/steel if using) and bake for about 15-20 minutes, until the top is golden and crisp.

- If desired, for extra crispness, you can flip the pizza over and bake for an additional 5 minutes to crisp the bottom.

Serve:

- Remove the pizza from the oven and let it cool for a few minutes before slicing.

- Pizza Bianca is fantastic on its own but can also be served with vegan cheeses, grilled vegetables, or a light salad to make a more substantial meal.

Enjoy this Roman delicacy right at home, warm and fresh out of the oven!

Fagioli con le Cotiche (Bean Soup)

Traditionally, this hearty soup usually includes pork rinds.

Originating from a time and place where nothing went to waste, this dish is a testament to the resourcefulness of Italian home cooking. You can easily enjoy a vegan version of this classic from the Lazio region by substituting ingredients without compromising on the authentic flavors.

Here is how to match the traditional taste and texture without using animal products.

Ingredients:

- 1 pound (about 2 cups) dried cannellini beans (or other white beans), soaked overnight
- 6 cups vegetable broth (more if needed)
- 2-3 tablespoons olive oil
- 1 large onion, finely chopped
- 2-3 garlic cloves, minced
- 2 medium carrots, chopped
- 2 celery stalks, chopped
- 1-2 bay leaves
- 1 teaspoon fresh or dried rosemary
- Salt and black pepper to taste
- 1 piece of kombu seaweed or a few dried shiitake mushrooms (optional, for the 'umami' flavor that comes from the pork rinds)
- Fresh parsley, chopped (for garnish)
- Extra virgin olive oil (for serving)

Instructions:

Prepare the Beans:

- After soaking the beans overnight, drain and rinse them well. This process reduces the cooking time and makes it easier to digest.

Cook the Aromatics:

- In a large pot, heat the olive oil over medium heat.
- Add the onion, carrots, celery, and a pinch of salt.
- Sauté until the vegetables are soft, about 5-7 minutes.
- Add the minced garlic and continue to cook for another minute until fragrant.

Simmer the Beans:

- Add the soaked beans, bay leaves, rosemary, and the piece of kombu seaweed or dried shiitake mushrooms if using.
- These ingredients serve as a vegan alternative to pork, providing a depth of flavor similar to the original recipe.
- Pour in the vegetable broth, ensuring the beans are completely covered with liquid.
- You can adjust the amount of broth depending on how brothy you prefer your soup.
- Bring the mixture to a boil, then reduce the heat to low and let it simmer.
- Cook with the lid slightly ajar for approximately 1.5 to 2 hours or until the beans are tender.

Season and Blend (optional):

- Once the beans are cooked and tender, remove the bay leaves, kombu, or shiitake mushrooms.
- Season the soup with salt and pepper to taste.

- If you prefer a creamier texture, you can blend part of the soup using an immersion blender or by transferring a portion of the beans to a blender, blending until smooth, and then reintegrating the mix into the pot.

Serve:

- Serve the soup in bowls, garnished with fresh parsley and a generous drizzle of extra virgin olive oil.
- This dish goes well with crusty bread, perfect for dipping.

By replacing the pork rinds with ingredients like kombu or shiitake mushrooms, you can maintain the savory depth that makes Fagioli con le Cotiche so satisfying while keeping the dish completely plant-based. Enjoy your vegan version of this classic comfort food from Lazio!

Puntarelle alla Romana

Puntarelle alla Romana is a classic salad from Rome, part of the Lazio region, and it's naturally vegan.

Puntarelle is a type of chicory with a bitter flavor that's often mellowed by a dressing of anchovies, garlic, and olive oil.

However, since we're making a vegan version, we'll omit the anchovies and use an alternative to achieve a similar savory depth.

Here's how you can make a vegan Puntarelle alla Romana:

- 1 large head of Puntarelle (You can also use chicory or endive if Puntarelle is not available, but Puntarelle is the most authentic.)
- Salt

For the vegan "anchovy" dressing:

- 1 tablespoon capers, rinsed and drained
- 2 tablespoons of nutritional yeast (for the umami flavor)
- 1 small garlic clove, minced
- 1/2 cup extra virgin olive oil
- 2 tablespoons red wine vinegar or apple cider vinegar
- Salt and black pepper to taste

- Optional: a few drops of soy sauce or tamari for extra umami flavor

Instructions:

Prepare the Puntarelle:

- Clean the Puntarelle by removing the outer leaves to reveal the light green shoots within.
- Cut the shoots into long, thin strips.
- If you're using a type of chicory or another green, try to slice it to resemble Puntarelle as closely as possible.
- Soak the Puntarelle strips in a bowl of ice water for about one hour.
- They will curl up and lose some of their bitterness.
- This step is essential as it gives the Puntarelle its characteristic texture and slightly milder taste.

Prepare the Vegan "Anchovy" Dressing:

- Using a mortar and pestle, crush the capers and garlic into a paste.
- If you don't have a mortar and pestle, you can finely mince them together with a knife.
- Transfer the caper and garlic mixture to a bowl.
- Add the nutritional yeast, and if using, the soy sauce or tamari.
- Mix well.
- The nutritional yeast and soy sauce provide the umami flavor typically offered by anchovies.
- Whisk in the olive oil and vinegar until well combined. Season with salt and pepper to taste.

- The dressing should be bold and tangy, complementing the bitterness of the Puntarelle.

Assemble the Salad:

- Drain the Puntarelle from the ice water and pat them dry with a clean kitchen or paper towel.
- Place them in a large bowl and toss with the vegan "anchovy" dressing until well coated.

Serve:

- Puntarelle alla Romana is best served fresh, right after tossing with the dressing.
- It makes a refreshing appetizer or side dish, embodying the simple elegance and bold flavors of Roman cuisine.

Enjoy your traditional Roman salad with the satisfaction of keeping it completely plant-based!

Maritozzi con la Panna (without the cream)

Maritozzi con la Panna are sweet buns that are typically split open and filled with whipped cream, a traditional treat from Rome.

Making a vegan version of Maritozzi is straightforward, as you can substitute standard ingredients with plant-based alternatives.

Instead of regular whipped cream, we'll use a vegan cream made from coconut milk or another plant-based cream.

Here's how:

Ingredients

for Maritozzi:

- 500 grams (approx. 4 cups) all-purpose flour
- 100 grams (approx. 1/2 cup) granulated sugar
- 100 grams (approx. 1/2 cup) plant-based butter, melted
- 200 ml (approx. 3/4 cup plus 1 tablespoon) soy or almond milk, lukewarm
- 1 packet (7 grams, or 2 1/4 teaspoons) active dry yeast
- Zest of 1 organic orange
- 1/2 teaspoon salt
- 75 grams (approx. 1/2 cup) raisins or sultanas (optional)
- Powdered sugar for dusting (optional)

- 1 can (400 ml, or approx. 1 3/4 cups) full-fat coconut milk, chilled overnight, or a similar quantity of commercial vegan whipping cream
- 1-2 tablespoons powdered sugar (adjust based on your preferred sweetness)
- 1 teaspoon vanilla extract

Instructions:

Prepare the Dough:

- In a large bowl, combine the lukewarm plant-based milk with the sugar and yeast. Stir until the yeast is dissolved, then let it sit for 5-10 minutes until it starts to froth.

- Add in the melted plant-based butter, orange zest, and salt, then gradually add the flour, kneading it until the dough comes together. You can use a stand mixer with a dough hook attachment or your hands.

- If using raisins, add them at the end of the kneading process. Ensure they are evenly distributed throughout the dough.

- Cover the dough with a damp cloth and let it rise in a warm place for about 2 hours or until it doubles in size.

Shape the Maritozzi:

- Once the dough has risen, punch it down on a lightly floured surface.

- Divide it into 10-12 equal pieces and roll each piece into an oval shape.

- Place the rolls on a baking sheet lined with parchment paper, leaving enough space between them to expand.

- Cover with a clean kitchen towel and let them rise again for about 1 hour.

Bake:

- Preheat your oven to 180°C (350°F).

- Once the rolls have risen, bake them for about 20 minutes or until they're golden brown.

- Remove the Maritozzi from the oven and let them cool completely on a wire rack.

Prepare the Vegan Whipped Cream:

- If you're using coconut milk, open the can and scoop out the solid part at the top, placing it into a chilled mixing bowl.

- The remaining liquid can be saved for other recipes.

- With a hand mixer or a whisk, start whipping the coconut cream.

- Add the powdered sugar and vanilla extract, then continue to whip until the mixture is fluffy and holds peaks.

- If you're using a commercial vegan whipping cream, follow the whipping instructions on the product.

Assemble the Maritozzi:

- Once the Maritozzi are completely cool, slice each one horizontally, being careful not to cut all the way through.

- Fill with a generous dollop of your vegan whipped cream.

- Optionally, dust the Maritozzi with powdered sugar.

Serve:

- These are best served fresh, as the cream is at its fluffiest.

- Enjoy your vegan Maritozzi as a delightful dessert or a sweet, indulgent breakfast, true to the Roman tradition but tailored for a plant-based diet.

Crostata di Visciole (Sour Cherry Tart)

Crostata di Visciole, or Sour Cherry Tart, is a beloved dessert in the Lazio region, particularly in Rome.

It combines a sweet pastry crust with the tangy, vibrant flavor of sour cherries (visciole).

A vegan version of this traditional dessert involves substituting some standard ingredients with plant-based alternatives.

Ingredients:

For the Vegan Pastry Crust:

- 300 grams (approx. 2 1/2 cups) all-purpose flour
- 150 grams (approx. 3/4 cup) granulated sugar
- 150 grams (approx. 2/3 cup) cold vegan butter (cut into small cubes)
- Zest of 1 organic lemon
- A pinch of salt
- 6-8 tablespoons cold water (or as needed)

For the Sour Cherry Filling:

- 500 grams (approx. 18 oz) fresh or jarred sour cherries (visciole) in their juice
- 100-150 grams (approx. 1/2 to 3/4 cup) granulated sugar (adjust to taste based on the sourness of the cherries)
- 2 tablespoons cornstarch or arrowroot powder

Instructions:

Prepare the Vegan Pastry Crust:

- In a large mixing bowl, combine the flour, sugar, lemon zest, and a pinch of salt.

- Add the cold vegan butter to the flour mixture.

- Using a pastry cutter or your fingers, work the butter into the flour until the mixture resembles coarse breadcrumbs.

- Gradually add cold water, one tablespoon at a time, mixing until the dough starts to come together.

- You may not need all the water, so add it slowly until the dough forms.

- Once the dough is cohesive but not sticky, form it into a ball.

- Wrap it in plastic wrap and chill in the refrigerator for at least 30 minutes.
- This process helps the vegan butter solidify, making the dough easier to work with.

Prepare the Sour Cherry Filling:

- If you're using fresh cherries, pit them, and if you're using jarred cherries, drain them but keep the juice.
- You'll need the juice for the next steps.
- In a saucepan, combine the cherries, sugar, and about half of the reserved juice. Bring the mixture to a simmer over medium heat.
- Dissolve cornstarch or arrowroot powder in the remaining cherry juice, ensuring there are no lumps, and then stir this into the cherry mixture.
- Continue to cook, stirring constantly, until the mixture thickens, resembling a jam-like consistency.
- Once thickened, remove from heat and let it cool.

Preheat the Oven and Prepare the Tart Shell:

- Preheat your oven to 180°C (350°F).
- Remove the dough from the refrigerator and roll out about two-thirds of it on a floured surface, shaping it to fit your tart pan (typically around 9 inches in diameter).
- The dough should extend slightly over the edges of the pan.
- Gently press the dough into the pan, trimming any excess and repairing any cracks.
- Prick the bottom with a fork to prevent it from puffing up during baking.

- Pour the cooled cherry filling into the tart shell, spreading it evenly.

- With the remaining dough, roll it out and cut it into strips to create a lattice top over the cherries.

- You can also opt for a simpler design and cover the tart with shapes cut from the dough.

- This step is where you can get creative.

- If desired, you can brush the top of the pastry with a bit of plant-based milk or melted vegan butter to give it a golden color while baking.

Bake:

- Bake the crostata in the preheated oven for approximately 30-40 minutes or until the crust is golden brown and the filling is bubbly.

- Once done, remove it from the oven and allow it to cool before serving. The filling will continue to thicken as it cools.

Enjoy your vegan Crostata di Visciole! This dessert is a delightful representation of Lazio's regional cuisine, offering a harmonious balance of sweet pastry and tart cherries, all without any animal products.

These dishes exemplify how vegan adaptations can honor the culinary traditions of Lazio, highlighting local produce and traditional flavors while adhering to vegan principles. They prove that with a few thoughtful substitutions, you can enjoy the region's culinary delights without straying from a plant-based diet.

Abruzzo

Abruzzo, known for its diverse culinary landscape where mountainous and coastal cuisines blend, offers a variety of dishes that celebrate the rich agricultural bounty of the region.

Traditional Abruzzese cuisine is marked by its use of simple, honest ingredients. For vegans, many of these dishes can either be enjoyed in their original form or require minimal modification to fit within a plant-based diet. Here are some vegan-friendly dishes and adaptations from the Abruzzo region:

Pasta e Ceci (Pasta with Chickpeas)

Pasta e Ceci (Pasta with Chickpeas) is a hearty, flavorful dish popular throughout Italy, with variations seen in different regions, including Abruzzo.

While the recipe traditionally might include non-vegan ingredients like anchovies or animal-based broth, it's easily adaptable to a vegan preference without sacrificing flavor.

Ingredients:

- 1 cup dried chickpeas, soaked overnight (or two 15-ounce cans of chickpeas if you're short on time)
- 1/4 cup olive oil, plus extra for drizzling
- 1 large onion, finely chopped
- 2-3 garlic cloves, minced
- 1 sprig rosemary (or 1/2 teaspoon dried rosemary)

- 1/4 teaspoon red pepper flakes (optional, for heat)
- 2 tablespoons tomato paste
- 4 cups vegetable broth (or water, as needed)
- 8 ounces (225g) ditalini pasta or another small pasta shape
- Salt and black pepper to taste
- Fresh parsley, chopped (for garnish)

Instructions:

Prepare the Chickpeas:

- If you're using dried chickpeas, after soaking them overnight, drain and rinse them.
- Place them in a large pot, cover with water, and bring to a boil.
- Reduce the heat and simmer until they're tender, which could take around 1.5-2 hours.
- Skip this step if you're using canned chickpeas.

Cook the Base:

- In a large pot or Dutch oven, heat the olive oil over medium heat.
- Add the onion, and cook until it starts to become translucent about 5 minutes.
- Add the garlic, rosemary sprig, and red pepper flakes (if using) to the pot.
- Sauté for another 1-2 minutes, until the garlic is fragrant, being careful not to burn it.

Add the Chickpeas:

- If you're using canned chickpeas, rinse and drain them before this step.

- Add the chickpeas to the pot along with the tomato paste, stirring well to ensure the paste coats the chickpeas and veggies.

Simmer:

- Pour in the vegetable broth and increase the heat to bring the mixture to a boil.

- Once boiling, reduce the heat to a simmer.

- If you started with dried chickpeas, you could opt to add some of the water used for boiling them. It contains flavor and nutrients that can enhance the dish.

- Let the mixture simmer for about 20-30 minutes if you're using canned chickpeas (and up to an hour if you started with dried, cooked chickpeas).

- This process allows the flavors to meld.

Add the Pasta:

- Add the pasta to the pot and continue to simmer, stirring occasionally.

- The pasta should be done in about 10-12 minutes, but refer to the package instructions for the specific time.

- As the pasta cooks, it will absorb the broth, thickening the stew.

- If the mixture becomes too thick, you can add a bit more broth or water to reach your desired consistency.

- Taste the stew and add salt and black pepper as needed. Remember, the flavors should be robust and well-balanced, representing the simplicity of Abruzzo's cuisine.

Serve:

- Once the pasta is cooked to your liking, remove the rosemary sprig.

- Serve the Pasta e Ceci hot, garnished with fresh parsley and a drizzle of olive oil, if desired.

This warm, comforting dish is perfect for any season, offering a rich tapestry of flavors with every spoonful while staying true to vegan dietary preferences. Enjoy your meal, or as they say in Italy, "Buon appetito!"

Minestra di Ceci (Chickpea Soup)

This comforting soup enjoyed in its vegan form, is made by slow-cooking chickpeas with garlic, rosemary, and a pinch of spicy pepperoncino.

Extra virgin olive oil is often used to finish the dish, adding a layer of richness.

- 1 cup dried chickpeas, soaked overnight (or two 15-ounce cans of chickpeas if you're short on time)
- 3 tablespoons olive oil
- 1 large onion, finely chopped
- 2-3 garlic cloves, minced
- 2 medium carrots, peeled and chopped
- 2 celery stalks, chopped

- 1 medium potato, peeled and diced (optional for added heartiness)
- 1 teaspoon rosemary, finely chopped (fresh) or 1/2 teaspoon (dried)
- 1 can (400g or 14 oz) of diced tomatoes (or fresh tomatoes peeled and chopped)
- 5-6 cups vegetable broth or water (more if you prefer a thinner soup)
- Salt and black pepper to taste
- Fresh parsley or basil, chopped (for garnish)

Instructions:

Prepare the Chickpeas:

- If using dried chickpeas, after their overnight soak, drain and rinse them.
- Place them in a large pot, cover with several inches of water, and bring to a boil.
- Reduce the heat and let them simmer until tender, which could take about 1.5-2 hours.
- If you're using canned chickpeas, you can skip this step.

Sauté Vegetables:

- In a large pot or Dutch oven, heat the olive oil over medium heat.
- Add the onions, carrots, and celery, and sauté until the onions are translucent and the vegetables are tender, about 5-7 minutes.
- Add the garlic and rosemary, cooking for another 1-2 minutes until the garlic is aromatic but not browned.

Add the Remaining Ingredients:

- Stir in the diced tomatoes (with their juice) and cook for a few minutes to combine the flavors.

- If you're using canned chickpeas, rinse and drain them before adding them to the pot.

- If using chickpeas you've cooked from dried, you can add them now.

- Add the diced potato if you're using it.

- Pour in the vegetable broth or water.

- The amount of liquid depends on how thick you want your soup to be.

Simmer the Soup:

- Bring the mixture to a boil and then reduce the heat to let it simmer.

- Cover the pot and let the soup cook for 20-30 minutes, allowing the flavors to meld together.

- The chickpeas should be very tender, and the potato should break down slightly, naturally thickening the soup.

Season and Serve:

- Taste the soup and adjust the seasoning with salt and black pepper as desired.

- If you prefer a creamier texture, you can use an immersion blender to slightly puree the soup in the pot. Be careful not to turn it entirely into a puree (unless that's your preference).

- Serve the hot soup in bowls, garnished with chopped parsley or basil and a drizzle of olive oil if desired.

This simple yet flavorful dish reflects the essence of Abruzzese cuisine, focusing on the natural flavors of quality ingredients.

It's a versatile recipe that can be adapted to any season or personal preference. Enjoy your vegan Minestra di Ceci!

Arrosticini

Arrosticini are a special kind of traditional skewered meat from the Abruzzo region.

They are typically made of lamb or sheep meat. Creating a vegan version of Arrosticini involves replacing the meat with plant-based ingredients that can mimic the texture and absorb the flavors characteristic of the original dish.

Ingredients:

For the Vegan Arrosticini:

- 500g (approx. 1lb) homemade or store-bought plain seitan (ensure it's in a block or large piece)
- Olive oil for brushing and drizzling
- Salt to taste

For the Marinade:

- 3-4 garlic cloves, minced
- 1 sprig of fresh rosemary, leaves removed and finely chopped (or 1 teaspoon dried rosemary)
- Juice of 1 lemon
- 1/4 cup of olive oil
- Salt and black pepper to taste

Instructions:

Prepare the Seitan:

- If the seitan is homemade and raw, cook it first according to your preferred method (boiling, steaming) until it's firm and chewy. Allow it to cool down.
- Cut the seitan into cubes roughly the size of large dice, aiming to make them uniform for even cooking.

Marinate:

- In a bowl, mix the olive oil, lemon juice, minced garlic, chopped rosemary, salt, and black pepper to prepare the marinade.
- Add the seitan cubes to the bowl, ensuring they are well-coated with the marinade.
- Cover the bowl with plastic wrap and refrigerate.
- Let the seitan marinate for at least 2 hours or, for best results, overnight.

Prepare the Skewers:

- If using wooden skewers, soak them in water for at least 30 minutes before use to prevent burning.
- Thread the marinated seitan cubes onto the skewers.
- Press them together nicely to mimic the traditional look of Arrosticini.

Cooking:

- Preheat a grill or grill pan over medium-high heat.
- Once hot, place the skewers on the grill. They will cook quickly, so keep an eye on them.
- Grill the skewers for approximately 2-3 minutes on each side until they are nicely browned and have grill marks.
- The high heat will help the seitan develop a crust similar to what you'd find in traditional Arrosticini.

Serving:

- Once off the grill, season the skewers with a bit more salt (optional) and drizzle them with a little olive oil for extra flavor and shine.
- Serve the vegan Arrosticini immediately while they are still hot.
- They are typically eaten directly off the skewer, accompanied by slices of crusty bread and a salad or grilled vegetables.

This approach offers a plant-based alternative to traditional Arrosticini, respecting the flavors and presentation of the Abruzzese classic while making it accessible for those following a vegan diet.

Sagne e Fagioli (Pasta and Beans)

"Sagne e Fagioli" is a traditional pasta and bean dish from the Abruzzo region. It is renowned for its hearty and rustic flavors.

The dish is naturally vegetarian and can easily be adapted to a vegan diet by ensuring that the pasta used doesn't contain eggs and by avoiding any dairy toppings. Here's how.

Ingredients:

- 250g (about 1/2 lb) of sagne pasta (a short, flat, and wide pasta, often with a ruffled edge; if unavailable, tagliatelle or fettuccine cut into shorter lengths can be used)
- 400g (about 14 oz) of cooked borlotti beans (canned is fine; rinse and drain)
- 3 tablespoons of olive oil
- 1 large onion, finely chopped
- 2-3 cloves of garlic, minced
- 1 carrot, finely chopped
- 1 celery stalk, finely chopped
- 400g (about 14 oz) of tomato passata or crushed tomatoes
- 1 teaspoon of dried thyme or oregano
- Salt and pepper to taste
- A pinch of red pepper flakes (optional)
- Fresh parsley, chopped (for garnish)
- 1 liter (about 4 cups) of vegetable broth or water

Instructions:

Prepare the Base:

- Heat the olive oil in a large pot over medium heat.
- Add the onion, carrot, and celery, and sauté until the vegetables are soft and the onion is translucent, around 5-7 minutes.
- Add the minced garlic (and red pepper flakes if you're using them for a bit of heat) and sauté for another minute until fragrant, making sure not to burn the garlic.

Add the Beans and Tomatoes:

- If using canned beans, ensure they're rinsed and drained to remove excess salt and other preservatives.

- Add the beans to the pot and stir well to combine with the vegetables.
- Pour in the tomato passata or crushed tomatoes, followed by the dried thyme or oregano, and stir to mix.
- Allow the mixture to cook for a few minutes so the flavors can meld.

Cook the Pasta:

- Pour in the vegetable broth or water and bring the mixture to a gentle boil.
- Once it's boiling, add the sagne pasta.
- If you can't find sagne, you can use another type of pasta like tagliatelle or fettuccine. Still, traditionally, a flat pasta works best.
- Stir the mixture occasionally to prevent the pasta from sticking together or to the bottom of the pot.
- The pasta will absorb a lot of the broth as it cooks.

Simmer:

- Reduce the heat and let your Sagne e Fagioli simmer until the pasta is cooked to your liking and the broth has thickened slightly.
- This process usually takes around 10-15 minutes, depending on the pasta used.
- If the soup seems too thick, add a bit more broth or water until it reaches your preferred consistency.
- Taste and adjust the seasoning with salt and pepper.

Serve:

- Once the pasta is tender and the beans are heated through, turn off the heat.

- Let the soup sit for a few minutes to cool slightly, allowing the flavors to come together even more.

- Ladle the Sagne e Fagioli into bowls, garnish with fresh parsley, and drizzle with a little extra virgin olive oil if desired.

This recipe keeps the integrity of the traditional flavors while ensuring that the ingredients are entirely plant-based. It's a warming, nutritious dish, perfect for cold days and for anyone seeking the comforting flavors of Italian home cooking. Enjoy your vegan meal!

Peperonata Abruzzese

Peperonata is a classic Italian dish made primarily from sweet bell peppers alongside onions and tomatoes. There are various regional variations, as discussed throughout this book. The Abruzzese version usually includes additional local ingredients and methods. However, the core of the recipe remains focused on the sweet, slow-cooked peppers. The good news for vegans is that Peperonata is traditionally a vegan-friendly dish, so you don't need to make significant substitutions. Here's how you can prepare it:

Ingredients:

- 4 large bell peppers (preferably a mix of colors - red, yellow, and green) sliced into thin strips
- 2 medium-sized onions, thinly sliced
- 2-3 garlic cloves, minced
- 400g (about 14 oz) of ripe tomatoes (diced) or canned crushed tomatoes
- 3 tablespoons of olive oil
- Salt and pepper to taste
- Optional: 1-2 tablespoons of capers or sliced black olives
- Optional: a pinch of red pepper flakes for heat
- Optional: a few leaves of fresh basil, torn, or 1 teaspoon of dried oregano

Instructions:

Preparation of Vegetables:

- Clean the peppers by removing the cores, seeds, and membranes and slicing them into thin strips.

- Peel the onions and slice them thinly.

- If using fresh tomatoes, dice them into small pieces (you can remove the seeds if you prefer, but it's not necessary).

Cooking Process:

- In a large skillet or sauté pan, heat the olive oil over medium heat.

- Add the sliced onions and a pinch of salt, cooking until they're soft and translucent but not browned, about 5-7 minutes.
- Add the minced garlic (and red pepper flakes if you want a spicy kick), cooking for another 1-2 minutes until fragrant.
- Introduce the sliced peppers to the pan.
- Stir to combine with the onions and garlic, then cover and reduce the heat.
- You want the peppers to cook slowly and release their natural juices, about 10-15 minutes.

Adding Tomatoes:

- Once the peppers are soft, add your diced or canned tomatoes to the pan.
- If using canned tomatoes, make sure to include the juice as well.
- At this stage, you can also add the capers or olives if you're using them, which give a nice salty, tangy touch to the dish.
- Stir everything together, then re-cover the pan and let it all simmer for another 10-15 minutes.
- The tomatoes should break down, and the flavors will meld.

Final Seasoning:

- Uncover the pan and stir. If the mixture looks too watery, you can increase the heat slightly to reduce the liquid and thicken your Peperonata.
- Taste the mixture and add salt and pepper as needed.

- If you're using fresh basil, add it at the end of the cooking process to maintain its flavor and color.

Serving:

- Peperonata can be served in various ways: as a side dish, as a topping for bruschetta, or even as a sauce for pasta.
- It's delicious, both hot and at room temperature. Store any leftovers in the refrigerator. The flavors often improve the next day!

Enjoy your authentic vegan Peperonata Abruzzese! This dish is a celebration of simple ingredients and flavors, emblematic of traditional Italian home cooking.

Frittata di Patate

Frittata di Patate, a classic dish, originally hinges on eggs to achieve its signature texture.

However, the culinary world's evolving landscape has introduced innovative vegan versions, successfully capturing the dish's essence without eggs.

Using chickpea flour combined with assorted vegetables, this adaptation delivers a dense, omelet-like consistency that pays homage to the traditional frittata.

At the heart of this vegan variant lie the robust flavors of extra-virgin olive oil, gently caramelized onions, and delicate slices of potato. These ingredients synergize, ensuring the Frittata di Patate remains a testament to timeless taste, even in its plant-based form.

The focus remains on the flavors of extra-virgin olive oil, onions, and thinly sliced potatoes.

Ingredients:

- 4-5 medium potatoes, peeled and thinly sliced
- 1 cup chickpea flour (also known as gram flour or besan)
- 2 cups water
- 1/4 cup nutritional yeast (optional, for a cheesy flavor)
- 1 tsp turmeric (for color)
- 1/2 tsp baking soda
- Salt and black pepper, to taste
- 3-4 tbsp olive oil
- 1 medium onion, finely chopped
- 2-3 cloves garlic, minced

- Optional: chopped fresh herbs (like parsley or basil), vegan cheese, or other vegetables for added flavor

Instructions:

Prepare the Batter:

- In a mixing bowl, whisk together the chickpea flour, water, nutritional yeast (if using), turmeric, baking soda, salt, and pepper until smooth.
- Let the batter sit for at least half an hour to ensure the chickpea flour fully absorbs the water, which enhances the texture.

Cook the Potatoes:

- In a non-stick or well-seasoned cast-iron skillet, heat about 2 tablespoons of olive oil over medium heat.
- Add the sliced potatoes and cook, stirring occasionally, until they are slightly golden and almost cooked through.
- Season with salt and pepper during cooking.
- Once done, remove the potatoes from the skillet and set aside.

Sauté Onions and Garlic:

- In the same skillet, add a bit more olive oil if needed, and sauté the onions and garlic until they are soft and fragrant.
- If you're adding any other vegetables, now would be the time to do so.

Combine Ingredients:

- Add the cooked potatoes back into the skillet with the onions and garlic, arranging them in an even layer.
- You can add other optional ingredients (like chopped fresh herbs or vegan cheese) at this stage.

- Pour the chickpea batter over the vegetables in the skillet, ensuring an even distribution.
- Tilt the pan if needed to spread the batter evenly.

Cook the Frittata:

- Cook the frittata over medium-low heat for approximately 10-15 minutes or until the edges are firm and the bottom is golden.
- You can cover the skillet with a lid to help the cooking process.
- Once the bottom is done, you need to cook the top.
- You can either place the skillet in a preheated oven (if it's oven-safe) and broil for a few minutes (watching carefully to prevent burning), or you can flip the frittata using a plate or lid and cook the other side on the stovetop for another 5-7 minutes.

Serve:

- Once cooked through and golden brown on both sides, remove your vegan Frittata di Patate from the skillet and let it cool for a few minutes before slicing.
- It can be served hot or at room temperature and pairs wonderfully with a fresh salad or roasted vegetables.

This recipe is a fantastic way to enjoy a classic Italian dish without straying from a vegan diet, offering a satisfying and flavorful meal.

Pizze dei Morti (Cookie of the Dead) - Vegan Version

"Pizze dei Morti," or "Cookies of the Dead," are traditional Italian cookies that are typically made in certain regions of Italy to commemorate the Day of the Dead, known as "Festa dei Morti" or "Commemorazione dei Defunti," celebrated in early November.

These cookies often contain nuts, raisins, and chocolate, providing a rich, dense texture and flavor.

The following recipe is a vegan interpretation of this commemorative delicacy, adapted to exclude any animal products without sacrificing its authentic taste and texture. Since regional variations abound, this considers common ingredients found in the Abruzzo style.

Ingredients:

- 1 cup (150g) of all-purpose flour
- 3/4 cup (100g) of whole wheat flour
- 1/2 cup (50g) of almond flour or ground almonds
- 3/4 cup (75g) of powdered sugar
- 1/3 cup (75g) of cocoa powder
- 1 tsp of baking powder
- 1/2 tsp of baking soda
- A pinch of salt
- 1 tsp of ground cinnamon
- 1/2 tsp of ground cloves (optional, adjust according to preference)
- 1/2 cup (120ml) of plant-based milk (almond, soy, oat)
- 1/4 cup (60ml) of vegetable oil (like canola or sunflower) or melted coconut oil
- 1/4 cup (60ml) of agave syrup, maple syrup, or another liquid sweetener
- 1/2 cup (75g) of raisins or chopped dried figs
- 1/2 cup (50g) of chopped walnuts or hazelnuts
- Optional: Vegan dark chocolate chips or chunks

Instructions:

Preheat the Oven and Prepare the Baking Sheet:

- Preheat your oven to 350°F (175°C).
- Line a baking sheet with parchment paper or use a silicone baking mat.

Mix Dry Ingredients:

- In a large bowl, whisk together the all-purpose flour, whole wheat flour, almond flour, powdered sugar, cocoa powder, baking powder, baking soda, salt, cinnamon, and cloves (if using).
- These dry ingredients form the base of your cookies.

Combine Wet Ingredients:

- In another bowl, combine the plant-based milk, oil, and agave or maple syrup. Mix well to ensure everything is well incorporated.

Combine Wet and Dry Mixtures:

- Gradually add the wet mixture to the dry ingredients, stirring as you go. Mix until you have a cohesive, sticky dough.
- If the dough is too dry, add a little more plant-based milk; if too wet, add a bit more flour.

Add Fruits and Nuts:

- Fold in the raisins or dried figs and chopped nuts, ensuring they're evenly distributed throughout the dough.
- If you're using vegan chocolate chips or chunks, add them at this stage.

Form the Cookies:

- Using your hands, form the dough into small cookie shapes (they can be round, oval, or slightly flattened) and place them on the prepared baking sheet.
- These cookies do not spread much, so you can keep them relatively close together.

Bake:

- Place the cookies in the preheated oven and bake for 12-15 minutes, depending on their size.

- They should be set and slightly firm to the touch but not hard; they will firm up more as they cool.

Cool and Serve:

- Remove the cookies from the oven and allow them to cool on the baking sheet for several minutes before transferring them to a wire rack to cool completely. They will be quite soft initially but will harden into a more traditional, dense texture as they cool down.

Storage:

- Store the completely cooled "Pizze dei Morti" in an airtight container. They will keep well for up to 2 weeks and are said to become better over a few days as the flavors meld.

Enjoy these vegan "Pizze dei Morti" as a way to partake in the cultural observance of the Day of the Dead, honoring this Italian tradition in a compassionate, plant-based manner.

Calzone di Cipolla (Onion Pie)

"Calzone di Cipolla," or Onion Pie, is a savory pastry with different variations across various regions.

The dish is particularly noted for its filling, typically involving onions, olives, and sometimes anchovies or sardines, enclosed in a pizza dough-like crust. Here's how you can make a vegan version of the Calzone di Cipolla, inspired by the flavors commonly found in the Abruzzo region's cooking:

Ingredients

for the Dough:

- 2 1/4 teaspoons (1 packet) of active dry yeast

- 1 1/2 cups warm water
- 4 cups all-purpose flour, plus extra for dusting
- 1 1/2 teaspoons salt
- 1 tablespoon olive oil, plus extra for coating

For the Filling:

- 3 tablespoons olive oil
- 4 large white onions, thinly sliced
- Salt, to taste
- 1 tablespoon sugar (optional for caramelizing the onions)
- 1/4 cup white wine (vegan)
- 1 tablespoon capers, rinsed and chopped
- A handful of black olives, pitted and halved
- Red pepper flakes, to taste (optional)
- Black pepper, to taste
- A small handful of fresh parsley, chopped

Instructions:

Prepare the Dough:

- In a small bowl, dissolve the yeast in warm water.
- Set aside for about 10 minutes until frothy.
- In a large bowl or a stand mixer, combine the flour and salt.
- Make a well in the center and add the yeast mixture and olive oil.
- Stir until a soft dough forms.
- Transfer the dough to a floured surface.
- Knead for about 6-8 minutes until smooth and elastic. Alternatively, use the dough hook attachment on your stand mixer.

- Place the dough in a lightly oiled bowl, cover it with a clean kitchen towel, and let it rise in a warm place for about 1-1.5 hours or until doubled in size.

Cook the Filling:

- While the dough is rising, heat olive oil in a large skillet over medium heat.

- Add the sliced onions and a pinch of salt, and cook until they begin to soften.

- If you prefer sweeter, caramelized onions, add sugar at this stage. Cook, stirring occasionally, until the onions are translucent and golden brown.

- This process might take around 25-30 minutes.

- Pour in the white wine to deglaze the pan, scraping up any browned bits.

- Allow the mixture to simmer until the wine has mostly evaporated.

- Remove from heat. Stir in capers, olives, red pepper flakes (if using), and black pepper.

- Allow the mixture to cool. Stir in the fresh parsley before using.

Assemble the Calzone:

- Preheat your oven to 425°F (220°C). If you have a pizza stone, put it in the oven now to heat.

- Punch down your risen dough and divide it in half.

- On a lightly floured surface, roll out one-half into a circle about 12 inches in diameter.

- On one half of the dough circle, spread half of the onion mixture, leaving about an inch from the edge.

- Fold the dough over the filling to create a half-moon shape, pinching the edges to seal.
- Repeat with the second half of the dough and filling.
- If you don't have a pizza stone, transfer the calzone to a baking sheet lined with parchment paper.

Bake the Calzone:
- Place the calzone in the preheated oven and bake for about 18-20 minutes, or until the crust is golden and sounds hollow when tapped.
- Remove from oven and let it cool for a few minutes before slicing.

Serving:
- Serve your vegan Calzone di Cipolla hot, accompanied by a green salad or your choice of a vegan side.
- This dish celebrates the simple yet flavorful essence of Italian cuisine from the Abruzzo region.

Enjoy your compassionate culinary journey through Italy with this authentic regional dish, adapted to a vegan lifestyle.

Broccoli Rabe all'Abruzzese

Broccoli rabe, also known as rapini, is a traditional Italian vegetable that's commonly used in a variety of dishes.

In the Abruzzo region, it's often prepared simply with garlic, chili, and olive oil, sometimes with the addition of pasta or served alongside sausages. Here's how you can make a vegan "Broccoli Rabe all'Abruzzese," maintaining the dish's authenticity while ensuring it's free of animal products.

Ingredients:

- 1 large bunch of broccoli rabe (rapini), washed and trimmed
- 3-4 tablespoons of extra-virgin olive oil
- 3-4 cloves of garlic, thinly sliced or minced
- 1 red chili pepper, finely chopped, or 1/2 teaspoon of red pepper flakes (adjust to taste)
- Salt, to taste
- Optional: 1-2 tablespoons of white wine vinegar or a squeeze of fresh lemon juice

- Optional: Toasted breadcrumbs or vegan Italian sausage for additional texture and protein

Instructions:

Prepare the Broccoli Rabe:

- Bring a large pot of salted water to a boil.
- Blanche the broccoli rabe in the boiling water for about 1-2 minutes until it becomes bright green and slightly tender.
- This process helps remove some of the vegetable's natural bitterness.
- Immediately transfer the blanched broccoli rabe to a bowl of ice water to stop the cooking process and retain its vibrant color.
- Once the broccoli rabe is cool, drain well and gently squeeze out any excess water.
- Roughly chop into bite-sized pieces.

Cook Garlic and Chili:

- In a large skillet, heat the olive oil over medium heat.
- Add the garlic and red chili or chili flakes.
- Sauté for a couple of minutes until the garlic is lightly golden and fragrant.
- Be careful not to burn the garlic, as it can become bitter.

Sauté the Broccoli Rabe:

- Add the drained and chopped broccoli rabe to the skillet.
- Stir well to coat the greens in the garlic-chili oil. Season with salt to taste.
- Cook on medium-high heat for 5-10 minutes, stirring occasionally.

- The broccoli rabe should become tender but should retain some bite and a slightly crisp texture.

Adjust the Flavors:

- Optional: If you want to add a bit of acidity to balance the dish's bitterness, you can stir in a small amount of white wine vinegar or fresh lemon juice at this stage.

- Adjust the seasoning with more salt if necessary.

- If you're including vegan sausage, add it to the pan now, allowing it to heat through and absorb some flavors from the dish.

- If using toasted breadcrumbs, they will be used as a garnish.

Serve:

- Once everything is well combined, and the greens are cooked to your liking, transfer the broccoli rabe to a serving dish.

- If using, sprinkle with toasted breadcrumbs for added crunch.

- Serve your vegan "Broccoli Rabe all'Abruzzese" hot as a side dish to complement your main course, or incorporate it into a pasta dish for a hearty vegan meal.

This dish highlights the natural flavors of the ingredients. It reflects the simplicity of traditional Italian cooking from the Abruzzo region.

Maccheroni alla Chitarra con Pomodori Secchi

This iconic Abruzzo pasta can be paired with a simple sauce of sun-dried tomatoes, garlic, and chili flakes for a vegan-friendly, flavorful dish.

"Maccheroni alla Chitarra" is an iconic pasta from the Abruzzo region. It is known for its square-shaped spaghetti-type noodles, typically made with a tool known as a 'chitarra' (guitar). The strings of the 'chitarra' create the unique shape of the pasta as the dough is pushed through them. This vegan recipe maintains the authentic essence of the dish, incorporating sun-dried tomatoes for a flavorful twist.

Ingredients:

For the pasta (if making from scratch):

- 400 grams (about 14 ounces) of semolina flour
- 200 ml (about 7 ounces) of warm water
- A pinch of salt

For the Sauce:

- 1/2 cup sun-dried tomatoes (not in oil), chopped
- 1/4 cup olive oil
- 2-3 garlic cloves, minced
- 1 small chili pepper, finely chopped or red pepper flakes, as per taste
- 1/2 cup of fresh parsley, chopped
- Salt, to taste
- Optional: capers or olives for an extra burst of flavor

Instructions:

Making the pasta (optional):

- On a clean surface, make a mound with the flour and a well in the center.
- Sprinkle a pinch of salt over the top.
- Gradually add warm water to the well and mix with the flour until it starts to come together.
- If you need slightly more water, add it slowly.
- Knead the dough for about 10 minutes until it's smooth and elastic.
- Cover with a clean kitchen towel and let it rest for 30 minutes.
- If you have a 'chitarra,' roll the dough into a sheet about 1/8 inch thick.

- Place the sheet on the 'chitarra' and roll it with a rolling pin so the strings cut the pasta.
- Alternatively, you can use a sharp knife to cut the pasta into thin, square-shaped spaghetti strands.

Preparing the Sun-Dried Tomatoes:

- If you're using dried sun-dried tomatoes, rehydrate them by soaking them in warm water for about 30 minutes, then drain and chop.
- If they're sun-dried tomatoes preserved in oil, you can skip this step.

Cooking the Pasta:

- Bring a large pot of salted water to a boil.
- Cook the pasta until 'al dente.' If you're using fresh pasta, it will cook faster (approximately 3-4 minutes).
- Drain and reserve about a cup of pasta water.

Making the Sauce:

- While the pasta is cooking, heat the olive oil in a large skillet over medium heat.
- Add the minced garlic and chili pepper, sautéing until the garlic is slightly golden and fragrant.
- Add the chopped sun-dried tomatoes to the skillet and sauté for an additional 2-3 minutes.
- Optional: If you're using capers or olives, add them at this stage.

Combining Pasta and Sauce:

- Add the drained pasta to the skillet with the sauce, tossing to combine.

- Add a little bit of reserved pasta water if necessary to loosen things up and help the sauce coat the pasta.
- Cook for an additional 2 minutes, allowing the pasta to soak up the flavors.

Serving:

- Remove from heat, stir in the fresh parsley, and adjust the salt to taste.
- Serve your "Maccheroni alla Chitarra con Pomodori Secchi" hot, garnishing with more parsley or chili flakes if desired.

This dish embodies the rich culinary traditions of the Abruzzo region, highlighting the simplicity and robust flavors that Italian cuisine is known for. Enjoy your vegan meal!

These dishes from Abruzzo's culinary repertoire show that traditional recipes can be adapted to a vegan diet without losing their essence, celebrating the region's culinary heritage and the natural bounty of its landscapes.

Molise

Molise, though one of Italy's smallest and less touristy regions, offers a unique culinary tradition that reflects its rural roots and the pureness of its locally sourced ingredients. The cuisine here is defined by its simplicity, with many dishes having only a few ingredients but still packed with flavor. This makes it easier to find or adapt recipes to suit a vegan lifestyle. Here are some vegan-friendly dishes from Molise:

Bruschetta Molinese

Bruschetta is a classic Italian appetizer that consists of grilled bread rubbed with garlic and topped with various ingredients. You may be familiar with the most familiar version, which is topped with a mixture of fresh tomatoes, basil, garlic, and olive oil.

Here's a recipe inspired by Molisan cuisine, adapted for a vegan diet, that I am certain you will enjoy.

This recipe includes a rich, flavorful topping that combines traditional bruschetta elements with a unique blend of Molisan-inspired ingredients.

Ingredients:

- 1 loaf of Italian bread or baguette
- 3-4 tablespoons extra-virgin olive oil
- 2-3 cloves of garlic, whole (for rubbing) plus 2 cloves minced (for the topping)
- 4-5 ripe tomatoes, finely chopped
- 1 small red onion, finely chopped
- 1-2 tablespoons capers, drained and rinsed
- A handful of fresh basil leaves, torn or roughly chopped
- Salt and black pepper to taste
- Optional: red pepper flakes, to taste (be careful, they are very spicy)
- Optional: 1-2 tablespoons balsamic vinegar (for a tangy twist)

Instructions:

Prepare the Bread:

- Slice the loaf of bread into 1/2-inch (about 1.3 cm) slices.
- Preheat your grill or broiler, or you can heat a grill pan on the stovetop over medium heat.

Grill the Bread:

- Brush one side of each bread slice lightly with some olive oil.
- Place the bread slices oil-side down on the grill, grill pan, or under the broiler.
- Toast the bread until it's golden and crisp (about 2 minutes per side).
- Remove the bread slices from the heat.

Garlic Rub:

- Once the bread slices are toasted and while they're still warm, rub one side of each slice with a whole clove of garlic.
- The rough surface of the toasted bread will grate the garlic slightly, infusing the bread with a subtle garlic flavor.

Prepare the Topping:

- In a bowl, combine the finely chopped tomatoes, red onion, and the additional minced garlic (2 cloves).
- If you're using capers, add them to the mixture.
- Add the torn basil leaves and drizzle the remaining olive oil over the top.
- If you're using balsamic vinegar, add it now for an extra layer of flavor.

- Season with salt, black pepper, and red pepper flakes if you want a bit of heat.
- Mix everything well.

Marinate (Optional Step):

- For enhanced flavor, you can let the tomato mixture marinate for about 15-30 minutes at room temperature.
- This step allows the flavors to meld beautifully.

Assemble the Bruschetta:

- Spoon generous amounts of the tomato mixture onto the garlic-rubbed side of each toasted bread slice.
- Allow some of the juices to dribble onto the bread as they add to the flavor.

Serving:

- Serve immediately as an appetizer, snack, or side dish.
- Bruschetta is best enjoyed fresh, as the bread retains its crispness, and the topping is juicy.

Variation:

- If you want to reflect more of Molise's agricultural products, consider adding finely chopped olives or a sprinkle of chili in homage to the region's famous chili harvest.

Enjoy your vegan Molisan-inspired Bruschetta! This simple yet flavorful dish is sure to delight your taste buds with its combination of fresh ingredients and cultural authenticity.

Cavatelli con Verdure

Cavatelli con Verdure (Cavatelli with Vegetables) is a classic Italian dish that highlights the simple flavors of fresh vegetables combined with small, shell-shaped pasta called cavatelli. This recipe can easily be adapted to a vegan version by omitting traditional cheese and using plant-based ingredients.

Here's how you can prepare a delightful, cruelty-free version of Cavatelli con Verdure:

Ingredients:

- 400g (approximately 14 oz) cavatelli pasta (ensure it's egg-free)
- 3-4 tablespoons olive oil
- 3 garlic cloves, thinly sliced or minced
- 1 small red chili (optional), deseeded and finely chopped or red pepper flakes to taste
- 1 medium zucchini, sliced into half-moons or diced
- 1 medium bell pepper (any color), chopped

- 1 small eggplant, diced
- 200g (approximately 7 oz) cherry tomatoes, halved
- Salt and black pepper, to taste
- A handful of fresh basil leaves, roughly torn, plus extra for garnish
- Optional: nutritional yeast or vegan Parmesan cheese for serving

Instructions:

Prepare the Vegetables:

- Clean and chop the zucchini, bell pepper, and eggplant into bite-sized pieces.
- Slice the cherry tomatoes in half. Set all the vegetables aside.

Cook the Cavatelli:

- Bring a large pot of salted water to a boil.
- Add the cavatelli and cook according to the package instructions until the pasta is al dente.
- Reserve about 1 cup of pasta cooking water, then drain the pasta and set aside.

Sauté the Vegetables:

- While the pasta is cooking, heat the olive oil in a large pan over medium heat.
- Add the sliced garlic and chopped chili (if using), sautéing for about 1-2 minutes or until the garlic is golden and fragrant.
- Be careful not to burn the garlic.
- Next, add the zucchini, bell pepper, and eggplant to the pan.

- Season with salt and pepper to taste.
- Cook, stirring occasionally, until the vegetables are tender, about 10-12 minutes.
- Add the cherry tomatoes to the pan and cook for an additional 3-5 minutes, until the tomatoes are just soft and their juices begin to release.
- This creates a natural sauce.

Combine Pasta and Vegetables:
- Add the cooked cavatelli to the pan with the vegetables, tossing everything together so the pasta is well-coated with the juices from the pan.
- If the mixture seems dry, add a bit of the reserved pasta water to create more of a sauce.
- Allow everything to cook together for 1-2 minutes so the flavors meld beautifully.

Add Fresh Basil:
- Remove the pan from heat and stir in the fresh basil leaves.
- Adjust seasoning with more salt and pepper if needed.

Serve:
- Dish out the cavatelli con verdure into serving bowls.
- If desired, sprinkle with nutritional yeast or vegan Parmesan cheese for a cheesy flavor boost and garnish with more fresh basil.

Optional Add-Ins:
- For extra protein, consider adding chickpeas or cooked lentils into the mix.

- If you want more greens, spinach or kale can be added just before you combine the pasta and vegetables, allowing them to wilt perfectly within the dish.

Enjoy your meal! This dish celebrates the flavors of fresh vegetables and simple seasonings, all combined with the delightful chewy texture of cavatelli pasta. It's a light yet satisfying dish that is perfect for any occasion.

Tarallucci al Finocchio

These are small, round, and crunchy biscuits, typically flavored with fennel seeds, white wine, and extra-virgin olive oil.

They make a great snack or an accompaniment to salads.

Ingredients:

- 3 cups (360g) all-purpose flour, plus more for dusting
- 3/4 cup (150g) granulated sugar
- 1/2 cup (120ml) olive oil or vegetable oil
- 1/2 cup (120ml) plant-based milk (such as almond, soy, or oat milk)
- 1 teaspoon baking powder
- 1-3 tablespoons fennel seeds (adjust according to preference)
- A pinch of salt

- Optional: Zest of 1 organic lemon or orange for added flavor
- Optional: Icing sugar for dusting

Instructions:

Preheat the Oven:

- Start by preheating your oven to 350°F (175°C).
- Line a baking sheet with parchment paper or a silicone baking mat.

Mix Dry Ingredients:

- In a large bowl, combine the all-purpose flour, granulated sugar, baking powder, fennel seeds, and salt.
- If you're using lemon or orange zest, add it to this mix.
- Whisk these ingredients together until well-mixed.

Add Wet Ingredients:

- Create a well in the center of your dry ingredients and pour in the olive oil and plant-based milk.
- Using a spoon or even your hands, mix everything together until it forms a smooth, cohesive dough.
- The dough should be pliable but not too sticky.
- If it's too dry, add a bit more plant-based milk; if it is too wet, add a little more flour.

Shape the Tarallucci:

- Pinch off small pieces of dough and roll them into balls (about the size of a walnut).
- Next, roll these balls into ropes, around 5 inches (13 cm) long.
- Shape these ropes into circles, crossing over the ends to form a "teardrop" shape or a traditional circular shape.

- Press the ends lightly to seal them.

Baking:

- Place the shaped cookies on your prepared baking sheet, leaving a bit of space between them for slight expansion.
- Bake in the preheated oven for around 15-20 minutes or until they're slightly golden and firm.
- They don't need to brown as much as other cookies might.

Cooling:

- Remove the tarallucci from the oven and allow them to cool on the baking sheet for a few minutes before transferring them to a wire rack to cool completely.
- They will harden more as they cool.

Serving:

- If desired, dust the cookies with a bit of icing sugar before serving for presentation and a touch of extra sweetness.
- Serve them with coffee or tea, or enjoy them on their own!

Storing:

- Keep any leftover cookies in an airtight container at room temperature.
- They should last for up to 2 weeks.

Enjoy your vegan Tarallucci al Finocchio! These delightful cookies are a treat within vegan dietary restrictions, embracing the traditional flavors that make this Italian biscuit so beloved.

Insalata di Ceci (Chickpea Salad)

A refreshing salad made with chickpeas, it's often mixed with parsley, tomatoes, onions, and a dressing of extra-virgin olive oil and lemon juice or vinegar.

This recipe incorporates traditional Italian flavors, adjusted for a vegan diet, and influenced by the culinary preferences of the Molise region.

Ingredients:

- 2 cups cooked chickpeas (if using canned, choose a 15-ounce can and rinse and drain the chickpeas)
- 1 small red onion, finely sliced
- 1-2 ripe tomatoes, diced (consider using cherry tomatoes for extra sweetness)
- A handful of fresh basil leaves, torn, or fresh parsley, chopped

- 2-3 tablespoons extra virgin olive oil (preferably of Italian origin, as it's a central flavor in the dish)
- 1 tablespoon red wine vinegar or fresh lemon juice (for that necessary tang in the salad)
- Salt, to taste
- Freshly ground black pepper, to taste
- Optional: 1-2 cloves of garlic, minced
- Optional: a pinch of red pepper flakes (peperoncino)

Instructions:

Prepare the Ingredients:

- Ensure your chickpeas are rinsed and drained if you're using canned.
- Clean and dice your tomatoes, finely slice the red onion, and prepare your herbs and optional garlic.

Assemble the Salad:

- In a mixing bowl, combine the chickpeas, red onion slices, diced tomatoes, and fresh basil or parsley.
- If you're using garlic, add it to the mix now.

Dress the Salad:

- Drizzle the salad with a generous amount of extra virgin olive oil, which will bring a rich flavor to the dish.
- Add red wine vinegar or lemon juice, salt, and freshly ground black pepper.

Mix Thoroughly:

- Toss all the ingredients together until everything is well coated in the dressing.
- Taste and adjust the seasoning as necessary, adding more salt, pepper, or vinegar/lemon juice if needed.

- If you prefer a bit of heat, consider adding a pinch of red pepper flakes.

Let the Salad Marinate:

- For the best flavor, cover your salad and let it marinate in the refrigerator for at least 30 minutes.
- This step allows all the beautiful flavors to meld.

Serve:

- Give the salad one more quick toss before serving.
- This dish can be served cold or at room temperature, making it a versatile option for various meals or seasonal needs.

Garnish (optional):

- For a touch of color and fresh flavor, consider adding an extra sprinkle of herbs or a few thin slices of red pepper on top just before serving.

Serving Suggestions:

- This Insalata di Ceci can be enjoyed as a standalone light meal, perfect for warm days when cooking is less appealing.
- It's also an excellent accompaniment to heavier dishes, providing a refreshing balance.
- Consider adding it to a mixed greens salad for added protein and texture, or serve it alongside grilled vegetables and a crusty piece of Italian bread for a complete meal.

This salad reflects the simplicity of Molise's cuisine, focusing on fresh ingredients and clear, vibrant flavors. It's a testament to the region's agricultural roots and the Mediterranean diet.

Frittata di Bietole

A traditional frittata di bietole (Swiss chard frittata) usually contains eggs.

However, creating a vegan version of this dish that maintains the heartiness and flavor is certainly possible. This vegan adaptation uses chickpea flour as a substitute for eggs, providing a protein-rich base that creates a texture similar to the original dish. Here's how you can prepare a Vegan Frittata di Bietole inspired by the culinary style of Molise.

Ingredients:
- 1 bunch of Swiss chard (bietole), washed and roughly chopped (you can use both leaves and stems)
- 1 cup chickpea flour (also known as gram flour or besan)

- 1 1/4 cups water
- 2-3 tablespoons olive oil
- 1 medium onion, finely chopped
- 2-3 cloves garlic, minced
- Salt, to taste
- Black pepper, to taste
- 1/4 teaspoon turmeric (for color; optional)
- 1/2 teaspoon baking powder
- Optional herbs and spices: nutritional yeast (for a cheesy flavor), a pinch of smoked paprika, or Italian herbs like thyme or oregano
- Optional: red pepper flakes or finely chopped fresh chili (peperoncino)

Instructions:

Prep the Swiss Chard:

- In a large pan, heat a tablespoon of olive oil over medium heat.
- Add the chopped onion and sauté until it starts to become translucent.
- Add the garlic and, if you're using them, the red pepper flakes or fresh chili.
- Sauté for another minute until fragrant.
- Add the Swiss chard. You might need to do this in batches, depending on your pan size.
- Cook down the chard until it's wilted and tender, which should take about 5-7 minutes.
- Season with salt and pepper to taste, then remove from heat and set aside.

Create the Batter:

- In a mixing bowl, whisk together the chickpea flour, water, salt, pepper, and turmeric (if using) until smooth.
- Let the mixture sit for a few minutes to thicken slightly.
- Stir in the baking powder.
- Add optional herbs, spices, or nutritional yeast at this stage.
- Add the cooked Swiss chard mixture to the batter, ensuring it's evenly distributed.

Cook the Frittata:

- Preheat your oven to 350°F (175°C) if you plan to bake the frittata for a firmer texture.
- Heat a medium oven-safe, non-stick skillet or cast-iron pan over medium heat with a tablespoon or so of olive oil.
- Once hot, pour in the frittata mixture, spreading it evenly in the pan.
- Reduce the heat to low and cover.
- Let it cook for 10-12 minutes until the edges are set, but the top is still slightly runny.
- If you're baking the frittata, transfer the skillet to your preheated oven and bake for an additional 10-15 minutes or until the center is firm and fully cooked.
- Otherwise, you can flip the frittata in the skillet and cook the other side on the stovetop for another 5-10 minutes until set.

Serve Your Frittata:

- Once cooked, remove your frittata from the oven or stovetop and let it cool for a few minutes.

- Carefully slide or invert the frittata onto a serving plate.
- This dish can be enjoyed hot or at room temperature.
- It pairs well with a side salad, some crusty bread, or roasted vegetables.

This vegan frittata di bietole offers a flavorful, egg-free alternative to a traditional Italian dish, reflecting Molise's simple culinary traditions with an emphasis on plant-based ingredients.

Ciambotta

Ciambotta, sometimes referred to as the Italian version of ratatouille, is a hearty vegetable stew that originally came from southern Italy.

It's common across various regions, with different names and slight variations in ingredients and preparation. In Molise, this dish would traditionally center around the locally available produce, making it a celebration of the region's agricultural bounty.

Here's a vegan version of Ciambotta, keeping true to the Molisan way — simple, rustic, and flavorful.

Ingredients:

- 2-3 tablespoons olive oil
- 1 large onion, chopped
- 2-3 cloves garlic, minced
- 1 medium eggplant, cut into 1-inch cubes
- 1-2 medium zucchini, sliced into 1-inch rounds
- 2 bell peppers, any color, seeded and chopped
- 3-4 large ripe tomatoes, chopped (or one 28-ounce can of whole or diced tomatoes)
- 1/4 cup fresh basil, torn or roughly chopped
- 1 teaspoon dried oregano
- Salt and pepper, to taste
- Optional: 1-2 potatoes, cut into 1-inch cubes
- Optional: red pepper flakes, to taste
- Optional: 1/4 cup of water or vegetable broth (as needed)

Instructions:

Prep the Vegetables:

- Wash and chop all your vegetables as indicated above.
- If you're using fresh tomatoes, consider removing the skins by blanching them in hot water.

Sauté Onions and Garlic:

- Heat the olive oil in a large pot or large, deep skillet over medium heat.
- Add the onions and a pinch of salt, cooking until they're soft and translucent, about 5-7 minutes.
- Add the garlic and cook for another 1-2 minutes until fragrant.

Cook the Hardier Vegetables:

- If you're using potatoes, add them first, cooking for a few minutes, as they'll take longer to soften.
- Add the eggplant next, stirring and cooking until it starts to soften and brown, around 5-7 minutes.
- If the vegetables start to stick, you can add a bit more olive oil or a few tablespoons of water to help deglaze the pan.

Add the Rest of the Vegetables:

- Add the zucchini, bell peppers, and tomatoes.
- Stir in the oregano and, if using, a pinch of red pepper flakes.
- At this point, if your vegetables are producing too little liquid, you can add some vegetable broth or water.
- However, the tomatoes should break down and provide quite a bit of liquid on their own.

Simmer the Stew:

- Reduce the heat, cover, and let your ciambotta simmer for 25-30 minutes, stirring occasionally.
- You're looking for all the vegetables to be very tender and the flavors to meld together.
- The longer it cooks, the more the flavors will develop.

Final Seasonings:

- Stir in the fresh basil and season your stew with more salt and pepper to taste.
- Simmer for an additional 5 minutes to let the new seasonings integrate.

Serving Your Ciambotta:

- Ciambotta can be served hot or at room temperature.
- It's often even better the next day after the flavors have had more time to blend.
- Serve it as a main dish with a loaf of crusty bread or as a side dish to complement other entrees.
- It's also traditional to top the stew with a drizzle of olive oil and a sprinkle of fresh basil.

This vegan ciambotta recipe highlights the simplicity of Molise cuisine, focusing on fresh, locally sourced ingredients and the region's agricultural roots. It's a versatile dish that showcases the flavorful produce found in this area of Italy.

In Molise, like much of Italy, the key to their cuisine is high-quality, locally sourced ingredients prepared in a way that highlights their natural flavors. This approach fits well with a vegan diet, focusing on the freshness and seasonality of vegetables and legumes.

Campania

Campania, a southern Italian region, is home to iconic dishes that are cherished worldwide. The region's fertile land produces an abundance of fresh vegetables, fruits, and herbs, making it a fantastic area to explore vegan dishes. Here are some traditional and adapted vegan specialties from Campania:

Pizza Marinara

Pizza Marinara is a classic Italian dish originating from Naples in the Campania region. It's one of the simplest and oldest kinds of pizza, and it's naturally vegan, containing no animal products in its traditional form.

The name "marinara" doesn't come from the sea (as one might think because of "marine") but rather from the "marinieri," translated to "sailors," who reportedly ate this type of pizza because it was a food that could be easily preserved.

The key to a good Pizza Marinara, like any traditional Neapolitan pizza, is the quality of the ingredients and the method of cooking.

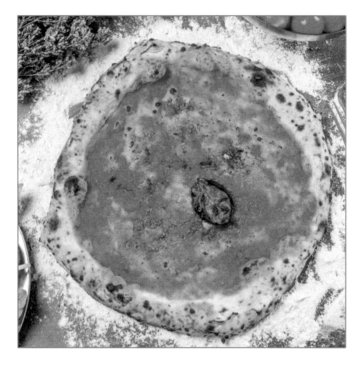

Traditionally, it's cooked in a wood-fired oven, which gives it a unique flavor.

Ingredients:

For the dough:

- 4 cups (about 500 grams) 00 flour (Italian high-protein flour) or strong bread flour
- 1 1/2 cups (350 ml) water
- 2 tsp (7 grams) salt
- 1/2 tsp (2 grams) fresh yeast (if using dry yeast, follow the package's conversion instructions)

For the topping:

- 1 1/2 cups (350 ml) of high-quality tomato sauce (pureed tomatoes)

- 2-3 cloves of garlic, thinly sliced or finely minced
- A small handful of fresh basil leaves
- Extra virgin olive oil
- Salt, to taste
- Optional: a pinch of oregano or red pepper flakes

Instructions:

Preparing the Dough:

- In a large bowl, dissolve the yeast in the water (ideally at about 68°F or 20°C).
- Start adding the flour gradually, mixing continuously.
- Once you've added about half the flour, add the salt.
- Continue adding the flour until you've formed a dough.
- Move it to a floured surface and knead for 10-15 minutes until smooth and elastic. (I usually prefer using the KitchenAid mixer.)
- Shape the dough into a ball, place it in a lightly floured bowl, cover it with a damp cloth, and let it rise for about 8 hours at room temperature or for about 2 hours if you can expose it to the sun and warm outside temperature.

Forming the Pizza Base:

- After the first rise, punch the dough down and divide it into 3-4 balls. Cover them with a hot-water-damped cloth and allow them to rise for another 1-2 hours.
- Preheat your oven to the highest setting, typically 475 - 550°F (245 - 290°C).
- If you have a pizza stone, put it in the oven now to heat up.
- Hand-stretch your dough into a round shape, creating a slightly thicker rim around the edge.

- Avoid using a rolling pin as it pushes the air out of the dough.

Preparing the Topping:

- Prepare your sauce by ensuring it's well-seasoned.
- You can cook a garlic clove in a bit of olive oil and mix this flavored oil into your sauce, if you prefer, instead of having bits of garlic on your pizza.
- If you're using minced garlic or sliced garlic, mix it directly into the sauce.

Assembling the Pizza:

- Place your stretched dough on a piece of parchment paper.
- With a ladle or spoon, spread a thin layer of tomato sauce over the dough, leaving a small border around the edge.
- Drizzle a little olive oil over the sauce and scatter a few basil leaves on top.
- If you're using them, also add your oregano or red pepper flakes.

Baking the Pizza:

- Transfer the pizza (with the parchment paper) onto the preheated pizza stone or place it on a baking sheet in the oven.
- Bake for about 7-10 minutes (depending on your oven's heat) until the crust is golden and crisp and the sauce is bubbling.

Serving:

- Carefully remove the pizza from the oven, drizzle with a little more olive oil if desired, and let it sit for a couple of minutes before slicing.

- Serve immediately, garnishing with more fresh basil if preferred.

Remember, the secret of Neapolitan pizza is in its simplicity and the quality of the ingredients used. Each flavor should be vivid and in harmony with the others. This vegan Pizza Marinara is a celebration of that simplicity, embodying the rich culinary traditions of Campania.

Spaghetti al Pomodoro

Spaghetti al Pomodoro stands as a testament to Italian culinary philosophy: Less is often more. Rooted deeply in the Campania region, especially Naples, this dish is a celebration of simplicity and purity.

At its heart, Spaghetti al Pomodoro is undeniably vegan, allowing the individual flavors of its minimal ingredients to shine through without any distractions. The key is in the selection: sun-ripened tomatoes bursting with juiciness, extra-virgin olive oil that carries a hint of the Mediterranean, and perfectly al dente spaghetti that holds onto the sauce just right. Preparation honors tradition, often involving hand-crushed tomatoes and garlic sautéed gently in olive oil.

The magic lies in the harmonious blend of these ingredients, coming together to create a plate that, while simple, resonates deeply with Italy's culinary soul. Dive into this timeless recipe and experience the very essence of Neapolitan cuisine.

Ingredients:

- 400 grams (about 14 ounces) of high-quality spaghetti (preferably bronze-cut)

- 800 grams (about 28 ounces) of fresh ripe plum tomatoes (San Marzano, if you can find them, as they are traditional to Campania) or high-quality canned San Marzano tomatoes if you're out of season
- 2-3 cloves of garlic, peeled and lightly smashed (but kept whole)
- A handful of fresh basil leaves
- 3-4 tablespoons of extra virgin olive oil (plus extra for drizzling)
- Salt, to taste
- Optional: a pinch of sugar (if your tomatoes are overly acidic)
- Optional: a pinch of red pepper flakes

Instructions:

Prepare the Tomatoes:

- If using fresh tomatoes, start by blanching them.
- Make small X-shaped incisions at the bottom of your tomatoes. Place them in boiling water for about 30 seconds until the skins loosen.
- Transfer to a bowl of ice water, then peel off the skins, remove the seeds, and roughly chop.
- If using canned tomatoes, open the can and crush the tomatoes with your hands or a fork for a rougher sauce.
- For a smoother sauce, you can blend them slightly.

Cook the Garlic:

- In a large skillet or saucepan, heat the olive oil over medium heat.
- Add the whole garlic cloves and red pepper flakes if you're using them.

- Sauté until the garlic is golden and fragrant but not browned (as that turns it bitter).
- This infuses the oil with a garlic flavor that forms the base of your sauce.
- Once ready, you can remove and discard the garlic or leave it in for a stronger flavor.

Simmer the Tomatoes:

- Add the prepared fresh or canned tomatoes to the skillet. Stir well and bring the mixture to a simmer.
- Lower the heat and continue to simmer the sauce, uncovered, for about 15-20 minutes, or until it thickens and the flavors concentrate.
- If your tomatoes are too acidic, consider adding just a pinch of sugar to balance the flavor.
- Season with salt to taste and add a few fresh basil leaves (keeping some for garnish).
- Let these cook in the sauce for the last few minutes.

Cook the Spaghetti:

- While your sauce is simmering, bring a large pot of salted water to a boil.
- Add your spaghetti and cook according to the package instructions until "al dente" (cooked to be firm to the bite).
- Reserve a cup of pasta cooking water and then drain the spaghetti.

Combine Pasta and Sauce:

- Add the drained pasta directly to your skillet with the sauce or return the pasta to the pot and add the amount of sauce you prefer.

- Toss the pasta with the sauce over medium heat, adding a little pasta cooking water if needed to loosen things up and allow the sauce to coat the spaghetti evenly.
- Do this for about 2 minutes; the pasta will finish cooking in the sauce and absorb the flavors.

Serving Your Dish:
- Serve the pasta hot, drizzled with a bit more extra virgin olive oil, and topped with fresh basil leaves.
- If desired, add a sprinkling of vegan parmesan cheese to enhance the flavor further.

In Campania, particularly around Naples, the quality of the local San Marzano tomatoes, grown in volcanic soil, makes a simple dish like Spaghetti al Pomodoro stand out. It's a celebration of natural flavors, and in its simplicity, it's a true culinary delight.

Caprese Salad

The traditional Caprese salad from Campania, known as "Insalata Caprese," is simplicity at its finest, traditionally showcasing fresh slices of mozzarella cheese with ripe tomatoes, basil, salt, and olive oil. However, making a vegan version of this dish involves substituting the mozzarella with a plant-based alternative.

There are several options for this, including using a store-bought vegan mozzarella or making your own from nuts (like cashews or almonds) or tofu.

Here's how you can create a Vegan Caprese Salad.

Ingredients:

- 2-3 large ripe tomatoes, sliced
- Vegan mozzarella cheese, sliced (available in stores or homemade)
- Fresh basil leaves
- High-quality extra virgin olive oil
- Sea salt, to taste
- Fresh ground black pepper, to taste (optional)
- Optional: balsamic glaze or vinegar for drizzling

Instructions:

Prepare the Ingredients:

- Begin by washing the tomatoes and basil.
- Slice the tomatoes into approximately 1/4-inch thick slices.

- If you haven't pre-sliced your vegan mozzarella, do so, trying to match the size of your tomato slices.

Assemble the Salad:

- Start with a slice of tomato, followed by a slice of vegan mozzarella, and then a basil leaf.
- Repeat this process until your plate is filled.
- You can create a stacked tower or arrange them in a circle or back-and-forth pattern on a platter.
- Be creative with your presentation based on the serving number and plate shape.
- Sprinkle the assembled salad with sea salt and fresh ground black pepper (if using) to taste.
- Remember, the key to this salad is the freshness of the ingredients, so each one brings its own rich flavor.

Adding the Final Touches:

- Drizzle the high-quality extra virgin olive oil generously over the top of the slices.
- The oil serves as a flavor enhancer, bringing the creamy vegan cheese and juicy tomatoes together in a harmonious blend.
- If you prefer, a drizzle of balsamic glaze or vinegar can add a nice tang that complements the sweetness of the tomatoes beautifully.

Serving the Salad:

- Serve your Insalata Caprese immediately as a refreshing starter or side dish.
- This salad is all about freshness, so it's best enjoyed right away and not stored for long periods.

If you choose to make homemade vegan mozzarella, here's a simplified recipe. Please note that there are more complex versions that can result in different textures and flavors.

- 1 cup of raw cashews (soaked for several hours or boiled for 10 minutes)
- 2 tablespoons of nutritional yeast
- 1 tablespoon of lemon juice
- 1/2 teaspoon of sea salt
- 1/2 cup of water (used for soaking the cashews)
- 2 tablespoons of agar agar flakes (or 2 teaspoons of agar agar powder)

Blend Ingredients:

- In a blender, combine the soaked cashews, nutritional yeast, lemon juice, salt, and the cashew-soaking water.
- Blend until smooth.

Prepare Agar Agar:

- In a small saucepan, dissolve the agar agar in 1/2 cup of water (if using flakes, you'll need to simmer and stir for about 5-8 minutes; the powder will dissolve faster).

Combine and Set:

- Quickly mix the agar mixture with the cashew blend and stir until well combined.
- Pour the mixture into a mold or container and refrigerate for at least 2 hours.

Once it's set, you can slice your vegan mozzarella for the Caprese salad, as mentioned in the steps above. The texture will be somewhat different from traditional mozzarella. Still, it will offer a creamy, satisfying element to your vegan dish.

By choosing high-quality ingredients, you can maintain the integrity of the traditional Caprese salad's flavors and experience, even with the substitution for vegan mozzarella.

Minestra Maritata

Minestra Maritata, or "Wedding Soup," is a traditional dish from the Campania region in Italy, particularly popular in and around Naples. Its name, translating to "married soup," refers to the "marriage" or a perfect blend of its ingredients — meats and green vegetables, traditionally endive and escarole, along with meat broth. To create a vegan version of Minestra Maritata, we'll substitute plant-based ingredients for the meats and broth while maintaining the hearty characteristics and rich flavors of the classic preparation.

Ingredients:

- 2 tablespoons olive oil
- 1 large onion, finely chopped
- 2-3 garlic cloves, minced
- 2 medium carrots, diced
- 2 celery stalks, diced
- 1 small fennel bulb, diced (optional)
- 8 cups vegetable broth (homemade or store-bought)
- 1 bunch of kale, chopped (traditional recipes use escarole; you may also use endive, collard greens, or a mix)
- 1 bunch of Swiss chard, chopped
- 1 can (15 ounces) of cannellini beans, rinsed and drained
- 1 teaspoon dried thyme
- 1 teaspoon dried oregano
- Salt and black pepper, to taste
- Fresh parsley, chopped, for garnish
- Vegan Italian sausage or meatballs (store-bought or homemade), optional
- Crushed red pepper flakes, optional, for added heat

Instructions:

Prepare the Base:

- In a large pot, heat the olive oil over medium heat.
- Add the onion, garlic, carrots, celery, and fennel (if using), sautéing until the vegetables are tender, about 5-7 minutes.
- If you're using vegan sausage or meatballs, add them to the pot and cook for an additional 5-7 minutes or until

they're browned and cooked through, stirring frequently to ensure they don't stick.

Add Greens and Broth:

- Add the chopped kale and Swiss chard (or escarole/endive) to the pot, stirring for 2-3 minutes until they start to wilt.

- Pour in the vegetable broth, bringing the mixture to a gentle boil.

- If you're using store-bought broth, opt for a low-sodium variety, as it gives you better control over the salt level in your soup.

Seasoning and Beans:

- Add the dried thyme, dried oregano, salt, and black pepper, adjusting the quantities to suit your taste.

- Incorporate the cannellini beans into the soup.

- These add protein and heartiness, complementing the greens' bitterness.

Simmer the Soup:

- Reduce the heat, allowing the soup to simmer for about 20-30 minutes, uncovered.

- This process melds the flavors together and ensures the greens are well-cooked and tender.

- Taste the soup, adjusting the seasoning, as necessary. If you prefer a spicier soup, consider adding a pinch of crushed red pepper flakes.

Serving:

- Ladle the hot soup into bowls, garnishing with fresh chopped parsley.

- If you want to add an extra touch, serve with crusty bread on the side to soak up the flavorful broth.
- For those desiring a cheesy flavor reminiscent of traditional recipes, sprinkle nutritional yeast or vegan Parmesan cheese on top before serving.

This vegan version of Minestra Maritata maintains the spirit of the traditional dish, celebrating the "marriage" of flavors between rich greens and savory broth, all without animal products. It's a nourishing, comforting soup perfect for cold days or whenever you need a hearty meal.

Melanzane a Funghetto

"Melanzane a Funghetto" (eggplants cooked in the style of mushrooms) is a simple yet flavorful dish from Southern Italy, particularly popular in the Campania region.

The name refers to the method of cooking the eggplants (melanzane), similarly to how one would sauté mushrooms (funghi). This vegan-friendly dish focuses on fresh ingredients and the rich, natural flavors of eggplant.

Here's how you can prepare it:

- 2-3 medium eggplants (about 1 kg in total)
- Salt, to draw out the water from the eggplants
- 4 tablespoons of extra virgin olive oil, more if needed
- 3-4 cloves garlic, finely sliced or minced
- 1 small bunch of fresh basil, leaves picked, plus extra for garnish
- 1-2 cups of tomato passata or crushed tomatoes (adjust according to how saucy you prefer the dish)
- Salt and black pepper, to taste
- Red pepper flakes, optional, for heat

Instructions:

Prep the Eggplant:

- Begin by washing the eggplants and cutting them into small cubes or bite-sized pieces.
- The skin can be left on for extra texture and nutrition.

- Place the chopped eggplant in a colander and sprinkle with salt, tossing to coat.
- Allow them to sit for about 30 minutes to draw out the bitterness and excess water.
- Afterward, rinse thoroughly and pat dry with paper towels.

Sauté Garlic:

- In a large skillet, heat the olive oil over medium heat.
- Add the sliced or minced garlic to the skillet.
- If you like a bit of heat, you can also add some red pepper flakes at this stage.
- Sauté until the garlic is just starting to turn golden, being careful not to burn it.

Cook Eggplant:

- Add the eggplant pieces to the skillet, increasing the heat to medium-high.
- Cook, stirring occasionally, until the eggplants start to brown and become soft, approximately 10-15 minutes.
- If the eggplants absorb all the oil and the pan seems too dry, you can add a little more olive oil to prevent sticking.

Add Tomatoes and Basil:

- Once the eggplants are nicely browned and softened, pour in the tomato passata or crushed tomatoes over the eggplant.
- Add most of the fresh basil leaves, reserving a few for garnish.
- Reduce the heat to low and let the mixture simmer for about 10-15 minutes, or until the sauce has thickened slightly and the eggplants are very tender.

- Stir occasionally to ensure the sauce doesn't stick to the skillet.

Season and Serve:

- Taste the mixture and add salt and black pepper, adjusting to your preference.

- Remove the skillet from the heat.

- Let it sit for a couple of minutes, allowing the flavors to meld together.

- Serve hot or at room temperature, garnished with the remaining basil leaves.

- This dish can be served as a side or even a main course, often accompanied by fresh bread to soak up the sauce.

- It's also a fantastic addition to pasta if you prefer a more substantial meal.

This rustic and delightful preparation of "Melanzane a Funghetto" is a celebration of simplicity, allowing the natural flavors of fresh, high-quality ingredients to shine through. It's a staple in Neapolitan cuisine and a testament to the region's culinary philosophy.

Insalata di Tarocco (Orange Salad)

Particularly popular in the winter, "Insalata di Tarocco" is a refreshing salad known for its vibrant colors and the delightful combination of sweet and savory flavors. Originating in Southern Italy, particularly in regions like Campania, this salad typically features Tarocco oranges, which are famous for their sweet taste, juiciness, and bright red flesh.

However, if Tarocco oranges are not available, any sweet, ripe blood orange variety can work in this recipe. Here's how to create a vegan version of Insalata di Tarocco.

Ingredients:

- 3-4 Tarocco oranges (or any other sweet blood oranges if Tarocco is unavailable)
- 1 small red onion, thinly sliced
- 2-3 tablespoons of extra virgin olive oil
- Salt, to taste
- Black pepper, to taste
- A handful of black olives, preferably of the Gaeta variety (common in Campania)
- A few fresh mint leaves or fresh basil leaves for garnish
- Optional: fennel bulb, thinly sliced
- Optional: chili flakes or a small fresh chili, thinly sliced

Instructions:

Prep the Oranges:

- Start by peeling the oranges. Using a sharp knife, carefully remove the skin and white pith, exposing the flesh of the oranges. You can do this by cutting off the top and bottom of the orange and then slicing the skin away from the flesh, following the curve of the fruit.

- Once peeled, slice the oranges into roughly 1/4-inch rounds. If you prefer, you can also segment the oranges by cutting between the membranes.

Arrange the Salad:

- On a serving platter, arrange the orange slices or segments in a single layer, slightly overlapping.

- Distribute the thinly sliced red onions over the oranges.

- If you're using fennel, you would add the slices at this stage as well.

- The anise-like flavor of fennel complements the sweetness of the oranges beautifully.

- Scatter the black olives around the platter.

- The olives add a savory counterpoint to the sweetness of the oranges.

Dressing and Seasoning:

- Drizzle the extra virgin olive oil evenly over the salad. The quality of the olive oil is crucial here, as it contributes significantly to the flavor of the dish.

- Season with salt and black pepper to taste.

- If you're using chili flakes or fresh chili, sprinkle them on now for a bit of heat.

- Tear the fresh mint leaves or basil leaves and sprinkle them over the top of the salad for a burst of fresh, aromatic flavor.

Serving:

- Serve the salad fresh, allowing it to sit for a few minutes before serving to let the flavors meld together slightly.
- This dish is excellent paired with crusty bread and a selection of other antipasti.

This Insalata di Tarocco is a celebration of Campanian produce, showcasing the region's prized citrus in a simple yet flavorful dish. It makes for a perfect start to a meal or as a palate-cleansing side dish, embodying the freshness and vibrancy of Southern Italian cuisine.

Pasta alla Sorrentina

Pasta alla Sorrentina is a classic dish from Campania, specifically from the town of Sorrento, as the name suggests.

It traditionally features pasta tossed in a simple tomato sauce, fresh mozzarella, and basil.

To adapt this to a vegan diet, we'll substitute regular mozzarella with a vegan alternative.

The key to this dish lies in the quality of the tomatoes and the freshness of the basil, giving the sauce a vibrant, aromatic flavor that's unmistakably Italian.

Ingredients:

- 400 grams (about 14 ounces) of pasta (penne, fusilli, or spaghetti)
- 2 tablespoons of extra virgin olive oil
- 2-3 cloves of garlic, minced
- 1 small onion, finely chopped (optional)
- 400 grams (about 14 ounces) of high-quality canned or fresh peeled tomatoes, crushed/chopped
- A handful of fresh basil leaves, plus extra for garnish
- Salt and black pepper, to taste

- 200 grams (about 7 ounces) of vegan mozzarella cheese, diced or shredded
- Vegan Parmesan cheese for serving (optional)
- Red pepper flakes (optional)

Instructions:

Prepare the Pasta:

- Bring a large pot of salted water to a boil.
- Cook the pasta according to the package instructions until it is al dente.
- Drain and set aside, reserving some pasta water.

Make the Tomato Sauce:

- While the pasta is cooking, heat the olive oil in a large skillet over medium heat.
- Add the minced garlic (and onion if you're using it), sautéing until fragrant and golden.
- Be careful not to burn the garlic.
- Add the crushed tomatoes to the skillet.
- If using canned tomatoes, include the juice as well.
- If using fresh tomatoes, add a small amount of water or reserved pasta water to get the desired sauce consistency.
- Season with salt and black pepper to taste.
- Add red pepper flakes if you prefer a bit of heat.
- Let the sauce simmer for 10-15 minutes or until it thickens slightly.
- Tear a handful of basil leaves and stir them into the sauce for the last few minutes of simmering.

- Add the drained pasta to the skillet with the sauce, tossing to combine.

- If the sauce is too thick, add a bit of the reserved pasta water to loosen it.

- Let it cook for a minute so that the pasta absorbs the flavors of the sauce.

Add Vegan Mozzarella:

- Turn off the heat.

- Add the vegan mozzarella to the skillet with the hot pasta and sauce, stirring gently to combine.

- The heat from the pasta will soften the cheese.

- If your vegan cheese melts well, you can put the skillet over low heat, cover it, and let the cheese melt for a minute or two.

Serve:

- Transfer the pasta to serving plates.

- Garnish with additional fresh basil leaves and a sprinkle of vegan Parmesan cheese, if desired.

- Serve immediately, enjoying the harmonious blend of the simple yet robust flavors.

This vegan version of Pasta alla Sorrentina retains the essence of the sunny Amalfi Coast, with the freshness of basil and the rich flavor of tomatoes. It's comfort food that pairs perfectly with a green salad and a crisp white wine, ideal for a cozy dinner or a summer meal.

Sartù di Riso

Sartù di Riso is a luxurious Italian rice dish that hails from Campania, with a rich culinary history influenced by French cuisine from when the French ruled Naples. The traditional recipe calls for meat and cheese, but we can easily make an exquisite vegan version that maintains the heart and soul of this comforting dish.

This layered, baked rice dish is typically filled with a flavorful tomato sauce, peas, mushrooms, and vegan cheese, all encased in a shell of creamy Arborio rice. It's a bit elaborate, perfect for special occasions or weekend cooking.

Ingredients:

For the rice:

- 500 grams (about 2 1/2 cups) Arborio rice
- 1 liter (about 4 cups) vegetable broth
- 2 tablespoons nutritional yeast (optional for cheesy flavor)
- Salt, to taste

For the filling:

- 2 tablespoons olive oil
- 1 small onion, finely chopped
- 2 garlic cloves, minced
- 400 grams (about 14 ounces) of chopped tomatoes (canned or fresh)
- 200 grams (7 ounces) mixed mushrooms, sliced (like button or cremini)
- 150 grams (5 ounces) frozen peas, thawed
- Salt and pepper, to taste
- A handful of fresh basil, chopped
- 100 grams (about 3 1/2 ounces) vegan mozzarella, grated
- 100 grams (about 3 1/2 ounces) vegan Parmesan cheese, grated

Instructions:

Precook the Rice:

- In a large saucepan, bring the vegetable broth to a boil.
- Add the Arborio rice and simmer until it's just al dente (it should still have a bit of chew because it will cook more in the oven).
- During the last minute of cooking, stir in the nutritional yeast and a pinch of salt.
- Drain any excess broth and set aside.

Prepare the Filling:

- Heat olive oil in a large skillet over medium heat.
- Add the onion and garlic, cooking until they're soft and fragrant.
- Add the sliced mushrooms and cook until they're tender and lightly browned.
- Stir in the chopped tomatoes (along with their juices if using canned).
- Let the mixture simmer for about 10-15 minutes or until the sauce thickens.
- Add the peas, then season with salt and pepper.
- Remove the skillet from the heat and stir in the fresh basil.

Assemble the Sartù:

- Preheat your oven to 180 degrees Celsius (356 degrees Fahrenheit).
- Lightly oil a round baking dish (preferably a springform pan for easy removal).
- Take about two-thirds of the precooked rice and press it into the bottom and up the sides of the pan, creating a "crust" that's sturdy enough to hold the filling.
- This step requires a bit of patience to get the rice even on all sides.
- Pour the tomato and mushroom mixture into the rice shell.
- Sprinkle the grated vegan mozzarella over the sauce, followed by a layer of vegan Parmesan.
- Cover the filling with the remaining rice, pressing it gently to seal the edges.

Bake:

- Cover the dish with foil and bake in the preheated oven for about 30 minutes.

- Then, remove the foil and bake for an additional 10-15 minutes or until the top is golden and crisp.

Serve:

- Remove the sartù from the oven and allow it to rest for about 15 minutes to set, which makes it easier to slice.

- If you used a springform pan, now's the time to release and remove the sides.

- Carefully cut the sartù into wedges, like a cake, and serve warm.

This vegan Sartù di Riso is a showstopper, perfect for impressing guests or enjoying a special family dinner. Each layer is packed with flavor, making every bite a rich experience. Though it's a bit of a project, the result is more than worth the effort!

In these dishes, the quality of the ingredients is paramount. Fortunately, Campania's rich volcanic soil, especially around Mount Vesuvius, produces some of Italy's best fruit and vegetables, particularly tomatoes, which are integral to the local cuisine. By focusing on these fresh ingredients, it's easy to adapt many Campanian dishes to a vegan diet without compromising on flavor.

Apulia (Puglia)

Apulia (or Puglia, in Italian), the sun-drenched region located in the heel of Italy's boot, is a paradise for food lovers, especially those adhering to a plant-based diet. Its agricultural richness is reflected in the variety of vegetables and legumes used in local cuisine, making it a favorable terrain for vegans. Here are some traditional dishes from Apulia that are vegan or can easily be adapted for a vegan diet:

Orecchiette con Cime di Rapa

Orecchiette con Cime di Rapa is a signature dish from the Apulia region. It combines "little ears" pasta with a type of leafy green. The traditional recipe often includes anchovies, but we'll omit these for a vegan version while still achieving a robust flavor.

Ingredients:

- 400 grams (14 ounces) orecchiette pasta
- 500 grams (18 ounces) of cime di rapa (also known as rapini or broccoli rabe), washed and chopped
- 3-4 tablespoons of extra virgin olive oil
- 3 cloves of garlic, thinly sliced or minced

- A pinch of red pepper flakes (adjust to taste)
- Salt, to taste
- Optional: 2 tablespoons of nutritional yeast or vegan Parmesan cheese for a cheesy flavor
- Optional: a handful of cherry tomatoes, halved

Instructions:

Prepare the Cime di Rapa:

- Clean the cime di rapa by removing the toughest parts of the stems; you can use the more tender stems, leaves, and florets.
- Bring a large pot of salted water to a boil.
- Blanch the cime di rapa in the boiling water for about 5 minutes, then remove with a slotted spoon, reserving the cooking water.
- This process removes some of the bitterness.
- Set the cime di rapa aside.

Cook the Pasta:

- In the same water used for the cime di rapa, cook the orecchiette pasta according to the package instructions (usually about 9-12 minutes) until it is al dente.

Create the Sauce:

- While the pasta is cooking, heat the olive oil in a large skillet over medium heat.
- Add the garlic and red pepper flakes, sautéing until the garlic is golden brown.
- Be careful not to burn the garlic, as it can become bitter.
- If you're using cherry tomatoes, add them now and cook for a few minutes until they're just softened.

- Add the blanched cime di rapa to the skillet and sauté it with the garlic and oil, cooking for a few more minutes until the flavors meld together.
- If the skillet becomes too dry, you can add a little bit of the pasta water.
- Season with salt according to your preference.

Combine Pasta and Sauce:
- Reserve a cup of the pasta cooking water, then drain the pasta.
- Add the orecchiette directly to the skillet with the cime di rapa mixture, tossing to combine over medium heat.
- Add a splash of the reserved pasta water if necessary to keep everything moist and help the sauce cling to the pasta.

Serve:
- If using nutritional yeast or vegan Parmesan, stir it in just before serving.
- Serve the pasta hot and divide onto plates.
- Drizzle with a little extra virgin olive oil if desired.

This dish shines in its simplicity, emphasizing the slightly bitter taste of the greens balanced with the richness of garlic and olive oil. It's a true Puglian delight, vegan style!

Fave e Cicoria

Fave e Cicoria (Fava Beans and Chicory) is a traditional Puglian dish known for its simplicity and deliciousness.

It pairs creamy pureed fava beans with the slightly bitter taste of sautéed chicory greens.

This peasant dish has been a staple in Southern Italian diets for centuries, mainly due to the accessibility and affordability of its ingredients. Here's how you can make the vegan version, which doesn't deviate from the traditional preparation.

Ingredients:

For the Fava Bean Puree:

- 500 grams (approximately 18 ounces or 1 pound) dried fava beans, peeled
- Cold water to cover the beans for soaking and cooking

- 3-4 tablespoons extra-virgin olive oil, plus extra for drizzling
- Salt, to taste

For the Chicory:

- 800 grams (approximately 28 ounces or 1.75 pounds) chicory (you can also use dandelion greens or another bitter green if chicory is hard to find)
- 2-3 garlic cloves, minced
- 3 tablespoons extra-virgin olive oil
- Salt and red chili flakes to taste

Instructions:

Prepare the Fava Beans:

- Begin by soaking the dried fava beans in plenty of cold water overnight to soften them.

- The next day, drain the beans and place them in a large pot.

- Cover with fresh, cold water.

- Bring the water to a boil and then reduce the heat to allow the beans to simmer.

- Cook for about 1-1.5 hours or until they are very tender, almost falling apart.

- Ensure the beans are always covered with water during cooking, adding more if necessary.

- Once cooked, drain the beans, reserving some of the cooking water.

- While still warm, puree the beans using a food processor, adding olive oil and salt to taste.

- If the mixture is too thick, add a bit of the cooking water to achieve a creamy consistency.

- While the beans are cooking, prepare the chicory.
- Clean the greens well and boil them in salted water for 4-5 minutes or until tender.
- Drain and let cool. Squeeze out any excess water.
- In a large skillet, heat the olive oil over medium heat.
- Add the garlic and red chili flakes, and sauté for a minute or until the garlic is fragrant but not browned.
- Add the boiled chicory to the skillet, tossing it with the garlic and oil. Sauté for a few more minutes and season with salt to taste.

Serve:

- To serve, place a generous portion of the warm fava bean puree on each plate, creating a well in the center.
- Fill with the sautéed chicory.
- Drizzle with a little more extra-virgin olive oil and serve warm.

This hearty and rustic dish offers a mix of textures and flavors — the smoothness of the beans contrasts with the bitterness of the greens. At the same time, the olive oil ties everything together with a rich, fruity undertone. It's a nourishing, comforting meal perfect for any season.

Friselle

Friselle, sometimes referred to as "frise," is a traditional type of hard bread from Puglia. They are usually made from durum wheat, baked twice, and come in the form of a ring. The unique aspect of friselle is that they need to be softened before eating, typically by being briefly soaked in water or topped with juicy vegetables.

They're a fantastic base for various toppings, akin to an open-faced sandwich. They can easily be incorporated into a vegan diet.

Here's a simple and traditional recipe to make vegan friselle.

for Making Friselle:

- 500 grams (about 1.1 pounds) of durum wheat flour
- 300 ml (about 10 fl. oz) of water (adjust as needed)
- 1 packet (7 grams or 1.5 teaspoons) of active dry yeast
- 1 teaspoon of salt
- 1 teaspoon of sugar (optional, for helping the yeast activate)

For Topping:

- Cherry tomatoes, chopped
- Olives (optional)
- 1 red or white onion (thinly sliced)
- Fresh basil leaves, torn
- High-quality extra-virgin olive oil
- Salt, to taste
- Freshly ground black pepper, to taste
- Red pepper flakes (optional)

Instructions:

Prepare the Dough:

- In a small bowl, dissolve the yeast in warm water (about 110°F or 45°C) with the sugar.
- Let it sit for a few minutes until frothy.
- In a larger bowl, mix the flour and salt.
- Add the activated yeast mixture.

- Work the mixture into a dough, adding more water or flour, as necessary.
- Transfer the dough to a floured surface and knead it for about 10 minutes until it becomes smooth and elastic.
- Place the dough in a lightly oiled bowl, cover it with a clean cloth, and let it rise in a warm place for approximately 2 hours or until it has doubled in size.

Shape and First Bake:

- Preheat your oven to 400°F (200°C).
- Punch down the dough and divide it into smaller pieces.
- Roll each piece into a ball, then shape it into a ring with a hole in the middle, similar to a bagel.
- Place the rings on a baking sheet lined with parchment paper.
- Cover with a cloth and allow them to rise for an additional 20-30 minutes.
- Bake the rings in the preheated oven for about 10-15 minutes or until they're just starting to become golden.
- They will not be fully cooked at this point.

Second Bake:

- Remove the partially baked friselle from the oven and carefully cut them horizontally into two thinner rings.
- You should now have two round, flat-bread pieces from each original ring.
- Spread these out on the baking sheet cut-side up and return them to the oven.
- Bake for an additional 10-20 minutes or until they're crispy and fully dried out, similar to a crouton's texture.

- Keep an eye on them to prevent burning.

Prepare Toppings:
- While the friselle are baking, chop the cherry tomatoes and tear the basil leaves. Set aside.

Serving the Friselle:
- To serve, briefly soak the crispy friselle in water to slightly soften them (this is traditionally done in seawater in Puglia, but regular water will work fine).
- Top the dampened friselle with the chopped tomatoes, basil, and a generous drizzle of olive oil.
- Add salt, freshly ground black pepper, and red pepper flakes (if using) to taste.

The result is a delicious and satisfying dish, where the crispness of the bread contrasts with the juicy freshness of the tomato and the aromatic hint of basil, all tied together by the richness of the olive oil. It's a delightful representation of Mediterranean flavors and Puglian culinary tradition.

Cialledda

Cialledda is a traditional dish from Puglia, specifically from the city of Bari. It's a type of bread salad similar to the Tuscan panzanella, and it's especially popular during the spring and summer months when the ingredients are fresh and abundant.

This dish is inherently vegan, focusing on vegetables, stale bread, and a dressing based on olive oil and vinegar. Here's how you can make your own Vegan Cialledda.

Ingredients:

- Stale bread (preferably a rustic Italian style bread), enough to make about 4 cups once torn into pieces
- 4 ripe tomatoes, large dice
- 1 cucumber, sliced
- 1 red onion, thinly sliced
- A handful of fresh basil leaves, roughly torn

- Salt, to taste
- Black pepper, to taste
- Extra virgin olive oil for dressing
- Red wine vinegar for dressing (quantity depends on your taste preference)
- Optional: Red chili flakes, capers, or sliced black olives for extra flavor

Instructions:

Prepare the Bread:

- If the bread is not stale enough, you can dry it out by placing it in a low oven until it's dry and slightly toasted.
- However, it shouldn't become too crispy or take on too much color.
- Tear the bread into bite-sized pieces and set aside.
- Some versions of cialledda soak the bread in water, squeeze it dry, and then crumble it into the salad.
- Choose the method based on your texture preference.

Mix the Vegetables:

- In a large bowl, combine the diced tomatoes, sliced cucumber, and sliced onion.
- If you're using capers, olives, or other additional ingredients, add them to the mix now.

Compose the Salad:

- Add the torn bread to the bowl with the vegetables, mixing it in well.
- If you've soaked your bread, ensure it is well-drained and slightly crumbled before adding.

- Sprinkle in the fresh basil, tearing the leaves with your hands to release more of their oils and flavor.
- Add salt and black pepper to taste.
- If you're using chili flakes, add them according to your spice preference.

Dress the Salad:

- Drizzle a generous amount of extra virgin olive oil over the salad.
- The oil is a key flavor component, so use the best quality you can find.
- Add red wine vinegar to taste.
- The salad should have a pleasant tang but not be overwhelmingly sour.

Let the Salad Rest:

- Cover the bowl with plastic wrap or a clean kitchen towel and let it sit at room temperature for at least 30 minutes to an hour.
- This resting period allows the flavors to meld and the bread to soak up the dressing and tomato juices, becoming delightfully tender.

Final Adjustments and Serving:

- Give the salad a final stir and taste for seasoning adjustments.
- Add more salt, pepper, or vinegar if needed.
- Serve the salad on its own as a light meal or as a side dish with other summer favorites.

Cialledda is a perfect example of Mediterranean cuisine, highlighting the flavors of fresh, ripe vegetables with the simple seasoning of olive oil, vinegar, and herbs. It's a refreshing dish to enjoy on warm, sunny days and a wonderful way to use up bread that's past its prime.

Basilicata

Basilicata, also known as Lucania, is a region in Southern Italy that boasts a rich agricultural landscape and a history steeped in tradition, both of which influence its unique cuisine. While many traditional dishes are centered around animal products, several meals are naturally vegan or can be easily modified. Here are some vegan dishes from the Basilicata region:

Cavatelli con Sugo di Pomodoro e Melanzane

"Cavatelli con Sugo di Pomodoro e Melanzane" is a delightful pasta dish that combines the richness of tomato sauce with the deep, earthy flavor of eggplants (melanzane in Italian).

Below is a vegan version of this traditional dish from Basilicata, ensuring no animal products are used without compromising on the authentic taste.

Ingredients:

- 400 grams (about 14 ounces) of cavatelli pasta (ensure it's egg-free)
- 1 large eggplant
- 2-3 tablespoons of olive oil
- 1 small onion, finely chopped
- 2-3 cloves of garlic, minced
- 400 grams (about 14 ounces) of chopped tomatoes (fresh or canned)
- A handful of fresh basil leaves
- Salt and black pepper, to taste
- Optional: red pepper flakes, to taste
- Optional: vegan cheese (like cashew Parmesan) for garnish

Instructions:

Prepare the Eggplant:

- Cut the eggplant into small cubes or slices, as you prefer.
- Sprinkle some salt on the eggplant pieces and place them in a colander.
- Let them sit for about 20-30 minutes to draw out the bitterness.
- Rinse the eggplant under cold water and dry with a clean kitchen towel.

Cook the Eggplant:

- Heat a tablespoon of olive oil in a large skillet over medium heat.
- Add the eggplant pieces and sauté until they are soft and nicely browned.
- This process might take around 10-15 minutes.
- Remove the eggplant from the skillet and set aside.

Prepare the Tomato Sauce:

- In the same skillet, add another tablespoon of olive oil.
- Add the chopped onion and sauté until translucent.
- Add the minced garlic and cook for another minute until fragrant.
- If you like your sauce spicy, you may add some red pepper flakes at this stage.
- Add the chopped tomatoes to the skillet.
- If using fresh tomatoes, ensure they're ripe and finely chopped.
- Season with salt and black pepper to taste.

- Lower the heat and let the sauce simmer for about 20-30 minutes until it thickens.
- Stir occasionally to prevent sticking.

Cook the Cavatelli:

- While the sauce is simmering, prepare the cavatelli. Bring a large pot of salted water to a boil.
- Add the cavatelli and cook according to the package instructions until they are 'al dente.'
- Drain the pasta, reserving a cup of the pasta cooking water.

Combine Pasta and Sauce:

- Add the cooked eggplant and fresh basil to the tomato sauce, stirring gently to combine.
- Add the cavatelli to the skillet with the sauce and toss to combine thoroughly.
- Add a bit of the reserved pasta water if necessary to lighten the sauce and help it adhere to the pasta.

Serve:

- Serve hot, garnished with a sprinkle of vegan cheese if desired.
- You can also add a few fresh basil leaves or a drizzle of olive oil on top for extra flavor.

This dish celebrates the simple yet profound flavors of Southern Italian cuisine, particularly of the Basilicata region. Each ingredient contributes to a depth of flavor, creating a hearty, satisfying meal that's perfect for any occasion.

Minestra di Farro Lucana

"Minestra di Farro" is a traditional Italian dish that often combines farro with beans, vegetables, and sometimes tomato sauce, creating a hearty soup. Farro is a grain, a bit nutty, usually cooked to soft, but with a toothsome body. In Basilicata, this dish would be prepared with locally sourced ingredients and simple seasonings, reflecting the region's culinary tradition.

Here's a vegan version of Minestra di Farro Lucana, keeping to the basics but allowing for the flavors to shine.

Ingredients:
- 1 cup farro (uncooked, rinsed) – available online
- 1 onion (chopped)
- 2 cloves of garlic (minced)
- 1 carrot (chopped)
- 1 celery stalk (chopped)

- 1 can (approximately 400g or 14 oz) cannellini beans (rinsed and drained) or similar white beans
- 1 can (approximately 400g or 14 oz) chopped tomatoes
- 6 cups vegetable broth
- 1 teaspoon dried thyme (or 1 tablespoon fresh thyme leaves)
- 2-3 tablespoons olive oil
- Salt and pepper to taste
- Optional: fresh parsley or basil for garnish
- Optional: red pepper flakes for a bit of heat

Instructions:

Prepare the Base:

- In a large pot, heat the olive oil over medium heat.

- Add the onion, carrot, and celery, and sauté until the vegetables are soft and the onion is translucent, about 5-7 minutes.

- Add the minced garlic (and red pepper flakes if you're using them) and sauté for another 1-2 minutes until the garlic is fragrant.

Cook the Farro:

- Add the rinsed farro to the pot and stir for a minute to allow the grains to toast slightly and absorb the flavors.

- Pour in the chopped tomatoes, including their juices, and stir to combine.

Add Liquids and Beans:

- Add the vegetable broth and the cannellini beans.

- If using dried thyme, add it now. Increase the heat to bring the mixture to a boil.

- Simmer the Soup

Melanzane Ripiene alla Lucana (without cheese)

"Melanzane Ripiene" translates to stuffed eggplants, a dish appreciated for its hearty flavors and satisfying nature. In the Basilicata region of Italy, traditional recipes often include various cheeses and sometimes meats, but it's possible to make a delightful vegan version of Melanzane Ripiene alla Lucana that maintains the essence of Lucanian cuisine's flavors and heartiness.

Ingredients:

- 2 large eggplants
- 1 cup cooked or canned chickpeas, drained and rinsed
- 1 onion, finely chopped

- 2-3 garlic cloves, minced
- 1 cup chopped tomatoes (fresh or canned)
- 1/2 cup breadcrumbs (ensure they're vegan)
- 1/4 cup chopped fresh basil
- 1/4 cup chopped fresh parsley
- 3 tablespoons nutritional yeast (optional for a cheesy flavor)
- Salt and pepper to taste
- Olive oil
- Optional: 1/4 teaspoon red pepper flakes

Instructions:

Prepare the Eggplants:

- Preheat your oven to 375°F (190°C).

- Cut the eggplants in half lengthwise.

- Using a spoon or melon baller, scoop out the flesh of the eggplants, leaving about a 1/4-inch shell so they hold their shape.

- Chop the removed flesh and set aside.

- Brush the inside of the eggplant shells with a little olive oil and season with salt.

- Place them on a baking sheet, cut side down, and bake for about 20-25 minutes until they are tender but still hold their shape.

Prepare the Filling:

- While the eggplant shells are baking, heat a bit of olive oil in a large skillet over medium heat.

- Add the onion and garlic and sauté until the onion is translucent.

- Add the chopped eggplant flesh to the skillet and cook until it is soft about 5-7 minutes.
- Add the chopped tomatoes and cook for another 5 minutes until the tomatoes are soft.
- If using, add the red pepper flakes at this stage.
- Stir in the chickpeas, cooking for a few more minutes.
- Use a fork or potato masher to partially mash the chickpeas so that some remain whole for texture.

Combine the Filling:
- Remove the skillet from heat.
- Stir in the breadcrumbs, nutritional yeast (if using), chopped basil, and parsley until well combined.
- If the mixture seems too dry, add a tiny bit of water or some more olive oil. Season with salt and pepper to taste.

Stuff the Eggplants:
- By now, the eggplant shells should be baked and slightly cooled.
- Flip them over so they are cut side up on the baking sheet.
- Spoon the filling into the eggplant shells, mounding it slightly. You should use all the filling.
- Drizzle the tops with a bit more olive oil. This helps the top get nicely browned.

Bake the Stuffed Eggplants:
- Put the stuffed eggplants back into the 375°F (190°C) oven and bake for another 20-30 minutes, until the tops are golden and the filling is heated through.

- Serve the Melanzane Ripiene hot, garnished with more fresh herbs if desired.

- They are often accompanied by a green salad or some fresh bread.

This vegan interpretation of Melanzane Ripiene alla Lucana captures the rich flavors and textures of the traditional dish while keeping it plant-based. It's a versatile recipe, allowing for different stuffings depending on available ingredients.

Pane di Matera

"Pane di Matera" is a renowned bread from the city of Matera in the Basilicata region of Italy. This bread has a distinct crust and flavor, typically attributed to the unique mineral properties of the water in the Matera area and the use of a natural fermentation process (sourdough).

The traditional recipe is inherently vegan, and making it at home can be a rewarding process.

However, it might not have the exact unique characteristics of the original Matera water and environment. Here's how you can make it:

Ingredients:

- 1 kg (about 2.2 lbs.) durum wheat flour (semolina), plus extra for dusting
- 600 ml (about 2.5 cups) water, room temperature (preferably mineral water to mimic Matera's natural water)
- 200 g (7 oz) sourdough starter
- 25 g (about 5 teaspoons) salt

Instructions:

For the Dough:

- Ensure your sourdough starter is active by feeding it 8-12 hours before you start your bread-making process.

- It should be bubbly and at its peak.

- In a large bowl, mix the flour with the water.

- Work it with your hands until all the water is absorbed.

- Cover with a damp cloth and let it rest for about 30 minutes to an hour.

- This process is called 'autolyse,' and it helps the flour absorb the water, aligns the gluten, and makes the dough easier to shape.

- After the resting phase, add your active sourdough starter and salt to the dough.

- Work the mixture in the bowl or on a work surface.

- Knead for about 10-15 minutes until you have a smooth and elastic dough.

- The dough will be a bit sticky, which is normal for sourdough.

- Place the dough in a lightly greased bowl, cover with a damp cloth, and let it rise until it doubles in size, about 3-6 hours, depending on the temperature of your room and the activity of your starter.

- The dough should be noticeably puffy and have increased in volume.

Shaping:

- Once risen, turn the dough out onto a lightly floured surface.

- Divide the dough into two parts for two loaves.

- Shape each half into an oval or round loaf, depending on your preference.

- Place each loaf on a baking sheet lined with parchment paper or a well-floured cloth, leaving enough space between them.

- Cover with a damp cloth.

- Allow the loaves to rise for another 2-4 hours until they have almost doubled in size again. Be careful not to let them over-proof; otherwise, they might collapse in the oven.

Baking:

- At least 30 minutes before baking, preheat your oven to the highest setting, typically between 475-500°F (245-260°C). I

- f you have a baking stone or steel, put it in the oven now. Otherwise, an overturned baking sheet will work.

- Before baking, you should make a few shallow slashes on the top of your bread with a sharp knife or a blade.

- This process, called 'scoring,' helps the bread expand in the oven.

- Transfer the loaves to the oven, either directly onto the preheated baking stone/steel or along with the baking sheet.

- To create steam, you can quickly spray some water onto the sides of the oven or place a baking tray with boiling water on the bottom rack.

- Bake the bread for about 30-40 minutes, or until the crust is golden brown and the loaves sound hollow when tapped on the bottom.

- Once baked, remove the loaves from the oven and let them cool on a wire rack for at least an hour before slicing.

Note: The unique characteristics of "Pane di Matera" are due to its environment's specific natural yeasts and the quality of the durum wheat used. The texture, flavor, and crust may vary based on your local ingredients, water mineral content, and oven. However, the process itself should give you delicious homemade bread that's crusty on the outside and soft on the inside, reminiscent of the traditional loaves from Matera.

Lagane e Ceci

"Lagane e Ceci" (Lagane and Chickpeas) is a traditional dish from Southern Italy, particularly from the

Basilicata region. "Lagane" are a type of pasta similar to tagliatelle but typically thicker and shorter, and they are traditionally made without eggs. This makes "Lagane e Ceci" an inherently vegan dish, focusing on simple ingredients with plenty of flavors. Below is a recipe that respects its traditional roots.

Ingredients:

- 300 g (about 10.5 oz) of dry lagane pasta (if you can't find lagane, you can use tagliatelle, fettuccine, or even pappardelle as a substitute).
- 400 g (14 oz) canned chickpeas, rinsed and drained (or use freshly cooked chickpeas if available)
- 1-2 garlic cloves, finely chopped
- 1 small onion or shallot, finely chopped
- 400 g (14 oz) canned chopped tomatoes or fresh ripe tomatoes, chopped
- Extra virgin olive oil
- Salt to taste
- Crushed red pepper flakes to taste (optional)
- Fresh parsley, chopped (optional for garnish)
- 1-2 sprigs of rosemary (optional)

Instructions:

Sauté the Aromatics:

- In a large skillet, heat a generous glug of extra virgin olive oil over medium heat.
- Add the chopped garlic and onion to the skillet.
- If you're using rosemary, add it now.

- Sauté until the onion becomes translucent and the garlic is fragrant but not browned.
- If you like a bit of heat, add some crushed red pepper flakes.

Cook the Chickpeas:

- Add the chickpeas to the skillet and stir to combine with the garlic and onion.
- Cook for a few minutes.
- Pour in the chopped tomatoes and add salt to taste. Stir well.
- Lower the heat, cover, and let everything simmer for about 15-20 minutes, stirring occasionally.
- If the mixture becomes too dry, you can add a little water. The goal is to have a relatively thick sauce.

Prepare the Pasta:

- While the sauce is simmering, bring a large pot of salted water to a boil.
- Add the lagane pasta and cook according to the package instructions until it is 'al dente.'
- If you're using fresh, homemade pasta, it will cook faster, usually in 2-4 minutes.
- Drain the pasta, reserving a cup of the pasta cooking water.

Combine Pasta and Sauce:

- Add the drained pasta to the skillet with the sauce.
- Toss to combine, adding a splash of pasta cooking water if needed to loosen things up and evenly coat the pasta.

- Cook together for a minute or two, allowing the pasta to absorb some of the sauce.
- If you used rosemary, remove the sprigs now.

Serve:

- Serve the dish hot, drizzled with a bit more extra virgin olive oil if desired.
- If you like, garnish with fresh chopped parsley for a burst of color and freshness.
- Offer some crusty bread on the side to mop up any remaining sauce.

This humble yet flavorful dish is a testament to the simple and healthy cuisine of the Basilicata region, relying on the quality of the ingredients and their combination for its satisfying character. It's a comforting meal that can be enjoyed year-round and is adaptable based on personal spice preferences and available ingredients.

Patate Arraganate

"Patate Arraganate" is a traditional Italian dish, particularly popular in Southern Italy, including the Basilicata region. The term "arraganate" comes from the word for "oregano" in the local dialect, highlighting the importance of this herb in the recipe.

This dish features potatoes baked with tomatoes, onions, and herbs, creating a flavorful, comforting side dish or main course. Here's how you can make a vegan version of "Patate Arraganate."

Ingredients:

- 4-5 large potatoes, peeled and thinly sliced
- 2-3 ripe tomatoes, thinly sliced
- 1 large onion, thinly sliced
- 3-4 garlic cloves, minced
- A handful of fresh oregano (or 2-3 teaspoons of dried oregano if fresh is unavailable)
- A handful of fresh basil leaves, torn
- Salt and black pepper, to taste
- Extra virgin olive oil
- Optional: red pepper flakes, to taste
- Optional: fresh parsley, chopped, for garnish

Instructions:

Preheat the Oven:

- Preheat your oven to 375°F (190°C).

Prepare the Vegetables:

- Ensure the potatoes, tomatoes, and onion are all thinly sliced. This helps them cook more evenly and absorb the flavors of the herbs and seasoning.

- In a baking dish, preferably a deep one, start by layering the slices of potato, slightly overlapping them.

- After the potato, add a layer of sliced onions and a layer of sliced tomatoes.

- Sprinkle a generous amount of minced garlic, chopped oregano, and basil over the tomatoes.

- If you're using red pepper flakes, add them now.

- Add salt and pepper to taste.
- Repeat the layers (potatoes, onions, tomatoes, garlic, herbs) until all ingredients are used, ending with a layer of herbs on top.
- Depending on the size of your baking dish, you should have about 2-3 layers.
- Generously drizzle extra virgin olive oil over the final layer.
- This will help everything cook evenly, prevent dryness, and add flavor.

Bake:

- Cover the baking dish with aluminum foil. This will prevent the top from burning and help the vegetables cook evenly.
- Place in the preheated oven and bake for about 30-40 minutes.
- After this time, remove the foil and bake for an additional 20-30 minutes, or until the top layer is golden and crispy and the potatoes are tender (you can test with a fork).

Garnish and Serve:

- Once cooked, remove it from the oven and let it cool for a few minutes.
- Garnish with fresh parsley if desired before serving.
- This dish is versatile and can be served as a main course for a light meal or as a side dish accompanying other dishes.

"Patate Arraganate" is a dish that celebrates the flavors of fresh herbs and vegetables. It's simple, yet the slow baking allows for the ingredients' flavors to meld beautifully, creating a deliciously aromatic and satisfying dish.

These dishes showcase the simplicity and flavor of Basilicata's cuisine, which relies heavily on local produce and traditional cooking methods. As with any regional cuisine, recipes can vary widely from one family or town to another, so there's a lot of room for exploration and adaptation to your vegan dietary needs.

Calabria

Calabria, the "toe" of Italy's "boot," is known for its rugged mountains, old-fashioned villages, and diverse cuisine influenced by its history of various settlers and conquerors. The region's Mediterranean climate makes it ideal for agriculture, especially olive and citrus trees, which heavily influence its traditional dishes. While many of these dishes incorporate fish and meat, there are also several options or recipes that can be adjusted to fit a vegan diet. Here are some vegan-friendly dishes originating from the Calabria region:

Calabrian Chili Paste Pasta

Calabrian chili paste Pasta, known for its vibrant color, smoky sweetness, and spicy heat, is a staple in Calabrian cuisine.

The paste is made from a blend of ground local hot chili peppers, sunflower and/or olive oil, vinegar, and salt. It's an excellent way to add a spicy depth to any dish, including pasta sauces. Below is a simple, flavorful recipe for Vegan Calabrian Chili Paste Pasta.

Ingredients:

- 400g (about 14 oz) of your preferred pasta (such as spaghetti, penne, or fusilli)
- 2-3 tablespoons of Calabrian chili paste (adjust according to your heat preference)
- 4-6 tablespoons of extra-virgin olive oil
- 2-3 large garlic cloves, thinly sliced or minced
- Salt, to taste
- A handful of fresh Italian parsley, finely chopped
- Optional: Crushed red pepper flakes for extra heat
- Optional: Zest of 1 lemon for freshness

Instructions:

Cook the Pasta:

- Bring a large pot of salted water to a boil.
- Add your pasta and cook according to the package instructions until it is 'al dente.'
- Reserve about 1 cup of pasta cooking water, then drain the pasta and set it aside.

Create the Sauce:

- While the pasta is cooking, heat the olive oil in a large pan over medium heat.
- Add the sliced or minced garlic, sautéing until just golden and fragrant. Be cautious not to burn the garlic, as it can become bitter.
- Reduce the heat and stir in the Calabrian chili paste, cooking for 1-2 minutes.
- The paste should become more aromatic and infuse into the oil, creating a unified color.

- Add the drained pasta directly into the pan with your chili paste mixture, tossing to combine thoroughly.

- Add a bit of the reserved pasta water as needed to loosen things up and create a light, cohesive sauce that coats your pasta. The starch in the water helps bind the pasta and sauce together.

- If using, add the lemon zest at this stage. It will provide a fresh, citrusy contrast to the deep, spicy flavors of the dish.

Season and Garnish:

- Taste your dish and add salt if necessary.

- Remember, the chili paste is already quite salty, so you may not need much.

- If you want your pasta to be spicier, consider sprinkling some crushed red pepper flakes on top for that extra kick.

- Remove your pan from the heat and stir in the fresh parsley for a touch of herbaceous freshness.

Serve:

- Serve your pasta hot, garnished with more parsley if desired.

- Each serving should be glossy, evenly coated with sauce, and sprinkled with herbs.

This Vegan Calabrian Chili Paste Pasta is a celebration of Calabrian flavors, adaptable based on your heat preferences. It's a dish best served with a side of crusty bread to sop up the flavorful oil and a fresh salad to balance the heat. Enjoy the simplicity and robust flavors that Calabrian cuisine has to offer!

Focaccia alla Calabrese

Focaccia alla Calabrese is a delicious and flavorful variant of the classic Italian bread, often enriched with traditional ingredients found in Calabria.

This vegan version maintains the rich flavors and textures without compromising on the authenticity of the experience. Here's how you can make it:

Ingredients:

For the Focaccia Dough:

- 500g (about 4 cups) all-purpose flour or bread flour
- 2 tsp salt
- 1 packet (7g or 1/4 oz) instant yeast
- 300 ml (about 1 1/4 cups) warm water

- 2 tbsp olive oil, plus extra for greasing and topping

- 1-2 tbsp Calabrian chili paste (adjust to your preference)
- A handful of cherry tomatoes, halved
- 1-2 red onions, thinly sliced
- A few sprigs of fresh rosemary
- Coarse sea salt, to taste
- Optional: Sliced black or green olives
- Optional: Drizzle of vegan pesto or a sprinkle of dried oregano

Instructions:

Prepare the Dough:

- In a large mixing bowl, combine the flour, salt, and instant yeast, mixing well.
- Gradually add the warm water and olive oil to the dry mixture, stirring continuously until the dough begins to come together.
- Transfer the dough to a floured surface.
- Knead by hand for about 10 minutes or until the dough becomes smooth and elastic.
- Add a little more flour if the dough is too sticky or a bit more water if it's too dry.
- Shape the dough into a ball and place it in a lightly oiled bowl, turning it to coat in the oil.
- Cover with a clean kitchen towel and let it rise in a warm place for about 1-2 hours or until doubled in size.

Preheat the Oven and Prepare the Toppings:

- When the dough is almost ready, preheat your oven to 200°C (about 400°F).

- Slice the cherry tomatoes and onions and have your Calabrian chili paste and other toppings ready.

Shape and Season the Dough:
- Once the dough has doubled, punch it down gently to release the air.
- Transfer it to a lightly oiled or parchment-lined baking sheet.
- With your hands, spread and flatten the dough into a rectangle or circle about 1/2 inch thick.
- Using your fingers, press down across the entire surface of the dough to create dimples.
- Brush the top generously with olive oil.
- This will help the toppings stick and give the finished focaccia a lovely sheen and rich flavor.
- Evenly spread the Calabrian chili paste over the surface.
- If it's very thick, try to mix it with a little olive oil to make it easier to spread.
- Arrange the cherry tomatoes, sliced onions, rosemary, and any other desired toppings (like olives) across the dough.
- Press them in slightly.

Bake the Focaccia:
- Sprinkle the top with coarse sea salt, remembering that the chili paste is already quite salty.
- Place your focaccia in the preheated oven and bake for 20-25 minutes, or until the bread is golden brown and the toppings look nicely roasted.
- If you're using vegan pesto or dried oregano, drizzle or sprinkle them on top in the last 10 minutes of baking to avoid burning them.

- Once done, remove the focaccia from the oven and let it cool slightly on a wire rack.
- Slice it into squares or wedges and serve warm or at room temperature.

This vegan Focaccia alla Calabrese combines the heat of Calabrian chilies with the freshness of herbs and vegetables, creating a flavorful experience that's perfect as an appetizer, side dish, or even a main course with a hearty salad. Enjoy the spicy, hearty goodness characteristic of Calabrian cuisine!

Patate e Peperoni al Forno

A simple, hearty dish of potatoes and peppers roasted until they're perfectly caramelized. The vegetables may be mixed with a hint of spicy Calabrian chili.

Ingredients:

- 4-5 large potatoes, peeled and cut into 1/2-inch slices or wedges
- 2-3 large bell peppers (red, yellow, or a mix), seeded and cut into strips
- 1 medium onion, thinly sliced
- 3-4 cloves of garlic, minced
- 4-5 tablespoons of extra-virgin olive oil
- Salt and pepper, to taste
- A handful of fresh parsley, chopped
- Optional: A pinch of red pepper flakes or Calabrian chili for heat
- Optional: A few cherry tomatoes for added sweetness and color

Instructions:

Preheat the Oven:

- Preheat your oven to 200°C (about 400°F).
- Adjust the rack to the middle position.

Prepare the Vegetables:

- After cleaning and cutting the potatoes, peppers, and onion, place them in a large mixing bowl.
- Add the minced garlic.
- Drizzle the vegetables with olive oil, enough to coat them lightly.
- Sprinkle with salt, pepper, and red pepper flakes or Calabrian chili if you're using them.
- Mix everything well to ensure the vegetables are evenly coated.

Bake the Dish:

- Transfer the vegetable mixture to a large baking dish or a sheet pan, spreading everything out in an even layer.
- If using, scatter the cherry tomatoes throughout the pan.
- Place the pan in your preheated oven, and bake for about 35-45 minutes, or until the potatoes are tender and golden brown.
- Halfway through the cooking time, stir the vegetables to ensure they cook evenly and don't stick to the pan.

Check for Doneness:

- Check the potatoes for doneness by piercing them with a fork. They should be easily pierced and soft on the inside.
- If the vegetables start to brown too quickly, but the potatoes are not yet done, you can cover the dish with aluminum foil and continue baking until ready.

Final Touches:

- Once the dish is done, remove it from the oven and let it cool for a few minutes.
- Sprinkle with fresh, chopped parsley for an added layer of flavor and a pop of color.

Serve:

- Serve your "Patate e Peperoni al Forno" hot or warm.
- It can be a main dish, served alongside a fresh salad and crusty bread, or it can serve as a side dish to complement other entrees.

This dish embodies the essence of Calabrian cuisine with its straightforward ingredients and flavors. The baking process brings out a beautiful sweetness in the peppers and a lovely texture in the potatoes, creating a satisfying dish that celebrates the vegan simplicity and deliciousness of Southern Italian cooking.

Melanzane a Beccafico (Vegan version)

"Melanzane a Beccafico" is a traditional Southern Italian dish with different variations across Sicily and Calabria.

Typically, the recipe involves stuffing rolled eggplant slices with a mixture that can include cheese, breadcrumbs, and sometimes fish like anchovies or sardines. In this vegan interpretation, we keep the essence of the dish but omit any animal products. Here's how you can make Vegan Melanzane a Beccafico, Calabrian style:

Ingredients:

- 2-3 large eggplants
- 1 cup breadcrumbs (ensure they're vegan)
- 3-4 tablespoons of extra-virgin olive oil, plus more for brushing
- 2 cloves of garlic, minced
- 1 small bunch of fresh parsley, chopped
- 2 tablespoons capers, drained and chopped
- 2 tablespoons raisins, soaked in warm water for 10 minutes and drained
- Salt and pepper, to taste
- A pinch of red pepper flakes (optional)
- Juice of 1 lemon
- Wooden toothpicks (for securing the rolls)

Instructions:

Prepare the Eggplants:

- Wash the eggplants and slice them lengthwise into about 1/4-inch thin slices.
- Lay out the slices on a tray, sprinkle them with salt, and let them sit for about 30 minutes to draw out the bitterness.
- Rinse the slices and pat them dry with paper towels.

Cook the Eggplant Slices:

- Preheat your oven to 375°F (190°C).

- Brush both sides of the eggplant slices with olive oil and place them in a single layer on a baking sheet lined with parchment paper.
- Bake for about 10-15 minutes until they are tender and slightly browned.
- Remove from the oven and let them cool enough to handle.

Prepare the Filling:

- In a skillet, heat 3-4 tablespoons of olive oil over medium heat.
- Add the minced garlic and red pepper flakes (if using), sautéing until the garlic is fragrant.
- Add the breadcrumbs and toast them, stirring constantly, until they're golden and crispy.
- Remove from the heat and transfer the mixture to a bowl.
- Stir in the chopped parsley, capers, and raisins. Season with salt and pepper to taste. Squeeze in the lemon juice and mix well.

Assemble the Eggplant Rolls:

- Lay an eggplant slice flat and place a spoonful of the breadcrumb mixture at one end.
- Don't overfill, or rolling will be difficult.
- Carefully roll the eggplant up around the filling, creating a small roll.
- Secure it with a wooden toothpick to ensure it stays in place.
- Repeat with the remaining eggplant slices and filling.

- Arrange the stuffed eggplant rolls on a baking sheet, leaving a bit of space between each roll.

- You can drizzle a little more olive oil on top if you prefer.

- Bake in the preheated oven for about 15-20 minutes or until the eggplant rolls are heated through and slightly crispy on the outside.

Serve:

- Serve your Vegan Melanzane in a Beccafico hot, garnished with additional fresh parsley or basil if desired.

- They can be served as an appetizer, side dish, or main course, often accompanied by a fresh salad or crusty bread.

This vegan adaptation maintains the heart and soul of the dish, focusing on the savory flavors of the filling, the tender juiciness of the eggplant, and the joy of sharing a handmade meal.

Calabrian cuisine is characterized by its use of spicy chilies and fresh vegetables, both of which are abundant in the region. Many of the traditional meals can be easily adapted to a vegan diet, allowing for the exploration and enjoyment of new flavors without having to compromise on dietary preferences.

The Islands

Sicily

Sicily's rich culinary tradition reflects the island's historical layers of various cultures, from the Greeks and Arabs to the Normans and Spanish, offering a diverse cuisine with an emphasis on fresh, local ingredients. Many traditional Sicilian dishes are based on vegetables, fruits, and grains, providing a variety of options that are either already vegan or can be easily adapted. Below are some vegan-friendly dishes and adaptations from the Sicily region:

Caponata

Perhaps one of the most iconic Sicilian dishes, Caponata is a classic Sicilian dish that epitomizes the flavors of the region, with its sweet, tangy, and slightly salty depth.

It is naturally vegan, containing no animal products.

While there are many variations of Caponata, each with its unique twist, here's a traditional version that's easy to prepare and loaded with flavor.

Ingredients:

- 1 large eggplant (about 1 lb), cut into 1/2-inch cubes
- Salt, for drawing water out of the eggplant
- 1/4 cup olive oil (you may need extra)
- 1 medium onion, chopped
- 2 celery stalks, chopped
- 3-4 ripe tomatoes, chopped (or one 14-oz can of chopped tomatoes)
- 2-3 cloves garlic, minced
- 2 tablespoons capers, rinsed and drained
- 1/4 cup green olives, pitted and halved
- 2 tablespoons red wine vinegar (or to taste)

- 1-2 tablespoons sugar (depending on your taste)
- 1/4 cup fresh basil, torn or roughly chopped
- 2 tablespoons pine nuts (optional)
- Freshly ground black pepper, to taste
- 2 tablespoons tomato paste (optional for a richer sauce)
- Red pepper flakes (optional, for heat)

Instructions:

Prep the Eggplant:

- Sprinkle the eggplant cubes generously with salt, put them in a colander, and let them sit for about 30 minutes.

- This process, known as "degorging," draws out the moisture and helps remove any bitterness.

- After 30 minutes, rinse the eggplant under cold water and pat dry with paper towels.

Cook the Eggplant:

- In a large skillet or sauté pan, heat the olive oil over medium heat.

- Add the eggplant cubes (in batches if necessary) and fry until they are golden brown and tender, about 10-12 minutes.

- Remove the eggplant from the pan and set aside.

Sauté the Aromatics:

- If needed, add a bit more olive oil to the pan.

- Add the chopped onion and celery, sautéing until they are softened, about 5-7 minutes.

- Add the minced garlic and cook for another minute until fragrant.

Add the Main Components:

- Stir in the chopped tomatoes (with their juice if canned), capers, and olives.

- Add the tomato paste if you're using it.

- Allow the mixture to simmer for 5-6 minutes, stirring occasionally.

- If you're using pine nuts, toast them in a separate, dry pan until golden, then add them to the mixture.

Combine Everything:

- Return the eggplant to the pan with the tomato mixture.

- Stir gently to combine.

- In a small bowl, whisk together the red wine vinegar and sugar until the sugar dissolves.

- Pour this over the eggplant mixture. This adds the characteristic sweet and sour flavor of traditional Caponata.

- Let everything simmer together for another 10-15 minutes until all the flavors have melded and the mixture is thick and stew-like.

- If you prefer a bit of heat, add a pinch or two of red pepper flakes.

Final Touches:

- Remove from heat and mix in the fresh basil.

- Taste and adjust the seasoning with salt, black pepper, and additional vinegar or sugar if necessary, depending on how sweet or tangy you want your Caponata.

- Caponata is best served at room temperature and can be even better the next day after the flavors have had more time to blend.
- It's traditionally served as an appetizer on crostini or rustic bread. Still, it also pairs wonderfully with pasta or as a side dish with other main courses.

Enjoy this quintessential Sicilian dish that perfectly balances the Mediterranean flavors!

Pasta alla Norma

This classic Sicilian pasta dish is made with fried eggplant tomato sauce and topped with grated Ricotta Salata cheese.

For a vegan version, skip the cheese or use a vegan cheese substitute. The key is in the richness of the tomato sauce and the eggplant's texture.

Ingredients:

- 1 large eggplant, cut into 1/2-inch cubes
- Salt
- Olive oil for frying (about 1/2 cup, as eggplant absorbs a lot of oil, but this is reduced in the method below)
- 1-2 cloves garlic, minced
- 1 28-oz can of good quality whole peeled tomatoes (or fresh ripe tomatoes, blanched, skins removed and chopped)
- 1 teaspoon red pepper flakes (optional, adjust to taste)
- Freshly ground black pepper, to taste
- 1 handful fresh basil leaves, roughly torn or chopped
- 1 lb pasta (traditionally macaroni or rigatoni, but spaghetti works well too)
- Vegan ricotta or parmesan cheese, or nutritional yeast (optional, for topping)

Instructions:

Prep the Eggplant:

- Sprinkle the eggplant cubes generously with salt and place them in a colander set over a bowl.
- Let them sit for about 30 minutes to an hour. This process will draw out the bitter liquid from the eggplant.
- After the time has elapsed, rinse the eggplant cubes under cold water and then thoroughly pat them dry with paper towels.

Fry the Eggplant:

- Heat a good amount of olive oil in a large frying pan over medium-high heat.

- You can shallow-fry the eggplant in batches, turning the pieces until golden brown on all sides.

- Because eggplants absorb a lot of oil, try not to add them until the oil is hot.

- Once the eggplant is fried, use a slotted spoon to transfer it to a plate lined with paper towels to drain the excess oil.

- Set aside.

Prepare the Tomato Sauce:

- In the same pan, reduce the heat to medium.

- You may remove some of the oil or add more if necessary.

- Add the minced garlic and red pepper flakes (if using) and sauté until the garlic is golden and fragrant.

- Add the tomatoes, crushing them with your hands if whole, along with their juice.

- Season with salt and black pepper to taste.

- Reduce the heat to low and simmer the sauce for about 15-20 minutes or until it thickens.

- Stir in the basil leaves, saving a few for garnish.

Cook the Pasta:

- While the sauce is simmering, cook the pasta according to the package instructions in a large pot of salted boiling water.

- Cook until al dente, then drain, reserving some of the pasta water.

Combine Pasta and Sauce:

- Add the fried eggplant to the tomato sauce and stir gently, cooking for a few more minutes until the eggplant is tender.
- Toss the drained pasta with the eggplant sauce.
- Add a little pasta water if necessary to loosen things up and evenly coat the pasta.

Serve:

- Serve the pasta hot, garnished with the remaining fresh basil.
- If desired, sprinkle with vegan cheese or nutritional yeast for a cheesy flavor.
- Some people enjoy adding a drizzle of extra virgin olive oil over the top for added richness.

This vegan version of Pasta alla Norma is a tribute to the simplicity and deliciousness of Sicilian cuisine, celebrating the region's love for fresh produce and hearty pasta dishes.

Arancini di Riso

Arancini di Riso, or simply Arancini, are delightful Sicilian rice balls that are stuffed, coated with breadcrumbs, and then deep fried. They are traditionally filled with meat sauce, mozzarella, and peas. However, a vegan version omits the cheese and meat, replacing them with vegan-friendly ingredients without compromising on the taste or texture. Here's how you can make Vegan Arancini.

Ingredients:

For the Rice:

- 2 cups Arborio rice
- 4 cups vegetable broth
- A pinch of saffron (optional for color and flavor)

- Salt, to taste

For the Vegan Filling:

- 1 cup cooked and seasoned vegetables (like mushrooms, peas, or finely diced vegan meat substitutes)
- Vegan cheese (optional, use a type that melts, like vegan mozzarella)
- Olive oil for sautéing
- 1 small onion, finely chopped
- 2 cloves garlic, minced
- 1/2 cup tomato sauce
- Salt and pepper, to taste
- Fresh herbs (like basil or parsley), optional

For the Coating:

- 1-1.5 cups breadcrumbs
- Flour (for dusting)
- Water or plant-based milk (for dipping)
- Seasonings like salt, pepper, and maybe some nutritional yeast (optional)

Instructions:

Prepare the Rice:

- In a pot, bring the vegetable broth to a boil. Stir in the rice, saffron, and salt.

- Reduce the heat to low and cover.

- Cook until the rice is tender and all the broth is absorbed about 20 minutes.

- Spread the cooked rice on a baking sheet to cool, then refrigerate for a few hours, as this will help in forming the balls.

Prepare the Filling:

- Heat a bit of olive oil in a pan over medium heat.

- Add onions and sauté until translucent.

- Add garlic and cook for an additional minute.

- Add your choice of vegetables or vegan meat, cooking until they're well-cooked.

- Stir in the tomato sauce and cook the mixture down until it's quite thick.

- If using herbs, add them at the end.

- Season to taste with salt and pepper.

- Let this mixture cool.

Form the Arancini:

- Once the rice has cooled and become very sticky, you're ready to form the arancini.

- Take a portion of rice and form a ball about the size of a large egg.

- Make an indent in the center with your thumb.

- Fill the indent with a small amount of vegetable filling and a piece of vegan cheese (if using).

- Cover the filling with a bit more rice and reshape it into a ball.

- Repeat until all rice and filling are used.

Coat the Arancini:

- Set up a station with flour, water, plant-based milk, and seasoned breadcrumbs in separate bowls.

- Roll each rice ball in flour, shaking off the excess, then dip it in the water or plant-based milk, and finally roll it in the breadcrumbs until well coated.

Fry the Arancini:

- Heat oil in a deep fryer or large, heavy-bottomed pan to 350°F (175°C).
- Fry the rice balls in batches so they are not crowded, turning occasionally until golden brown.
- This should take about 4-5 minutes per batch.
- Once done, remove them with a slotted spoon and drain on paper towels.

Serve:

- These are best served hot, but be careful, as the filling can be quite hot immediately after frying.
- Serve with marinara sauce or a vegan aioli for dipping if desired.

Enjoy your cruelty-free version of this classic Sicilian comfort food!

Panelle

Panelle (or Panella di Ceci) is a traditional Sicilian street food. It's a fritter made from chickpea flour, making it naturally vegan.

These fritters are crispy on the outside, soft on the inside, and are typically served inside a bread roll like a sandwich or enjoyed plain, often with a squeeze of lemon. Here's how you can make them:

- 2 cups chickpea flour (also known as gram flour or besan)
- 6 cups water
- 2-3 teaspoons of salt (or to taste)
- 1 teaspoon black pepper (or to taste)
- Optional herbs: parsley, rosemary, or thyme, finely chopped
- Olive oil for frying
- Lemon wedges for serving

Instructions:

Prepare the Batter:

- In a large pot, mix the chickpea flour, salt, and black pepper.

- If you're using any herbs, add them now.
- Gradually add the water to the chickpea flour mixture, whisking constantly to ensure there are no lumps. This step is crucial for the texture of the panelle.
- Once you've added all the water and the mixture is smooth, transfer the pot to the stove.

Cook the Mixture:
- Cook the mixture over medium-low heat, stirring constantly with a wooden spoon.
- The batter will start to thicken as it comes up to temperature.
- Continue cooking and stirring for approximately 10-15 minutes or until the mixture becomes very thick and starts to pull away from the sides of the pot.
- Be patient, as stopping too early can result in a panelle that doesn't hold together.

Shape the Panelle:
- Quickly pour and spread the thickened batter onto a flat, heat-resistant surface, such as a large baking tray or marble board.
- You want to spread it to a thickness of about 1/3 inch (just under a centimeter).
- Use a spatula or a palette knife to help spread the mixture evenly.
- Allow the mixture to cool completely. It will firm up significantly as it cools, making the next step easier.

- Once the mixture is set and firm, use a knife or a cookie cutter to cut it into shapes (traditionally rectangles or circles).

- Heat a generous amount of olive oil in a large frying pan over medium-high heat.

- Once the oil is hot, add the panelle in batches, frying until they are golden and crisp on both sides. This will take about 3-5 minutes per side.

- Transfer the cooked panelle to paper towels to drain any excess oil.

Serve:

- Panelle is best served hot, with lemon wedges on the side.

- Squeeze the lemon over the panelle just before eating.

- If you're serving them sandwich style, you can place them in a fresh bread roll, like a ciabatta, possibly with a sprinkle of salt and a drizzle of lemon juice.

Enjoy this simple, tasty, vegan Sicilian snack!

Fennel and Orange Salad (Insalata di Finocchi e Arance)

"Insalata di Finocchi e Arance" (Fennel and Orange Salad) is a refreshing and aromatic dish that hails from Sicily, combining the crispness of fennel with the sweetness of oranges.

This salad is inherently vegan, making it a perfect and easy dish to prepare for anyone following a vegan diet.

Here's how you can make it:

Ingredients:

- 2-3 large navel oranges
- 2 medium fennel bulbs
- 1 small red onion
- Extra virgin olive oil for dressing
- Salt, to taste
- Black pepper, to taste
- Optional: black olives for an extra salty bite and visual contrast
- Optional: a handful of fresh mint leaves or parsley for an added refreshing element

Instructions:

Prepare the Oranges:

- Cut the top and bottom off the oranges.

- With the orange sitting flat on one of the ends you just cut, use a sharp knife to slice off the peel and the white pith, following the curve of the fruit.

- Try to remove only the peel and pith, keeping as much of the orange flesh intact as possible.

- Once peeled, hold the orange over a bowl (to catch any juice) and cut along the membrane on both sides of each segment to free the segments from the orange.

- Alternatively, you can slice the oranges into rounds or half-moons if you prefer.

- Place the orange segments in the bowl and squeeze the membranes you're left holding to get any remaining juice into the bowl.

Prepare the Vegetables:

- Trim the stalks and fronds off the fennel bulbs, saving some of the dill-like fronds for garnish.

- If the outer layer of the fennel bulb is tough, you can remove and discard it.

- Cut the fennel bulb in half from top to bottom and remove the hard core at the base of each half.

- Use a mandolin or a very sharp knife to slice the fennel into thin, almost translucent slices.

- Peel the red onion and slice it into thin rings or half-moons, according to your preference.

- In a large serving bowl, combine the sliced fennel and red onion with the orange segments (including any juice collected).
- Drizzle with a generous amount of extra virgin olive oil, and season with salt and black pepper to taste.
- Toss everything together gently.

Garnish and Serve:

- If using, add the black olives and freshly torn mint leaves or parsley to the salad for extra flavor and visual appeal.
- Garnish with the reserved fennel fronds for a touch of green and a hint of aniseed flavor.
- Give the salad a final gentle toss, and it's ready to serve.

This salad is a celebration of simple, fresh flavors and is a beautiful addition to any meal. The crispness of the fennel, the sweetness of the oranges, and the sharpness of the onion create a delightful and refreshing combination. Enjoy this burst of Sicilian sunshine on a plate!

Carciofi Ripieni (Stuffed Artichokes)

Carciofi Ripieni, or Stuffed Artichokes, is a dish that showcases the flavors of fresh artichokes, often mixed with breadcrumbs, cheese, and anchovies.

For a vegan twist, we'll substitute the non-vegan ingredients while preserving the Mediterranean essence of this Sicilian classic.

Ingredients:

- 4 large fresh artichokes
- 1 cup breadcrumbs (consider whole wheat for extra nutrition)
- 3 cloves garlic, minced
- 1/4 cup fresh parsley, finely chopped
- 2 tablespoons nutritional yeast (as a cheese substitute, adds a cheesy flavor)
- 1/2 teaspoon crushed red pepper flakes (optional)
- Salt and black pepper, to taste

- Juice of 1 lemon, plus extra wedges for serving
- 1/4 cup extra virgin olive oil, plus more for drizzling
- Water or vegetable broth (for steaming)

Instructions:

Prepare the Artichokes:

- Rinse the artichokes under cold water.
- Using scissors, snip off the pointy ends of the artichoke leaves and cut off the top 1 inch of the artichoke.
- Remove the smaller leaves near the base and stem.
- If the stems are long, trim them to about 1 inch, peeling the tough outer layer of the stems.
- Rub the cut parts with lemon to prevent them from turning brown.
- Open up the leaves gently to make space for the stuffing.

Make the Stuffing:

- In a bowl, mix the breadcrumbs, minced garlic, chopped parsley, nutritional yeast, red pepper flakes (if using), salt, and pepper.
- Add the lemon juice and olive oil, combining everything well.
- The mixture should be evenly moist; if it seems too dry, add more oil or a splash of water.

Stuff the Artichokes:

- Hold an artichoke over the bowl, spoon the stuffing in between the leaf layers, and fill them generously.
- Start from the outer layers and move inward. Ensure the stuffing is distributed evenly among the artichokes.

Cook the Artichokes:

- Place the stuffed artichokes upright in a large pot.

- Add enough water or vegetable broth to cover the bottom of the pot by about 1.5 inches.

- Drizzle additional olive oil over the top of the artichokes if desired.

- Cover the pot with a lid and bring the water to a boil over high heat.

- Once boiling, reduce the heat to a simmer and let the artichokes cook for about 40-50 minutes or until the leaves can be easily pulled off.

- Be sure to check the water level occasionally, adding more as needed so the pot doesn't dry out.

Serving:

- Carefully remove the artichokes from the pot.

- Set each on a plate and serve warm, with extra lemon wedges on the side for squeezing over the top.

- To eat, pull off the outer petals one at a time, dip the white fleshy end in additional olive oil or lemon juice if desired, place in your mouth, and pull through teeth to remove the soft, pulpy portion.

- Discard the remaining petals.

- Continue until all petals are removed.

- Then, with a knife or spoon, scrape out and discard the inedible fuzzy part (called the "choke") covering the artichoke heart.

- The remaining bottom of the artichoke is the heart and is entirely edible.

Enjoy your vegan Carciofi Ripieni, a dish that brings a taste of Sicily right to your table!

Granita

Granita is a semi-frozen dessert that originated from Sicily and comes in various flavors. The most traditional ones are lemon, coffee, and almond.

For a vegan version of granita, we avoid any dairy products that are sometimes used in different variations of granita. Here, we'll go through a simple recipe for a refreshing lemon granita, but feel free to substitute the flavor with any fruit of your choice.

Ingredients:

- 1 cup (240 ml) water
- 1/2 cup (100 g) sugar
- 1 cup (240 ml) fresh lemon juice (approximately 4-6 lemons, depending on size and juiciness)
- 2-3 tablespoons lemon zest
- Fresh mint leaves (optional, for garnish)

Instructions:

Make the Simple Syrup:

- Combine the water and sugar in a saucepan.
- Bring to a simmer over medium heat, stirring occasionally until the sugar dissolves completely.
- Remove from heat and allow it to cool to room temperature. This is your simple syrup base.

Prepare the Lemon Mixture:

- While the syrup is cooling, zest the lemons until you have 2-3 tablespoons of zest, then juice them until you have about 1 cup of lemon juice.
- Combine the lemon juice and zest in a mixing bowl.
- Once the simple syrup is cool, add it to the lemon mixture and stir well.

Freeze the Mixture:

- Pour the mixture into a shallow, freezer-safe dish (a metal baking dish works well as it will speed up the freezing process).

- Place the dish in the freezer for about 30-40 minutes.
- Check the mixture, and once it begins to freeze around the edges, take a fork and stir the mixture, breaking up the frozen parts near the edges into smaller chunks and mixing them toward the center.
- Return the dish to the freezer, then check and stir every 30 minutes after that, breaking up any large chunks into small pieces with a fork for about 3-4 hours or until the mixture has a fluffy, snowy texture.
- The frequent stirring is what delivers the granita's classic flaky texture, so don't skip this step!

Serving:
- Once the granita is thoroughly frozen and flaked, serve it in chilled bowls or glasses.
- Garnish with fresh mint leaves if you like.
- If the granita becomes too hard in the freezer, give it a brief thaw at room temperature and break it up again with a fork before serving.

Storing:
- Granita can be stored in the freezer in a sealed container.
- It's best enjoyed within a few days of making it, as the texture will change over time.

This refreshing treat is perfect for hot weather. It can be customized with other flavors like strawberry, mint, coffee (using a strong, cooled espresso and reducing the sugar as needed), almond (using almond milk and almond extract), or other fruit juices. The method remains the same: replace the lemon juice with your chosen flavor base. Enjoy your Sicilian-style vegan granita!

Couscous alla Trapanese

Couscous alla Trapanese is a traditional dish from Trapani, in Sicily, Italy. This dish reflects the diverse cultural influences on Sicilian cuisine, as couscous is primarily associated with North African culinary traditions. Couscous is often served with fish or seafood but can be veganized using a spicy vegetable stew.

Here's how you can make a vegan version of Couscous alla Trapanese, keeping the essence of the dish but ensuring all ingredients are plant-based.

Ingredients:

For the Couscous:

- 2 cups (350 g) couscous
- 2 tablespoons olive oil
- 2 1/4 cups (530 ml) vegetable broth, boiling hot
- Salt, to taste

For the Vegetable Stew:

- 1/4 cup (60 ml) olive oil
- 1 medium onion, finely chopped
- 2-3 garlic cloves, minced
- 1 medium carrot, chopped
- 1 medium zucchini, chopped
- 1 medium bell pepper, red or yellow, chopped
- 1 cup (150 g) cherry tomatoes, halved
- 1/2 cup (75 g) green olives, pitted and sliced
- 2 tablespoons capers, rinsed and drained
- 1-2 teaspoons red chili flakes (adjust to taste)
- 1 teaspoon dried oregano or a handful of fresh basil, chopped
- Salt and black pepper, to taste
- 2 1/2 cups (590 ml) tomato sauce or crushed tomatoes

To Serve:

- Fresh parsley or basil, chopped (for garnish)
- Lemon wedges
- Chili flakes (optional)

Instructions:

Prepare the Couscous:

- Place the couscous in a large bowl.
- Stir in a pinch of salt and 2 tablespoons of olive oil.

- Pour the boiling vegetable broth over the couscous, making sure the couscous is completely covered.
- Cover the bowl with a plate or plastic wrap and set aside for about 10-15 minutes.
- After the couscous has absorbed all the liquid, fluff it with a fork to break up any lumps.
- Cover and set it aside.

Make the Vegetable Stew:
- Heat olive oil in a large saucepan over medium heat.
- Add the onion and garlic, sautéing until the onions are translucent, about 3-4 minutes.
- Add the carrot and cook for another 2-3 minutes, then add the zucchini and bell pepper.
- Continue cooking, stirring occasionally, until the vegetables start to soften, about 5-7 minutes.
- Stir in the cherry tomatoes, olives, capers, chili flakes, oregano or basil, and some salt and black pepper to taste.
- Cook for another 2-3 minutes.
- Pour in the tomato sauce or crushed tomatoes.
- Bring the mixture to a simmer and reduce the heat to low.
- Cover and let it simmer for about 15-20 minutes, allowing the flavors to meld together.

Combine the Couscous and Vegetable Stew:
- Once the vegetable stew is done, you can either mix the couscous directly into the pan of vegetables, stirring gently to combine, or you can serve the stew over the couscous in individual bowls.

- Serve the Couscous alla Trapanese hot, garnished with fresh parsley or basil.
- Provide lemon wedges for squeezing over the top and additional chili flakes for those who prefer extra heat.

This dish is a celebration of Mediterranean flavors, making the most of fresh vegetable produce and the distinctive texture of couscous. It's hearty and satisfying, even without the traditional fish or seafood— a perfect example of the versatility and inclusiveness of Sicilian cuisine.

When adapting traditional Sicilian recipes for vegans, the focus remains on the freshness and flavors of the ingredients. The island's cuisine is celebrated for its rich taste and the high quality of locally grown produce, making it a versatile option for vegan dishes.

Sardinia

Sardinia, one of Italy's most beautiful major islands, has a distinct cuisine that incorporates various ingredients abundant in the region, including grains, vegetables, fruits, and legumes.

While some traditional dishes include meat and dairy, there are several inherently vegan dishes, as well as others that can be adapted to a vegan diet. Here's a look at vegan-friendly options from Sardinian cuisine:

Pane Carasau

This traditional Sardinian flatbread, also known as "carta di musica" (music paper bread), due to its thinness, is naturally vegan. It's made with wheat flour, salt, yeast, and water and can be enjoyed as a snack or alongside main dishes.

Ingredients:

- 500g / 4 cups durum wheat flour (semolina)
- 1 teaspoon salt
- Around 300ml / 1 1/4 cups warm water (as needed)

- 1 teaspoon instant yeast (optional, it's traditionally made without yeast, but it helps with the bubbling aspect and is more forgiving for beginners)

Instructions:

Prepare the Dough:

- In a large mixing bowl, combine the durum wheat flour and salt.
- If you're using yeast, you should activate it first by dissolving it in a little warm water and then adding it to the flour mixture.
- Gradually add warm water to the flour mixture, kneading continuously until you have a smooth, elastic dough.
- The amount of water necessary may vary based on the flour's absorbency, so add it slowly until the desired consistency is reached.
- Cover the dough with a clean kitchen towel and let it rest for about an hour at room temperature.
- If you're in a hurry, you can shorten this resting period, but the dough becomes easier to work with the longer you let it rest.

Roll Out the Dough:

- After the resting period, preheat your oven to the highest setting, usually around 250°C (480°F).
- If you have a pizza stone, put it in the oven now to heat.
- Divide the dough into small balls about the size of a lemon.
- On a lightly floured surface, roll out each ball of dough as thinly as possible; they should be almost transparent.

- If the dough resists while rolling, let it rest for a few more minutes.

First Baking:

- Place the rolled-out dough onto the hot pizza stone or a baking sheet lined with parchment paper.
- Bake in the preheated oven until it's crispy and just starting to brown about 4-6 minutes.
- You'll see it start to bubble up in places, which is expected.
- Remove from the oven and let it cool for a minute.
- Then, with a very sharp knife or scissors, quickly slice or cut the bread horizontally through the middle of the bubble, creating two thin sheets from each piece of bread.
- Repeat the process with the remaining balls of dough.

Second Baking:

- Once all your bread is baked and halved, return the thinner sheets to the oven.
- This time, you'll bake them until they're fully crisped and golden, approximately 2-3 minutes. Watch them closely to prevent burning.
- Remove the bread from the oven and allow it to cool completely. They will continue to crisp up as they cool.

Serving and Storing:

- Serve immediately or store in an airtight container.
- Pane Carasau can be enjoyed as is or dampened (as is traditional) with a little bit of water, then drizzled with olive oil and a sprinkle of salt.
- This bread is versatile and can be used for dipping, as a base for pizza toppings, or accompanied by Sardinian wines and cheeses (or vegan alternatives).

Making Pane Carasau at home is a bit challenging due to the thinness of the dough, but it's worth the effort for the delicious, crispy result. It's a beautiful part of Sardinian food culture that you can now enjoy vegan-style at your own table.

Fregola con Verdure

Fregola (or fregula) is a type of pasta from Sardinia, similar to couscous but larger.

It's often served with clams or seafood. Still, a vegan version incorporates mixed vegetables, tomatoes, and aromatic herbs, creating a hearty and flavorful dish.

Fregola works wonderfully in soups and salads, but it's also excellent as a side or main dish when cooked with vegetables, as in this vegan recipe for Fregola con Verdure (Fregola with Vegetables).

Ingredients:

- 1 cup fregola pasta
- 2 tablespoons olive oil
- 1 small onion, finely chopped
- 2 garlic cloves, minced
- 1 medium zucchini, chopped
- 1 medium yellow bell pepper, chopped
- 1 cup cherry tomatoes, halved
- 1/2 cup frozen peas, thawed
- Salt and black pepper, to taste
- 2 cups vegetable broth or water
- Fresh herbs (such as parsley, basil, or thyme), chopped
- Vegan parmesan cheese for serving (optional)

Instructions:

Cook the Fregola:

- In a pot of boiling salted water, cook the fregola pasta for about 10-12 minutes (or according to the package instructions) until it's al dente.
- Since fregola sizes can vary, it's important to taste for doneness. Drain and set aside.

Sauté the Vegetables:

- While the fregola is cooking, heat the olive oil in a large skillet over medium heat.
- Add the onion and garlic and sauté until the onion is soft and translucent, about 2-3 minutes.
- Add the zucchini and bell pepper to the skillet.

- Cook, stirring occasionally, until the vegetables are tender, about 5-7 minutes.
- Stir in the cherry tomatoes and peas, then cook for an additional 3-5 minutes, until the tomatoes are just starting to break down but still retain their shape.
- Season with salt and black pepper to taste.

Combine Fregola and Vegetables:
- Add the cooked fregola to the skillet with the vegetables, stirring to combine.
- If the mixture seems dry, add a little vegetable broth or water; the amount required can depend on the exact heat of your stove and the size of your skillet.
- Let the fregola and vegetables cook together for a couple of minutes, allowing the flavors to meld.
- Adjust the seasoning with more salt and black pepper if needed.

Garnish and Serve:
- Remove the skillet from the heat. Stir in the fresh herbs, reserving a few for garnish.
- Serve the fregola hot, garnished with the reserved herbs and a sprinkle of vegan parmesan cheese if desired.

This dish is customizable based on the vegetables you have on hand. For instance, eggplant, asparagus, or broccoli would also be great additions or substitutes. Fregola con Verdure is a colorful, nutritious, and satisfying meal that highlights the simple flavors of fresh, high-quality ingredients characteristic of Sardinian cuisine.

Minestrone di Fave e Cicorie (Fava Bean and Chicory Soup)

"Minestrone di Fave e Cicorie" is a hearty and traditional Italian soup, particularly popular in Southern Italy and regions like Sardinia.

It combines fava beans (broad beans) and bitter greens like chicory, offering a nutritious and flavorful dish. Here's a vegan version of this classic soup, keeping true to its rustic roots.

Ingredients:

- 1 cup dried fava beans (broad beans), soaked overnight
- 2 tablespoons olive oil
- 1 large onion, chopped
- 2 garlic cloves, minced
- 2 carrots, diced
- 2 celery stalks, diced
- 1 small bulb of fennel, diced (optional)
- 1 potato, peeled and diced
- 1 bunch of chicory (you can substitute with other bitter greens like endive or escarole if chicory is unavailable), roughly chopped
- 1 can (14 oz) of chopped tomatoes
- 6 cups vegetable broth or water
- Salt and pepper, to taste
- A pinch of red pepper flakes (optional)
- Fresh herbs (like parsley or basil) for garnish

Instructions:

Prepare the Fava Beans:

- After soaking the fava beans overnight, drain and rinse them.
- If they're unpeeled, remove the outer skins by pinching the skin between your fingers and popping out the inner bean.

Cook the Base:

- In a large pot, heat olive oil over medium heat.
- Add the onion and garlic, sautéing until the onion is translucent, about 3-5 minutes.

- Add the carrots, celery, fennel (if using), and potato to the pot.
- Cook, stirring occasionally, until the vegetables begin to soften, around 5 minutes.

Add the Beans and Broth:

- Add the soaked and peeled fava beans to the pot, followed by the chopped tomatoes (with their juice) and vegetable broth.
- If you like your soup with a bit of a kick, add a pinch of red pepper flakes at this stage.
- Increase the heat and bring the mixture to a boil.
- Then, reduce the heat to a simmer, cover, and let it cook for about 30-40 minutes, or until the beans are close to tender.

Add the Greens:

- Once the beans are almost done, add the chopped chicory (or other bitter greens) to the pot.
- Stir them in, allowing them to wilt and become tender, about 5-10 minutes, depending on the greens' toughness.
- At this point, check the beans for doneness.
- They should be tender but not mushy, still holding their shape. If they're not yet done, let the soup simmer for a few more minutes.

Season and Serve:

- Taste the soup and adjust the seasoning with salt and pepper.
- The amount of salt needed may vary depending on the saltiness of your vegetable broth.

- Once everything is cooked and seasoned to your liking, turn off the heat.
- Ladle the soup into bowls, garnish with fresh herbs, and serve hot.

This minestrone is a celebration of simple, peasant-style cooking where fresh, local ingredients shine.

The fava beans provide heartiness, while the chicory brings a touch of bitterness that's wonderfully offset by the savory broth and sweet vegetables. This soup is even better the next day after the flavors have had more time to meld, making it a great option for meal prep as well.

Maccarrones de Busa with Tomato Sauce

"Maccarrones de Busa" is a traditional Sardinian pasta, similar to bucatini, which is often made using a knitting needle or a similarly shaped tool to form long, hollow strands.

This pasta is typically served with a robust meat sauce that complements its unique texture.

Below is a recipe for vegan Maccarrones de Busa with a simple yet flavorful tomato sauce.

Ingredients:

For the Maccarrones de Busa:

- Semolina flour (approximately 400g, but be prepared to adjust as needed)
- Water (as needed for the dough)
- A bit of salt

For the Tomato Sauce:

- 2 tablespoons olive oil
- 1 small onion, finely chopped
- 2-3 garlic cloves, minced
- 1 can (28 ounces) whole peeled tomatoes, crushed by hand
- Salt, to taste
- Pepper, to taste
- A pinch of sugar (optional)
- Fresh basil, torn (a handful)
- Red pepper flakes (optional)

Instructions:

Making the Pasta:

- Start by placing semolina flour in a mound on a clean surface.
- Make a well in the center.
- Gradually add water to the well and mix with your fingers, incorporating little by little until a dough starts to form.
- It should be firm and not sticky.
- Knead the dough for about 10 minutes until it's smooth and elastic.
- Then, cover it with a damp cloth and let it rest for at least 30 minutes.
- To shape the pasta, roll the dough into long, thin logs (about the thickness of spaghetti).
- Wrap each strand around a knitting needle or a metal skewer, and then roll back and forth on your work surface to create the hollow shape.
- Slide the pasta off the needle and place it on a semolina-dusted tray. Repeat with the remaining dough.

Preparing the Sauce:

- While the dough is resting, you can start the sauce.
- Heat the olive oil in a saucepan over medium heat.
- Add the chopped onion and cook until it's soft and translucent, not browned.
- Add the minced garlic and cook for another minute until fragrant.
- Add the crushed tomatoes and their juice to the saucepan.

- Bring the mixture to a simmer, allowing it to cook for about 20-30 minutes, stirring occasionally.
- The sauce should thicken, and the flavors will concentrate over time.
- Season with salt, pepper, and a pinch of sugar (if using) to balance the acidity of the tomatoes.
- If you like a bit of heat, add some red pepper flakes.

Cooking the Pasta:
- Bring a large pot of salted water to a boil.
- Cook the maccarrones de busa until al dente.
- Fresh pasta cooks much quicker than dried, so it should take about 3-4 minutes.
- Check frequently to avoid overcooking.
- Reserve a cup of pasta cooking water and then drain the pasta.

Combining Pasta and Sauce:
- Add the pasta to the saucepan with the tomato sauce.
- Toss to combine, adding a little pasta water if necessary to loosen things up and ensure the pasta is well-coated.
- Stir in the fresh basil just before serving.

Serving:
- Serve the pasta hot, garnished with more fresh basil.
- If desired, you can also sprinkle on some nutritional yeast or vegan Parmesan cheese for an extra layer of flavor.

Enjoy your authentic Sardinian dish! This meal is a celebration of simple ingredients coming together to create something truly special and delicious.

Insalata di Arance e Finocchi (Orange and Fennel Salad)

"Insalata di Arance e Finocchi" (Orange and Fennel Salad) is a refreshing and simple dish, often found in various parts of Italy, including the beautiful island of Sardinia.

This salad is known for its bright, fresh flavors and health benefits, making it a popular choice, especially during warmer weather. Here's how you can prepare it in a vegan way, which, given the nature of the original recipe, requires no modifications to make it plant-based.

Ingredients:

- 4 large oranges (preferably blood oranges if available)
- 2 fennel bulbs
- 1 red onion (small), thinly sliced
- 4 tablespoons of extra virgin olive oil
- Salt, to taste
- Black pepper, to taste
- 1-2 tablespoons of fresh lemon juice
- Fresh mint leaves or parsley for garnish (optional)
- Black olives (preferably Kalamata), pitted and sliced (optional)
- Chili flakes or finely chopped fresh chili (optional for a bit of heat)

Instructions:

Prepping the Oranges:

- Top and tail the oranges.
- With a sharp knife, remove the skin and white pith following the curve of the fruit, ensuring it's fully peeled and the flesh is exposed.
- Over a bowl to catch the juices, carefully slice between the membranes to segment the oranges, or you can slice the oranges into rounds if you prefer.
- Remove any seeds as you come across them.

Preparing the Fennel:

- Cut off the tops of the fennel bulbs and remove any tough or bruised outer layers.
- Slice the fennel very thinly, using a mandolin if you have one, for more uniform slices.

Assembling the Salad:

- In a large salad bowl, combine the orange segments (or slices) and any juice with the sliced fennel and red onion.
- If you're using olives or chili for an extra kick, add them now.
- Drizzle with the extra virgin olive oil and fresh lemon juice.
- Add salt and pepper to taste.
- Toss everything together gently to combine.

Garnishing:

- Just before serving, garnish with fresh mint leaves or parsley if you're using.
- These fresh herbs will give a burst of color and freshness to the dish.

Serving:

- This salad is best served fresh to maintain the crispness of the fennel and the juiciness of the oranges.
- It's a great side dish or starter and pairs wonderfully with a crusty loaf of bread or a main dish of your choice.

This vibrant salad is a celebration of Mediterranean flavors and offers a delightful texture contrast between the ingredients. It's not only visually appealing but also packed with nutrients, making it a fantastic addition to your healthy vegan repertoire.

Malloreddus alla Campidanese (vegan version)

"Malloreddus alla Campidanese" is a traditional pasta dish from Sardinia, specifically from the Campidano area. The dish is characterized by its small, shell-shaped pasta known as malloreddus (also referred to as gnocchetti sardi), which is typically paired with a rich tomato-based sauce and often features sausage and Pecorino cheese.

However, we'll create a vegan version of this classic Sardinian dish without compromising on the traditional flavors.

Ingredients:

For the Malloreddus:

- 400g malloreddus pasta (you can find this at Italian specialty stores or use a small shell pasta as a substitute)

For the Vegan Sauce:

- 2 tablespoons olive oil
- 1 small onion, finely chopped
- 2-3 cloves garlic, minced
- 1 medium carrot, finely chopped
- 1 stalk of celery, finely chopped
- 400g (about 14 oz) can of quality crushed tomatoes
- 1/3 cup sun-dried tomatoes, chopped
- Salt, to taste
- Black pepper, to taste
- 1 teaspoon fennel seeds (to mimic the flavor of traditional sausage)
- 1 teaspoon smoked paprika (for some smoky flavor)
- A pinch of chili flakes (optional)
- A splash of red wine (optional)
- A handful of fresh basil, torn
- Vegan sausage (optional), crumbled or chopped into small pieces

Instructions:

Preparing the Sauce:

- Start by heating the olive oil in a large saucepan over medium heat.
- Add the onion, and sauté until it becomes translucent, about 4-5 minutes.

437

- Add the minced garlic, carrot, and celery, and continue to sauté until all the vegetables are soft, about 5-7 minutes.

- If you're using vegan sausage, add it now and cook for a few more minutes, allowing it to brown slightly.

- Stir in the fennel seeds, smoked paprika, and chili flakes (if using).

- If you opt to use a splash of red wine for depth, add it now and let it cook off for a couple of minutes.

- Add the crushed and sun-dried tomatoes to the saucepan.

- Bring the mixture to a simmer, and let it cook for about 20-30 minutes until the sauce thickens and the flavors meld.

- Stir occasionally to prevent sticking.

- Season with salt and pepper to taste. Add most of the fresh basil, reserving some for garnish.

Cooking the Pasta:

- While the sauce is simmering, prepare the malloreddus pasta.

- Bring a large pot of salted water to a boil.

- Cook the pasta according to the package instructions until it is al dente.

- Once cooked, drain the pasta, reserving a cup of the pasta water.

Combining Pasta and Sauce:

- Add the drained pasta directly into the saucepan with the tomato sauce.

- Toss to combine thoroughly, adding a little pasta water if necessary to loosen the sauce and ensure it coats the pasta generously.

- Serve the malloreddus hot, garnished with the remaining fresh basil.
- You can also sprinkle on some nutritional yeast or vegan parmesan if desired for an extra cheesy flavor.

This vegan take on the classic Malloreddus alla Campidanese allows you to enjoy the rich, comforting flavors of Sardinian cuisine without the use of animal products.

Seadas (Sebadas)

Seadas or Sebadas is a traditional Sardinian dessert, often described as a large, sweet ravioli that's usually filled with a mild cheese such as Pecorino, deep-fried and served with honey. In adapting this recipe to be vegan, we'll substitute the cheese with a vegan alternative and use agave syrup or maple syrup instead of honey to keep the dessert plant-based.

Ingredients:

For the dough:

- 300g (about 2 1/2 cups) all-purpose flour
- 100ml (a little less than 1/2 cup) warm water
- 50ml (about 3 1/2 tablespoons) extra virgin olive oil or melted vegan margarine
- A pinch of salt

For the filling:

- 200g (about 7 oz) vegan cheese (choose a mild-flavored one, preferably one that melts well and is not too strong, like a vegan mozzarella)
- 2 tablespoons agave syrup or maple syrup, plus extra for serving
- Grated zest of 1 unwaxed lemon

For frying:

- Vegetable oil

Instructions:

Prepare the Dough:

- In a large mixing bowl, combine the flour and salt.
- Add the olive oil or melted vegan margarine and start mixing.
- Gradually add warm water and knead until the dough is smooth and elastic.
- If it's too dry, add a bit more water, one tablespoon at a time.

- Cover the dough with a clean kitchen towel and let it rest for about 30 minutes.

Prepare the Filling:

- In a bowl, combine the grated vegan cheese, lemon zest, and agave or maple syrup.
- Mix well.

Assemble the Seadas:

- On a lightly floured surface, roll out the dough into a thin sheet, about 1/8-inch thick.
- Using a round cutter or a glass, cut out circles about 10cm (4 inches) in diameter.
- Place a spoonful of the cheese mixture in the center of half of the circles, being careful not to overfill.
- Leave enough space around the edges to seal the dough.
- Moisten the edges of the dough with a little water and place another dough circle on top of each filled circle.
- Press the edges together firmly to seal, then use a fork to crimp the edges.

Fry the Seadas:

- Heat a generous amount of vegetable oil in a deep frying pan over medium heat.
- Once the oil is hot, carefully add the seadas one at a time, frying until golden brown on both sides. Be cautious with the hot oil, as it can splatter.
- Use a slotted spoon to transfer the fried seadas to a plate lined with paper towels to drain excess oil.

- Serve the seadas warm, drizzled with additional agave or maple syrup.

This vegan version of Seadas maintains the spirit and flavor profile of the traditional Sardinian dessert, allowing those following a plant-based diet to enjoy it. The result is a deliciously sweet, citrusy, and cheesy filling encased in a crispy, golden brown pastry.

Chapter 5
The Vegan Italian Wine Guide

Understanding labels

Italy, like many other wine-producing countries, has a long history of making wines that could be considered vegan by default, simply due to traditional production methods. However, "vegan" in the context of wine specifically refers to the fining process where animal-derived products are often used.

Italian wines, revered globally, offer an exquisite mosaic of flavors, styles, and traditions. Navigating their labels requires understanding specific indicators. "Organico" signifies organic cultivation, avoiding synthetic chemicals. For vegan-friendly assurance, look for

"Vegano" or certifications like the Vegan Society's trademark, indicating the absence of animal-derived substances in production.

Typically, wines are clarified through a process called fining, where agents are added to remove unwanted particles. Non-vegan fining agents can include gelatin (from animals), casein (a milk protein), albumin (egg whites), and isinglass (from fish). Vegan wines, on the other hand, either skip the fining process or use vegan-friendly agents such as bentonite clay, carbon, or vegetable plaques.

Here's the tricky part: not all wines from a particular region or variety in Italy (or elsewhere) will be vegan, as the vegan designation is more about the specific producer's practices rather than the wine type or region.

However, if you're looking for vegan wines, many producers nowadays label their bottles as vegan-friendly, especially with the growing demand for vegan products. Also, several wine databases and online retailers have begun to categorize wines by their vegan status, making it easier for consumers to make informed choices.

That said, you can't necessarily pinpoint specific "major Italian Vegan wines" in terms of varieties or regions because whether a wine is vegan or not depends on the individual producer. However, you can find vegan versions of major Italian wines like Chianti, Barolo, Prosecco, Pinot Grigio, and many others if you seek out producers who embrace vegan practices.

Suppose you're interested in specific brands or vineyards. In that case, it's best to research individual producers who are known for vegan practices or to consult vegan wine databases.

Pairing wine with vegan food

Pairing vegan wine with plant-based cuisine is an art, enhancing the dining experience. The key is balancing flavors. Light, crisp wines complement delicate vegetable dishes, while robust, full-bodied wines stand up to heartier fare. Consider acidity, sweetness, and tannins to ensure the wine and meal harmoniously enhance each other. My recommendation is to log on to an online wine seller, such as totalwine.com, and search for "Vegan Wines." The resulting suggestions will show you their grade, consumer reviews, and pricing. Each wine is described, revealing the regional origin, brand, wine type, varietal, style, % ABV (alcohol by volume), and taste.

Afterword

Italian cuisine is undergoing a revolutionary shift, with a surging vegan wave influencing its traditional dishes. Far from a fleeting trend, this movement emphasizes sustainability, health, and ethical food choices. Classic dishes like lasagna and risotto are being reimagined. Dairy and meat are replaced with plant-based alternatives like cashew cheese and lentil 'meats' without losing authentic flavors or textures. The focus is not just on replicating traditional flavors but enhancing them using innovative cooking techniques and a broader array of nutrients.

Sustainability is central to this transformation. The environmental toll of animal farming propels chefs and consumers towards plant-based diets. Italian cooking's age-old ethos of using local, seasonal produce is now seen through the lens of ecological responsibility and promoting local biodiversity. Coupled with the health advantages of a plant-dominant diet, veganism aligns with a comprehensive approach to well-being.

The horizon of Italian vegan cuisine is expanding, promising a cultural change where vegan dishes will become a norm, acclaimed for their sustainability, health benefits, and culinary depth. This evolution ensures Italian kitchens honor their ancestral, soulful cooking while addressing the ethical and environmental demands of today.

Veganism is more than a dietary choice; it's a transformative lifestyle journey. It introduces a world of novel flavors, healthier habits, and mindful living. Embracing veganism doesn't forsake traditional tastes but reimagines them. Every vegan meal, even if imperfect, contributes to environmental conservation, animal rights, and individual health. As you embrace this path, every dish becomes a beacon of positive change. Relish the culinary adventure, and savor the ethical, nutritious meals.

Made in United States
Troutdale, OR
12/12/2023

15762424R00255